BEAUFIGHTER ACE

The Night Fighter Career
of
Marshal of the Royal Air Force,
Sir Thomas Pike, GCB, CBE, DFC*

DO/TLM.

Headquarters, No. 11 Group,
Royal Air Force,
UXBRIDGE,
MIDDLESEX.

17th. March, 1941.

Dear *Pike*

      I would like to congratulate you on your success the other night.

2.   I am very glad you have started your period of Command so well, and wish you all the best of luck in the future.

      Yours *v sincerely*

T. Leigh-Mallory

Wing Commander T.G. Pike,
   Officer Commanding,
      No. 219 Squadron,
         R.A.F. Station,
           TANGMERE.

Congratulations from Air Marshal Sir Trafford Leigh-Mallory, Commander of No. 11 Group, RAF.

BEAUFIGHTER ACE

The Night Fighter Career
of
Marshal of the Royal Air Force,
Sir Thomas Pike, GCB, CBE, DFC*

Richard Pike

Pen & Sword
AVIATION

First published in Great Britain in 2004 by
Pen & Sword Aviation
an imprint of
Pen & Sword Books Ltd
47 Church Street
Barnsley
South Yorkshire
S70 2AS

ISBN 1 84415 123 9

Typeset in 10/12pt Palatino by
Phoenix Typesetting, Auldgirth, Dumfriesshire

Printed and bound in England by
CPI UK

Pen & Sword Books Ltd incorporates the imprints of Pen & Sword Aviation,
Pen & Sword Maritime, Pen & Sword Military, Wharncliffe Local History,
Pen & Sword Select, Pen & Sword Military Classics and Leo Cooper.

For a complete list of Pen & Sword titles please contact
PEN & SWORD BOOKS LIMITED
47 Church Street, Barnsley, South Yorkshire, S70 2AS, England
E-mail: enquiries@pen-and-sword.co.uk
Website: www.pen-and-sword.co.uk

To the memory of my father, Tom, whose
quietly spectacular achievements
should not be quietly forgotten, and to
the memory of my mother, Althea,
whose staunch support we forgot to thank.

Acknowledgements

For their help and for their illuminating comments, very many thanks
to: the Royal Air Force Museum, Hendon, for Fighter Command combat
reports and other archive material; Mr P. J. V. Elliott, Senior Keeper at
the Royal Air Force Museum, Hendon; Mr C. J. Weir MA, historian and
former World War Two anti-aircraft gunner; Mr S. Wright, former
World War Two Beaufighter navigator, now living in Australia; the
Bognor Regis Local History Society; Ms S. Endacott, Bognor Regis local
historian; the Tangmere Airfield Museum, West Sussex; the Manager,
The Royal Hotel, Bognor Regis; Mrs B. E. Watkinson (née Miss Caryl
Pike); Mrs A. C. Mayres (née Miss Ann Pike).

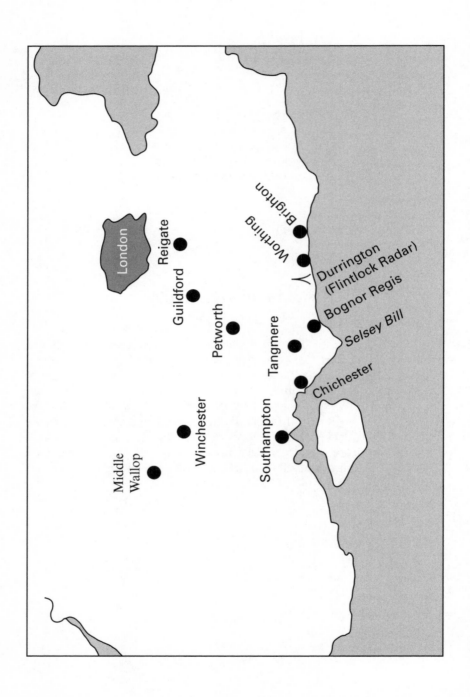

Contents

Prologue

A curious commotion stirs the crowds; people grow restless as they anticipate a high point of the day. The fine September morning is marked by a poignant atmosphere, a heady blend of nostalgia and entertainment. Massed bandsmen play melodies which tug at the massed hearts of sentimental souls. Later a flypast of military aircraft will cause the suspension of flights at Heathrow Airport, but for now everyone counts on a different distraction.

When there's a further surge from the crowds, and when I glance at my mother, I see her fidgeting uncomfortably in her seat placed next to mine on the grandstand. Our position is one of privilege; we are surrounded by Very Important Persons, although lesser mortals have to endure hours of standing close by.

The earlier gathering of personalities was impressive. Battle of Britain aces had mingled with squadrons of air marshals, the air filled with a clash of laughter and pathos as old colleagues met up. One gentleman had appeared especially ebullient in this rank-conscious environment. But then on the cuffs of his uniform jacket he carried the coveted insignia: a single thick ring at the foot of four thin ones. Like my late father he had risen through the hierarchy to become a 'Marshal of the Royal Air Force'.

I glance again at my mother. The determined set of her jaw and her resolute gaze clearly communicate the strength of character so deeply instilled in this eighty year-old lady. She has been a widow for seven years already, and she has confounded family worries about her ability to cope after my father's death. During his lifetime her artistic, if impractical, qualities had complemented her husband's talents with a powerful (if perplexing) ingenuity. However, she had managed to put to good use the versatility and the resilience picked up from the war years. In the staunch manner expected and taken for granted, she had perfected the role of a senior officer's wife. When he had died she had carried on in an unorthodox fashion to be sure, but nevertheless she had persevered with remarkable success as she insisted on handling life her own way.

I watch a group of VIPs as they climb the grandstand steps. Attendant ushers are efficient and urbane while they help the newcomers. As she notices this, I see my mother smile – that beautiful . . . that English rose smile, and I recall how she was visibly touched by the congenial manner of these ushers when we arrived earlier . . . 'Lady Pike . . . how are you? Wonderful to see you again. How sad that Sir Thomas could not have witnessed this special day . . .' we chatted comfortably as they took us to our VIP seats.

But now we sit for endless minutes waiting for the event to start. We listen to the band, wonder at the huge crowds, study our programmes, chat with our neighbours and watch the arrival of VIPs including Prime Minister Margaret Thatcher.

Coincident with another surge of people, a distinctive rumble, resembling the sound of a football crowd, starts to sweep through the area – 'there she is . . . look . . . there's Princess Di.' Children are hoisted onto shoulders as folk push for a better view. I even yearn for a pair of binoculars, but it strikes me that such impedimenta might be frowned upon in view of my pseudo-VIP status. Members of the Royal Family file slowly onto the balcony of Buckingham Palace. Observant crowds point and cheer. The atmosphere becomes agitated; nearby barriers are knocked in the general crush and excitement; even the grandstand appears to totter ominously in the swell of spectators. The greatest interest is directed towards Diana, The Princess of Wales with her shy look, her distinctive head posture . . . her winsome smile.

At length, when the Royal Family are in place, the massed bands strike up once more. The shuffling amongst the crowds dies down as another haunting tune is played. The mood becomes poignant, the air electric. Every immaculate note, practised to perfection, stimulates a further sense of pining nostalgia.

When the music ceases, a portly gentleman – an air commodore – stands up from the VIP area, walks to the front, turns around, and salutes the grandstand party in a somewhat ostentatious fashion.

"What's he up to?" can be heard from some child in the non-VIP area. There's a frozen hush amongst the VIP elements, but this contrasts with the humorous titter which sails through the crowds.

However, the massed bands soon begin to play another theme; the awkward moment is resolved; the aura of nostalgia returns, wafting across as if caught on the breeze, and the spectators quieten. The music lifts our spirits. The march past and the royal salute will take place shortly; everyone now becomes absorbed and subdued as the Battle of

Britain Fiftieth Anniversary celebrations proceed smoothly and efficiently once again.

A few days before the event in London, and while I made preparations to fly from my home in Scotland, one of my daughters, ten year-old Sally, with sacrilegious simplicity asked: 'Why do they go on about the Battle of Britain so much?'

We sat down by our kitchen table with my wife Sue. 'This one is kind of special,' I said.

'Why?'

'Because it's the fiftieth anniversary, that's why.'

'What happened in the Battle of Britain?'

I adopted a 'don't they teach you anything in school these days?' expression, and continued: 'The German Air Force – the *Luftwaffe* – was sent by Hitler and Göering in vast numbers to wipe out the Royal Air Force.' I glanced at a pamphlet on the Battle of Britain which has just arrived by post.

'We had over three thousand aircrew fighting in the battle, from fourteen different countries. Tragically, over five hundred aircrew were killed. Our pilots became so exhausted that more than one fell asleep at the controls after touchdown. When rescue crews raced up to the crashed machines, they would find the pilot slumped over the controls. At first they thought the man was dead.' Sally continued to gaze at me, her expression a mixture of puzzlement and amazement.

'Despite the gallantry of the pilots,' I said, 'only one Battle of Britain pilot, Flight Lieutenant J B Nicolson, was awarded the Victoria Cross.'

'What happened to him?' asked Sally.

'He was in a dogfight near Southampton when his aircraft was hit and set on fire. He was wounded, and he was preparing to abandon his aircraft because of the flames, when he sighted an enemy fighter. The man must have had astonishing courage. He managed to regain control of his aircraft, then he attacked and shot down the enemy before resuming his bale out procedures. As a result of the delay he was seriously burnt. After many months of medical treatment he returned to flying duties, but tragically he died in a flying accident later in the war.'

'Poor man,' said Sue. 'What courage . . .'

Sally's eyes had grown wide. She thought about this for a few moments, then asked: 'What other stories do you know about the Battle of Britain?'

'Well there was one incredible incident, witnessed by hundreds of picnickers in Hyde Park. The people were watching the dogfights in the

London skies above them; it was almost as if the battles were part of the afternoon's entertainment. Suddenly they could see that one of our pilots was in trouble. The engine of his aircraft had been hit by gunfire from a German Dornier bomber, and the British machine was crippled. The crowds didn't know at the time, of course, but as it turned out, the pilot, a man called Sergeant Holmes, had another problem: he'd run out of ammunition.'

I glanced out of the kitchen window and for a second or two contemplated the natural beauty of the surrounding trees and shrubs. I felt a shiver of emotion as I observed the placid scene, so far removed from the one I described. 'The next thing the picnickers saw,' I continued, 'absolutely horrified them: the pilot began to dive his aircraft deliberately and directly at the Dornier. He rammed the fuselage of the bomber with one of the wings of his fighter. The two aircraft became entangled, and then broke apart as each machine entered a dramatic, out-of-control dive. Shortly afterwards the Dornier crashed on Victoria Station; the crew baled out, and landed by parachute on the Oval cricket ground. Sergeant Holmes himself landed by parachute on a steep roof, slithered across the tiles, tumbled over the guttering, and smashed into a lidless dustbin beneath. He was badly hurt, but at least he was alive.'

Sally listened intently while I told her this tale. Her small face betrayed a mixture of different emotions. Eventually she angled her head to one side, and asked with a serious expression: 'When did you say the Battle of Britain was?'

'As I mentioned, this is the fiftieth anniversary, so it was fought in the summer of 1940. The most critical day was reckoned to be September the fifteenth, so it's around then that they normally have the remembrance events.'

'But you weren't even born then were you?' asked Sally.

'No, but your grandfather was. And I'm going to London as his representative for this special anniversary.'

'Did he fly in the Battle of Britain?'

'No. He worked in the Air Ministry in London at the time.'

'Oh,' says Sally.

'He was nevertheless a very brave and clever man. He flew night fighters later in the war, after the Battle of Britain. He became an 'ace'.'

'An 'ace'?'

'He shot down more than five enemy aircraft – although the aircrew themselves don't like the term, and it isn't recognised officially.'

'What else did he do?'

'Before the war he was part of an aerobatic team; they were forerunners of the 'Red Arrows'.'

'The Red Arrows!' said Sally. After a moment of reflection, she glanced at me in a particular manner. The youngest of his eleven grandchildren, she had hardly known her paternal grandfather. Just three years old when he died, she was unaware of his natural charm, his wry humour, his reluctance to talk about his war experiences. She did not realise how, later in his life, he became visibly upset if he witnessed signs of physical violence. She did not know about his stern characteristics, his distinguished air, his lack of pomposity. Then there was his look that I knew so well, the look which could give a feeling of sudden unease; that look of sheer determination which exposed the chip of ice in his heart.

Sally didn't say another word. She didn't need to. Her expression alone made it clear that she expected to be told more about her grandparents and about their remarkable lives.

CHAPTER ONE

Hendon
Summer 1930

H e's been warned, but Flying Officer Thomas Geoffrey Pike still finds the size of the crowds unnerving. He glances at his team-mates, who seem just as bemused. The five of them walk towards their aircraft, the machines neatly aligned on the airfield grass at Hendon.

'Isn't that your wife, Tom?' one of the other pilots says as he nudges his twenty-three-year-old colleague.

Tom looks in the direction of the crowd and experiences a sudden thrill when he spots his young wife waving vigorously from the crowd-line.

'You're right – that's her.'

'Lucky fellow. How long have you been a married man?'

'Three months already.'

The pilots continue to chat as they stroll to their aircraft, but soon they split up as each man goes to his individual machine. As he nears his allotted De Havilland Moth, Tom begins to examine the outside of the aircraft. Despite the crowd's gaze, as a newly qualified flying instructor he is keen to apply the disciplines recently learnt as part of his course at the Central Flying School.

Some six years have passed since his initial training at Cranwell, but the quality of the flying instruction at Cranwell still causes Tom concern: the standards were less than impressive to his meticulous mind. After Cranwell he spent three years with No. 56 Squadron flying Grebe aircraft at Biggin Hill, just south of London. Later, he moved to the other side of London to North Weald, where he flew Siskins.

While at North Weald, Tom was invited one day, along with some fellow officers, to afternoon tea at the mansion of a local family, Sir Godfrey and Lady Thomas. The young officers saw it as quite a lark; something different, anyway. The tea party, however, presented Tom with a bonus that was quite unexpected. Among the select number invited he soon noticed a particularly attractive young lady. It did not take long for him to introduce himself to Miss Althea Elwell, who lived not far from the Thomases. And it did not take long for Miss Elwell to fall for this quiet but charismatic fighter pilot. Within months the couple were married, despite the fact that Miss Elwell was still a teenager.

With another glance at the crowd, Tom stops near his gleaming Moth for a moment; with a discerning eye he gives the machine a general look-over. He can still see Althea, an enthusiastic figure waving happily. Tom then looks across at the other pilots as they, too, check around their machines. Ground crew stand nearby, wearing special suits with 'CFS' embroidered at chest level.

'All right, sir?' asks Tom's member of ground crew. 'It's a nice day for it. Good luck, anyway.'

Tom nods gratefully as he inspects the Moth's single propeller, feeling for damage along the edges. He looks up at the engine cowling, searching for signs of oil leaks. He moves towards the wings of the biplane, stooping to inspect the fixed undercarriage for any damage, and to scrutinise the bottom wing. When satisfied, he stands upright to check the wing's upper surface before gazing up at the top wing. He feels the tension of the wires, diagonally crossed between the wings. He then walks towards the vertical struts that connect the wings and checks for signs of fabric tear where the diagonal wires are fixed to the struts. He looks up at the probes of the pitot-static system – are they clear? He moves towards the wing-end. He bends low again to inspect the area around the Royal Air Force roundel on the under surface of the bottom wing.

As Tom continues his walk-around check of the Moth, he is aware of restlessness among the crowds. The five display aircraft flew from their base at Wittering earlier, to pre-position at Hendon for the air pageant. Now, along with the other pilots no doubt, Tom is feeling the nervous tension experienced by most performing artists. The CFS team have practised their routine to perfection, but the excitement of the day still puts them on edge. The crowds, however, are unconcerned about this; they are just eager for action.

Soon, Tom clambers aboard his aircraft. As he settles into the rear cockpit, his member of ground crew is close by to assist with the strapping-in process. Tom then nimbly goes through the cockpit drills before engine start. When these have been completed, he looks across at the lead aircraft, and awaits the agreed signal.

While he waits, Tom catches sight of his wife once more, but his attention is soon diverted towards the leader when he holds his hand in the air. The other four pilots return this signal with thumbs-up signs, at which point the leader makes a rotating motion with his hand. The five pilots look inside their cockpits again as they initiate engine-start procedures. In addition, they glance at the ground crew who are standing outside, fire extinguishers at the ready.

The clattering from the Moths' engines soon begins to excite the crowds as they see signs of activity at last: 'Ooh, look! They're starting up!' Althea herself feels quite queasy as she watches.

When the pilots have completed further checks, they look across at the lead aircraft again. The awaited signal comes promptly; the procedures agreed in training seem to be working well. In spite of his sense of apprehension, Tom feels happy with the proceedings. The professional standards of CFS are to the satisfaction of his demanding mind.

In the back of that mind, though, is something rather less satisfactory; something that is in fact altogether sinister. It is just twelve years since the end of the Great War, but already there are ominous signals from Germany. The runaway inflation of the Weimar Republic of the 1920s shocked the world. So did the implications of Herr Hitler's political testament *Mein Kampf*, written while he was in prison. Tom was at Cranwell then. He and his colleagues soon realised that the skills they practised and taught might well be needed operationally in another war against Germany. Only recently Tom's station commander at Wittering briefed, 'Gentlemen, we have to confront the unhappy reality.' As the prospect of armed conflict with Germany was discussed, the officers expressed doubts about international efforts to forestall further trouble after the 'war to end all wars'. The government's lack of resolve to properly supply the armed services worried them too: the squadrons of the Royal Air Force were ill equipped to take on another war.

Tom watches the lead aircraft begin to taxi forward from its parked position, closely followed by the number two. Tom, as number three, then opens the throttle of his machine. The engine note responds immediately. The Moth starts to move forward, and Tom applies the rudder pedals positively to manoeuvre the aircraft. The wind stirred up by the machine's propeller feels stimulating as he follows the two Moths in front. As the aircraft head towards the take-off area, he glances behind to check that the other machines are following in turn.

Before long, all five aircraft begin to arrange themselves on the grass take-off strip. The lead machine faces into the wind and moves slowly forward to allow the others room to take up their pre-briefed places. When happy with his position, the leader stops; two Moths then move close to his left wing, in a swept echelon; the other two taxi up to the leader's right wing. For later Hendon pageants, the formation will add to the crowd's delight by taking off and performing aerobatics with wings tied together. Today, however, the team members are unfettered.

The leader glances left and right over his shoulders. All the pilots experience a sense of rising anticipation; they face a period of intense concentration. The Hendon air pageants are events of huge public attraction, and the crowds will thrill to the daring exploits of the aerobatic teams.

'OK, matey, let's go,' thinks Tom as he shows a thumbs-up sign.

The leader checks that the surrounding airspace is clear before giving a pronounced nod of his head. He then smoothly and progressively advances his machine's throttle. The others follow, and the surge of noise causes a thrill to rush through the crowd. Althea stands on tiptoe to watch the Moths begin their take-off roll, though she retains a sense of giddiness.

The machines move forward swiftly. The leader sets his throttle a little below maximum power to allow the others margin for adjustment. As airspeed picks up, at just the right stage, all the pilots follow the leader when he applies forward pressure on the stick. The tail skids soon become airborne. The pilots make continual small control adjustments until airspeed has increased. At the due moment they apply backward stick pressure, and the formation lifts into the air.

The concentration of the pilots remains focused on the leader. As he turns while the aircraft gain height, the leader sees the large stretch of water known as the Welsh Harp. Sited to the south-west of Hendon, the reservoir is a distinctive feature in the midst of the urban sprawl of north London to help the leader with his navigation and orientation.

Quite quickly, the leader begins to tighten his turn; Tom and his teammates feel the increasing levels of gravitational force. As the formation enters the rehearsed routine, the pilots battle to counter the effects of 'g'. 'Keep focused . . . come on Tom . . . keep fighting.' He grits his teeth against the forces. He clenches his stomach muscles and orders his mind to fight the greying-out sensation. If he's not careful, he could black out altogether. At one stage the leader inverts his aircraft as the formation flies towards the crowds. The leader experiences powerful negative 'g' forces, and he's aware of a red-out sensation in his eyes. The other machines remain upright as they follow, and eventually the leader rolls through 180 degrees again. He then applies bank for a wing-over to return to the crowd-line. When satisfied with his position, he pulls back on the stick to take the formation into a loop.

As the team continue to turn and dive, to loop and roll, they eventually come towards the end of their planned routine. 'It's gone really well today,' thinks Tom. 'At least Althea will have been

impressed.' He cannot know, of course, that his young wife is in difficulty just at that moment.

As the leader takes the formation towards the crowd-line for the
team's finale, he eases his machine down to gain airspeed. The leader
glances at the other aircraft before taking his head back in a deliberate
action. At just the right moment, he brings his head forward again to
signal with a positive nod. Immediately the five aircraft turn outwards,
the pilots pulling their machines upwards as if for a loop. Some of the
watchers break into spontaneous applause as they see what looks like
an upwards bomb-burst.

Before long the formation regroups, as practised many times, and the
leader then takes the team towards Hendon for landing. As the Moths
make their approach for touchdown, the pilots become aware once more
of the crowds along one side of the airfield.

As the pilots taxi their machines back to their parking spots after
landing, the ground crew give positioning signals. Then, just as Tom
goes through the shut-down procedure for his Moth, he becomes aware
that his particular member of ground crew is running up to the aircraft.
Tom frowns; this is uncharacteristic of the normally reliable man.

'Excuse me, sir – sorry.' The ground crew man is flustered: he knows
that Tom is meticulous and wouldn't like any out-of-line behaviour. 'It's
just that – sorry, sir – I think there's a problem with your wife.'

Tom leaps out of his machine.

'She's over there, sir, by the first-aid people.'

Tom follows the ground crew member as he runs. Near the first-aid
area they slow their pace when they see someone lying on a stretcher.
As they get closer, and as Tom recognises his wife on the stretcher, a
medical orderly looks across at him.

'It's all right, sir. Nothing serious,' says the orderly. 'She just fainted
in the heat.'

'The heat?' says Tom. 'Is it just the heat, then?'

As he crouches next to the stretcher, Tom holds his wife's hand, but
there's a sense of embarrassment between them. He tries to console her
as she mumbles apologies: her husband's moment of glory has been
spoiled by her feebleness; she feels mortified, and her eyes start to brim.
When he helps her to sit up, her pale face glances about nervously, and
eventually she holds his arm when he assists her to her feet.

There's a din of aircraft overhead from machines in a mock dogfight,
the next programmed feature of the pageant that day. The crowds roar
and clap as the pilots perform extra-daring manoeuvres. Soon, other
aspects of modern aerial warfare will be displayed: a kite balloon will
be brought down in flames. The Hendon air pageants started some ten

years ago; in four years' time they will pass into history, replaced for a further few years by the Empire Air Days. By 1939, however, the air displays will cease altogether, exchanged for aerial warfare. Perhaps in the early 1930s most folk knew in their hearts that it was just a matter of time before these aerobatic antics would be turned to deadly conflict.

Althea still clings to her husband's arm as she recovers. In the vicinity, the kite balloon rises slowly.

'Look at that balloon,' she says, gazing up at the bulky contraption.

'It's an odd-looking thing.'

'It's so huge.'

As the balloon gains height, a shadow begins to cover them.

'At least this'll give you relief from the sun,' says Tom, 'if not the noise.'

Display aircraft continue to perform aerobatic stunts.

'It's such a strange mix,' says Althea.

'All the fun of the fair, using the objects of war?'

All around, folk stare in fascination at the kite balloon as it rises above them. As the device climbs, and as Tom and Althea's shade is about to disappear, they watch the approaching shadow line with a sense of alarm. The line has a remorselessness, an inevitability about it as it creeps along the ground.

'How curious,' Althea remarks.

She is still feeling giddy as she studies the shadow gliding gently over them across the grass, and she is still clutching her husband's arm. The din and the activity around them seem so powerful and overwhelming.

The couple blink when the shadow's movement re-exposes them, and their thoughts seem to coincide.

'It's as if we're observing some portent,' says Althea.

'It does look quite ominous.'

'It looks like the shadow of war.'

'That's apt, is it not?'

'Though nobody wants to face up to it.'

'The shadow of war,' says Tom quietly as they continue to gaze up at the kite balloon. He hesitates before going on. 'I suppose that's right, though. I suppose it's got to happen eventually.'

CHAPTER TWO

The New CO
Tangmere, Sussex,
February 1941

A n awkward silence falls across the briefing room. As their new
commanding officer enters, the pilots and navigators of No. 219
(Night Fighter) Squadron get to their feet. The new commanding
officer himself, thirty-four-year-old Wing Commander Thomas
Geoffrey Pike, senses a slight air of caginess as the men shuffle from
their seats. There's a cold February atmosphere on this late afternoon at
Tangmere in West Sussex.

'Good afternoon, gentlemen,' says the new commanding officer. He
notes that a number of the aircrew are wearing dark adaptation goggles
to allow their night vision to adjust in readiness for that evening's operations. 'Sit down, please.' There's a further shuffling of chairs, then a
resumption of the awkward silence. The aircrew are painfully aware
that their new CO has come to them from a desk job at the Air Ministry.
To make matters worse, he has a reputation as an austere man who is
practically teetotal.

When Tom introduces himself, the aircrew note the rather diffident,
retiring nature of the man who is their new CO. Tom speaks with a
quiet confidence; he has the aircrew's attention, but still he senses their
attitude of doubtful restraint. The new CO starts by mentioning the
growing importance of the night fighter role in the war. As Tom
continues, he does not mince his words. It is fewer than six months
since the conclusion of the Battle of Britain, and now the Germans are
concentrating on night operations. To help counter this menace, No.
219 Squadron (motto: 'From Dusk Till Dawn') has recently taken
delivery of the latest radar-equipped Beaufighters. To date, the

squadron's performance has been disappointing, to put it mildly.

The new commanding officer's talk does not take long; under the pressures of war time is always at a premium. The CO responds to a few individual questions following his talk, then he dismisses squadron personnel for their specific duties.

For the next few days and weeks Tom immerses himself in the technical and other details of his job. He flies familiarisation sorties to consolidate flying skills on the new aircraft; in particular, it takes time to get used to the Bristol Beaufighter's fast landing speed. The aircraft has other problems when it comes to the take-off and landing procedures; pilots are especially wary of the twin-engine aircraft's tendency to swing wildly in the event of an engine failure. Once airborne, however, the Beaufighter is a robust machine, and pilots praise the aircraft's good general handling attributes and overall stout character.

Brought into service in the middle of the previous year, Tom is mindful that the Beaufighter's prototype (the Bristol type 156) first flew only the year before that, in July 1939. The aircraft, the brainchild of Mr L. G. Frise of the Bristol company, is a modified version of the Bristol Beaufort bomber, the fighter version having been rushed into wartime service.

The Beaufighter is a large machine. With a wingspan of 57 feet and 10 inches, and a length of 41 feet and 8 inches, the aircraft stands at a height of 15 feet and 10 inches. Powered by twin Bristol Hercules fourteen-cylinder radials, exchanged on some versions for the Merlin engine, the aircraft has a maximum speed of over 320 knots. It can reach an altitude in excess of 26,000 feet, weighs over 20,000lb when full, and has a range of more than 1,500 miles. Tom is aware, however, that the key feature of the Beaufighter's night fighter version – the vital difference to the conventional 'cat's eyes' night fighters – is the revolutionary airborne radar. Learning to use the AI Mark IV radar system efficiently is high on his list of priorities. This will be crucial in directing the aircrews towards enemy bombers, allowing the Beaufighter's weaponry – including four 20mm Hispano cannon and six .303 Browning machine-guns – to be brought to bear.

Tom spends time with his fellow squadron members, getting to know his engineering teams and his back-up personnel, and sitting with the aircrew as they remain in their crew room awaiting the call to action. The crew room has a gloomy atmosphere; the lighting is kept deliberately dim. The crews on immediate standby wear dark adaptation goggles, and 'Mae West' lifejackets are placed over their flying suits. The flying suits themselves are heavy duty with long zips and fur collars. Hanging around the crew room are parachute packs, their weighty buckles at the ready. Many of the aircrew smoke cigarettes, including Tom.

Gradually, the squadron members begin to appreciate that beneath their new CO's austere nature lies an immensely strong and determined character. He also has a surprisingly light touch with subordinates of all ranks, and shows a sympathy for the weaknesses of others. Tom becomes firm friends at this time with the man in charge of Tangmere's day fighter wing, the famous Wing Commander Douglas Bader, whose legs were amputated following a flying accident in 1931.

After several weeks, Tom – in consultation with his flight commanders – decides that he is fit to fly on operational sorties. The previous year, at the height of the Battle of Britain, it was the practice in dire situations to thrust new pilots prematurely into active service, sometimes with tragic results. In general, such desperate attitudes have now been modified, and commanding officers of squadrons are more circumspect. Wartime pressures remain, but COs have been briefed to ensure that their aircrew reach an operational standard before flying on active duty.

On Monday, 10 March, Tom has his last training sortie before being declared fit for operational assignments with No. 219 (Night Fighter) Squadron.

TUESDAY, 11 MARCH 1941

For his first evening on operational standby, Tom is crewed with one of the squadron's most experienced navigator/radar operators (for convenience, designated just 'navigator' or 'navrad'), Flying Officer Duart. Unlike daytime procedures, when sometimes entire squadrons are scrambled en masse to meet an incoming threat, the night fighters operate as individuals. The duty operations officer manages a rota system; crews are ordered into the air in rotation as and when they are needed to respond to enemy activity.

The time is approaching 6.30 in the evening. Other fighters from 219 Squadron have been scrambled already; Tom and Flying Officer Duart are the next-in-line crew.

Aircrews have no inkling when they might be required; they have to react as instructed by radar controllers when an enemy approach has been identified. Sometimes the crews are not needed at all. This uncertainty adds to the tense atmosphere in the crew room.

The crews have listened to the 6 p.m. news on the wireless, featuring a report on President Roosevelt's Lease-Lend agreement. In a 'fireside chat' broadcast FDR used the homely analogy of lending a neighbour a hose to put out the fire. Now the news reader has finished and the crews are being entertained by background music.

Tom shivers. He pulls the fur collar of his flying suit closer to his neck and peers through his dark adaptation goggles, trying to acclimatise himself to the shadowy, melancholy atmosphere in the crew room. He thinks he sees his navigator yawn, and he appreciates that the queasiness he can feel in the pit of his stomach is the same for everyone. Tom lifts one hand and attempts to make his goggles fit more comfortably.

'I've had a trial,' he mutters to his navigator, 'but I'm still worried about running out to the aircraft with these things on.'

'The limited vision is just about enough,' says Flying Officer Duart.

Tom seems unconvinced as he continues to fiddle anxiously with the goggles. He can just make out the coats and the aircrew jackets piled onto a stand in one corner of the room. Behind is a special rack: the rows of rifles provide a stark reminder of wartime life.

'Look on the bright side,' Flying Officer Duart adds. 'The goggles can come off as soon as we reach the aircraft. And if we do get called out tonight, we can look forward to our ration of fried eggs in the mess.'

'That's all right if you like eggs,' grumbles another member of aircrew.

The wireless dominates the ambience; feet tap in time to the nostalgic melodies. The lilting voice of Forces' Sweetheart Vera Lynn arouses a feeling of fond familiarity. At intervals, further items of news are read out by the BBC announcer. Comment is made on Hitler's ultimatum, delivered yesterday, for Yugoslavia to join the Axis forces.

At length, during a musical interlude, Tom's navigator attempts to ease the new CO's evident apprehension. 'How's your family settling in, boss? Where do they live?'

When crewed with the CO, the aircrew have been briefed that officers, in particular, can drop the use of 'sir'. A less formal mode of address may be used, especially when in the airborne environment, although personnel would never call the CO by his first name. The term 'skipper', widely used by Bomber Command, tends not to be favoured by the fighter crews.

'They live in Bedford at the moment,' Tom replies. 'Caryl, my elder daughter, is eight, and she's just started school there. School's not a problem for my other daughter, Ann. She's only two.'

'Finding a decent school is a problem nowadays.'

Another lull in conversation develops as the two listen to the wireless again, but the navigator returns to aviation matters when he next speaks.

'Who was the Air Ministry mastermind behind this idea to re-calibrate our airspeed indicators from miles per hour to knots?'

'It'll take a while to complete the change-over,' says Tom, 'but it's going to happen eventually.'

'I was reading about it in *Tee Emm* magazine. Pilot Officer Prune was telling us to be prepared.'

'It's what you call progress, I suppose.'

The sporadic conversation dries up again. The navigator tries to stifle another nervous yawn. Eventually, he says, 'We've run out of milk, boss, but I can offer you some black tea if you'd like it.'

'Thanks,' says Tom, nodding gratefully as Flying Officer Duart stumbles towards the tea bar area, his dark adaptation goggles still in place.

While Flying Officer Duart deals with the makings, the crews suddenly jump when the telephone rings. The man nearest the phone picks up the receiver.

'It's for the CO.'

Tom gropes his way across the room

'Hello . . . yes? Oh, hello, Adj.'

As Tom talks with the squadron adjutant, the rest of the aircrew begin to relax again, though most of them are feeling exhausted as a result of the strain of war operations night after night. Some aircrew try to doze, even though they remain uneasy and in a state of high mental readiness. When Tom returns to his seat after the telephone call, he realises that he, too, is very tired. He has worked long hours settling into his new job.

Tom sinks back into his seat, and he thinks about his conversation with the adjutant. It was not good news. Tom was recently the president of a board of inquiry following an ill-disciplined flying incident involving a young pilot. The pilot was found guilty, and given a minor punishment. However, even a minor punishment would not be appropriate now. The adjutant was informing Tom that the pilot had been shot down and killed in operations.

'This bloody war . . .'

Tom shakes his head as he ponders another wasted life. He sinks lower into his chair. The effect of the dark adaptation goggles adds to a growing soporific feeling. Another haunting wartime melody sings out from the crew-room wireless.

'The old days seem like a different world now,' he thinks.

Tom begins to reflect on his early life, and the difficulties faced by his family. His father died following a freak accident, and his mother struggled to bring up three boys on her own. Tom's middle brother, Bill, was making a success of his army career. Tragedy, however, had hit the family a second time: the eldest son, Roy, a scientist, died from pneumonia shortly after his arrival in California. 'Such a disastrous loss of a brilliant mind,' thinks Tom. Then his thoughts pick up on his time in North Africa some three years before the start of the war. They were such pleasant times; Althea and young Caryl had been so happy with their life in Egypt. The flying was exceptionally good. Tom was a flying instructor with No. 4 Flying Training School, based at Abu Sueir near Cairo. His duties took him on flights all over the Middle East, including Jordan, Jerusalem, Baghdad and Sinai.

Tom smiles to himself when he remembers some of the escapades. There were few flying regulations in those days, and low-flying opportunities were pretty much unrestricted. He still has the photograph taken from another machine as he flew his aircraft at low level over the Gulf of Aqaba. In the spring of 1936, Tom flew with some others on a detachment to Baghdad. The crews landed at Rutbah after an early start, and Tom remembers the breakfast that morning, taken as a picnic as they sat beside their aircraft. Later, the crews visited some of the bazaars of Baghdad, and they were intrigued by the multitude of mosques, including the Blue Mosque and the Marjan Mosque. Tom was fascinated by the basic lifestyle of folk in Baghdad, exemplified by the sight of horse-traps plodding through the streets. He also recalls some of the spectacular flying in Egypt itself. In particular, he remembers the Colossi of Memnon, the giant figures striving to weather their passage through the ages. Then there was the incredible Montaza Palace with its eccentric towers and unusual forests in the grounds. Quite routinely the pilots flew past the Pyramids, which looked so dramatic from the air. Sometimes they organised formations of aircraft to overfly Abu Sueir. It was almost like the old days at Hendon.

The telephone rings again. The aircrew shift irritably in their chairs; if this is part of having the CO on standby with them, then it is unwelcome. As Tom manoeuvres towards the telephone once more, there are a few murmurs of dissent. Tom himself feels disinclined to take the call, especially if it is more bad news.

As Tom begins his telephone conversation, his navigator places a mug of tea on a nearby table. The CO nods in gratitude; he can just make out the navigator returning to his seat. As he speaks on the phone, Tom tries to adjust his goggles, peering at the tea mug. He feels thirsty; the tea will be welcome, even without milk. He reaches out to pick up the mug. The tiresome goggles make even the simplest action seem awkward. As he fumbles for the mug, he suddenly stops moving and his conversation is abruptly interrupted.

There's an unearthly din about the scramble bell as it clangs. It makes an almost ghostly sound, especially when it is rung with such urgency. Simultaneously, Tom hears the duty operations officer cry out, 'CO and Flying Officer Duart, Beaufighter number 2083 – scramble, scramble, scramble!'

CHAPTER THREE

Enemy within Range

Tom hastily replaces the telephone receiver. He then manoeuvres across the crew room towards the door, vaguely aware of soothing background sounds from the wireless. Tom's navigator has already leapt to his feet; both aircrew keep on their dark adaptation goggles as they move through the room as nimbly as they can.

As the men hurry outside, instantly their senses are assaulted by the chilly air. The aircrew impulsively tear off their goggles as they dash towards their waiting Beaufighter, number R2083. In the dark environment the aircraft's black, sinister outline is virtually invisible to the untrained eye.

The external checks were performed earlier, so the aircrew head directly for their entrance hatches on the underside of the aircraft which lead to their individual cockpits. Flying Officer Duart, just ahead of Tom, eases into the cramped space of his cockpit, placed on the top fuselage between the wings and the tailplane. Tom climbs the steps of his entrance hatch, then moves forward to his separate cockpit in the nose of the aircraft, 18 feet in front of the navigator. As soon as they reach their cockpits, the crew stow their goggles. The airfield's blackout safeguards their carefully prepared night vision, but even so there's always the worry of a random white light appearing inadvertently. Inside the cockpit, red lighting preserves their night vision, although the crew still set the level of brightness as low as possible.

Quickly, Tom straps himself in. He then dons his flying helmet and oxygen mask before checking round the cockpit. When satisfied, he sets the engine controls at their pre-start position: throttles at three-quarters of an inch open . . . carburettor air intake heat controls at cold . . . cowling grills open . . .

The ground crew reached the Beaufighter just ahead of the aircrew. Sometimes ordered to start engines before the arrival of the air- crew, tonight the ground crew watch the pilot expectantly, ready to assist him with the start procedures. When instructed by Tom, the ground personnel turn each three-bladed propeller for at least two revolutions before they operate the engine Ki-gass priming pumps. As the men move about, Tom is aware of flickers of faint light from the special red lenses fitted to their torches.

Soon, Tom is ready to start the Beaufighter's first engine. He ensures the ground starter battery is plugged in, switches on the ignition, then, having signalled to the ground crew, he presses the starter and booster- coil push-buttons. Immediately there's a clamour as the first engine fires up. The ground crew remain close by, ready to continue the priming process until the engine runs smoothly on the carburettor. 'Come on, come on . . .' Tom impatiently times one minute, then he gradually opens the throttle. He sets the engine revolutions at 1,000 rpm to allow the engine to warm up.

When satisfied with the first engine's readings, Tom quickly runs through additional checks. He gives a further signal to the ground crew, then begins the second engine's start routine.

Eventually, when both engines have stabilised, Tom runs through the before-take-off checks: hydraulic power lever on . . . inner tank fuel cocks set to on, suction balance off . . . flaps set at fifteen degrees down . . . As soon as he has completed the checks, he gives a prearranged visual signal (usually a flash of the navigation lights) to air traffic control. The radio is used sparingly by the individual night fighters; the system of as few transmissions as possible reduces the chances of interception by eavesdropping enemy agents.

A narrow beam of green light from the Aldis lamp in the air traffic control tower soon gives Tom clearance to taxi towards the main runway. He moves the Beaufighter cautiously. The taxiway is unlit, but his painstakingly prepared night vision allows him to make out the line of the taxiway as he progresses. Eventually, as he approaches the Tangmere runway, a further green signal from air traffic control gives him clearance to line up and take off.

Meticulous as ever, while he manoeuvres the Beaufighter onto the runway Tom rechecks certain items before take-off: elevator trim tabs confirmed at take-off . . . rudder and aileron at neutral . . . propeller speed controls fully forward.

As soon as he's aligned with the runway, he applies the brakes. Tom now opens up the throttles against the brakes. He ensures both engines respond evenly before he throttles back again.

'All set to go?' Tom speaks briskly to his navigator.

'All set, boss.'

Tom releases the brakes and begins to advance both throttles. At once there's a surge of acceleration and a roar from the potent engines. As Tom continues to push the throttles forward to their full power position he keeps them evenly matched, and he is pressed against the back of his cockpit seat as the machine gains airspeed.

During the take-off roll a line of 'dimlights' (a mix of paraffin flares and battery-operated 'glim' lights) marks the runway, and Tom monitors the flight instruments; as soon as he's airborne, he will rely on these instruments implicitly. In the blackout conditions, there are no external references to assist with orientation other than the natural light from the moon and the stars.

Directly the Beaufighter's wheels leave the runway, Tom concentrates on the airfield's correct departure procedures. He focuses on accurate instrument flying to ensure the wartime routine is followed precisely. As soon as possible, he goes through the after-take-off checks: undercarriage up . . . raise flaps at 300 feet . . . hydraulic power lever to off . . . maintain 150 knots (172mph) recommended climb speed . . .

At a predetermined height, Tom changes from Tangmere's air traffic control frequency to a fighter control frequency. Radio silence is not practical any more; the vital information from the fighter controller at the GCI (ground control intercept) station has to be given to the aircrews. Nevertheless, the messages are delivered in clipped terms and kept as brief as possible. Whenever feasible, codes are used to deceive enemy eavesdroppers.

Tom is instructed by the fighter controller to maintain a height of 16,000 feet, and to take up a combat patrol (sometimes, rather inappropriately, called a 'standing patrol'). He has to fly in a box-shaped orbit in the vicinity of a ground beacon that shines a light of specific colour. He is trying out a new system which, if successful, will be brought into general use; he must fly a radius of some five miles from the beacon, in a left-hand pattern. Indications of enemy raiders have been spotted across the Channel, and Tom will be given individual instructions when the bombers come closer.

Sometimes, following a scramble order, the aircrew go directly into urgent, aggressive air combat. It is becoming less usual, though; normally the ground radar will give warning of approaching air-raids. On this particular mid-March night, Tom and his navigator will orbit for an hour before entering into combat.

In the absence of immediate action, the crew mentally wind down from their high state of tension, and while they wait they use the aircraft's intercommunication system to speak to each other. 'This AI seems OK tonight,' says the navigator at one point. As he checks the AI (airborne intercept) radar's control switches, the navigator is conscious of his pilot's limited experience on the Beaufighter. Nevertheless, he knows that the new CO has the advantage of a technical background, and that he has made every effort to learn about the complex workings of the aircraft and its new radar system.

As Tom peers outside his cockpit from time to time, he's reminded of how wartime Britain seems so eerie at night. The entire area is in blackout. However, when the raiders eventually decide to cross the Channel, the spooky darkness will be broken quite promptly. The scene will appear dramatic from an airborne platform; the aircrews will watch with grievous fascination when the searchlights and the anti-aircraft artillery start up. Criss-cross patterns of illumination will brighten the night skies in a picturesque and desperate scene of affray. The follow-on sight of exploding bombs, and resulting fires, will have a surreal semblance when viewed from the air. The aircrew's minds, though, will be filled with dread when they think about the reality of what's happening below them.

Tom maintains the Beaufighter in the combat patrol pattern; he seldom speaks to the ground radar unit at this stage. The aircrew, though, continue to chat sporadically while they wait for further orders from the fighter controller. At one point the navigator says jauntily, 'My wife was ticked off by the ARP the other night. She'd forgotten her gas mask.' Tom wonders about this domestic banter at such an hour. But then life has to go on. Perhaps it is good to relieve the tension.

Tom adjusts his tight-fitting oxygen mask; soon he will make another turn to maintain the patrol box. As he looks in the direction of London from time to time, he recalls his experiences at the Air Ministry during the Battle of Britain. Often it proved impossible to travel home; he simply slept in his office at the Air Ministry, where he worked in the Directorate of Organisation. When he did manage the journey home, Tom was impressed by the way in which ordinary folk dealt with the aftermath of bombing. He passed many scenes of individual tragedy, but invariably people somehow seemed to cope. After a heavy air-raid there was always the incessant ring of burglar alarms, the crunch of glass inside and outside buildings, and such an unpleasant smell everywhere. And the odour of burning buildings and leaking gas would combine with another sense, less tangible perhaps but equally repugnant: the sense of shock and terror.

Tom glances outside as he initiates another turn. To the south, in times of peace, he would have been able to see the coastal outline of southern Britain. He would have identified lights marking the metropolis of Bognor Regis, with Worthing and Brighton to the east. To the north, Tom would have sighted Guildford, before the southern outreaches of London itself. In the wartime blackout, however, everywhere is darkened. Ahead of his aircraft, in an easterly direction, is the eastern part of Sussex, and beyond that is the county of Kent, areas guarded by other fighter squadrons. The entire scene is embraced by a giant shadow.

'Standby for trade . . . bandits approaching at angels one five.'

The terse message from the fighter controller focuses the minds of Tom and his navigator in an instant. Tom advances the Beaufighter's throttles as he follows the new procedures, which require him to achieve a height of 2,000 feet above the enemy raid. The navigator rechecks the settings on his airborne radar. Tom makes a further worried movement of his oxygen mask, and he makes occasional throttle adjustments while the Beaufighter gains altitude towards 17,000 feet.

'Make your vector zero seven five degrees . . . clear to smack.'

The word 'smack' is a coded order to the fighters: Tom's Beaufighter has been authorised to attack and destroy radar-identified enemy raiders. As he follows the controller's instructions, Tom quickly goes through pre-combat checks: confirm cannons . . . gun button selection made . . . check ring-sight . . .

Suddenly, the crew see that the veil of blackout has been violated. In the far distance towards Kent, excited beams of light start to strike at the night skies. The faraway light is relatively faint, but even so the crew's night vision inevitably begins to deteriorate at this stage.

'Maintain this heading . . . the bandits are at angels one five still.'

As Tom acknowledges this call, he's aware that the palms of his hands are quite damp, despite the cold. His mind, however, seems to take on a startling clarity. With calculated coolness and precision, he follows the controller's instructions. In the distance, the searchlight beams persistently probe and dance. Occasionally, the beams reveal the generally clear weather conditions of the night, although Tom notes a few scattered clouds at medium level.

'Your assigned target's range is thirty miles.'

The aircrew check and double-check their weapons and radar equipment, aware that in just a few minutes they'll be committed to air combat. Their training is about to be put to the ultimate test; they must not fail now. Of their many fears, a fear of failure, of letting down their colleagues, is probably the hardest to bear. The equipment has to be on top form. Both the crew have to be too.

'Stand by . . . your target's now at a range of twenty-five miles. Turn right ten degrees. Maintain present altitude.'

Tom concentrates on flying as accurately as possible. The probing of the searchlights appears closer now as large areas of the night sky begin to be illuminated by the crazy capers of brilliance. Occasionally, a barrage-balloon's bulky outline is revealed. Tom marginally increases the level of brightness of his red cockpit lighting.

'Your target's approaching fifteen miles. Turn right another ten degrees.'

Tom glances at the moon as he applies this next minor correction; its ghostly light seems so insipid, overpowered by the searchlights. Having made the demanded correction, he holds the new heading as precisely as possible; he has to facilitate the controller's complex task. Events from now on will develop at an accelerating pace, although the passage of time will feel unreal: in some ways quick, in others slow.

'Turn starboard a further ten degrees. I repeat, your clearance to smack has been authorised.' The controller's tone is insistent as he confirms Tom's orders. 'Your assigned target is now at ten miles. Maintain this vector. The bandit's height remains at angels one five.'

As Tom follows the commands, he experiences an ever-growing sense of apprehension. His mouth feels dry. He nervously runs through the pre-combat checks once more, and rechecks around his cockpit: engine settings, temperatures, pressures, oxygen, fuel.

'Your target is approaching a range of five miles. Stand by for right turn. Stand by . . . turn right NOW. Make your heading two eight five degrees.'

The controller's voice has taken on a new urgency. Tom feels a curious mix of emotions. He tries to focus on precise flying and turns the Beaufighter towards the enemy machine he will soon trail from astern. During the turn he advances the Beaufighter's throttles, anxious not to end up too far behind.

'You're clear to flash weapon.'

With this instruction, the controller tells the navigator to bring the Beaufighter's 'AI' radar into action from standby mode. For operational reasons, the radar is not normally brought into use until an appropriate stage in the interception.

'Stand by. You're now on the same vector as the bandit. He's two miles ahead. Stand by. You're rapidly overtaking.'

Tom throttles back immediately. As he checks his flight instruments, he forces himself to fly accurately. He is conscious of his lack of combat experience, and he is well aware of the dangers of inaccurate night flying induced by exuberance in the heat of battle.

As the navigator tries to identify the intruder's blip on the AI radar, and as the Beaufighter draws closer to the enemy, the controller continues to monitor his own radar screen. By now, Tom has slowed his aircraft, bringing the rate of closure under control. So far the bandit has taken no evasive action, apparently oblivious of the Beaufighter's presence. Tom searches ahead, desperately trying to spot the enemy machine.

'Radar contact!' cries the navigator suddenly. He tries to sound calm, but his voice seems breathless with excitement. 'He's seven to eight hundred yards ahead, and he's below us. Hold this heading, and descend as you continue to close.'

Tom peers ahead, but he still has no visual sight of the enemy.

'Turn left . . . roll out there . . . reduce speed, a little more.'

Tom's navigator gives a series of minor instructions as the Beaufighter draws closer. Tom monitors the airspeed, anxious to avoid another dangerous overtaking scene. He knows he will have to stalk the bandit from astern for several minutes, advancing with stealth.

'The bandit's range is four hundred and fifty yards.'

Tom scans the night sky looking for the enemy, though his carefully prepared night vision is still impaired by the searchlight activity. As he squints ahead, and as he manoeuvres the Beaufighter, he feels increasing frustration at his inability to spot the enemy machine.

However, by now the manoeuvres have placed the moon behind the Beaufighter in a useful position. The faint lunar glow helps Tom, and he begins to make out the shape of an aircraft. At last he is able to identify an enemy machine grimly profiled against cloud, although he must still rely on the Beaufighter's radar system and the efficiency of his navigator's instructions.

'Turn right ten degrees. The bandit's now at three hundred and fifty yards . . . still closing.'

In a short while, the enemy will be at optimum firing range for the Beaufighter's cannon.

With the navigator's next report – 'The bandit's approaching two hundred and fifty yards; his range is slowly reducing' – Tom has confirmation that he's within firing range. By this stage, the Beaufighter has been in pursuit of the target from astern for eight minutes.

The pale moon gives a deceptive impression of calm, but one feature of that dreadful night-time atmosphere is far from spurious: all around is a palpable sense of fear – an ugly and primeval type of fear.

As the bandit holds its course, and as the Beaufighter continues to shadow the machine, Tom makes a last check with his navigator. For a second or two both men experience a sense of hesitation: have they taken all necessary actions? Are they prepared – will their training have prepared them for what is about to occur? They must act soon: the enemy machine is now clearly silhouetted against cloud.

The crew's undoubted commitment to duty is confirmed when the navigator hears his pilot's next call.

'Here goes,' cries Tom. 'Opening fire!'

CHAPTER FOUR

The Fieriest
of Baptisms

A harsh vibration rocks the Beaufighter's airframe, and Tom sniffs the sour odour of explosives. He sees a flash, followed by a burst of sparks. He holds the gun button down for a short burst, then releases it, and maintains his position in order to observe. As arcs of fire from the mayhem ahead illuminate the sky, the sudden dazzles begin to spoil his night vision. It's still good enough, though, for him to see a dark item of wreckage hurtle towards the Beaufighter. He applies a high angle of bank and simultaneously pulls back on the stick. He feels high 'g' forces as he takes this emergency avoiding action, and when he next catches sight of the enemy the bomber is below him, on the right side. Flames some three feet in length are stretching from the aircraft's starboard engine.

As Tom holds a nose-up attitude, he and his navigator try to keep the enemy in sight. However, the Beaufighter's altimeter is showing a fast rate of climb and within moments the enemy is out of view. The Beaufighter continues to climb, and as the airspeed decreases the machine starts to shake as it approaches stall speed. The airframe vibration becomes more pronounced as the airspeed and rate of climb reduce even further, and soon Tom finds himself in a deteriorating scenario – 'nose up and nothing much on the clock'. Within moments he is struggling to keep control of the aircraft.

Tom has to concentrate on his flight instruments. His night vision has been damaged, and the light from the moon and the stars is too feeble to be of use; he has to rely on the information inside the cockpit. This affirms his exact height, his reducing rate of climb, and his low airspeed. He focuses on the artificial horizon, the altimeter, the airspeed indicator, the turn and slip indicator; he has to depend on these instruments, combined with smooth and judicious flying, in order to recover.

As the aircraft shakes persistently, his instrument scan is disciplined, and he applies the basic techniques deeply instilled over the years. The airspeed indicator hovers at a dangerously low reading as he repeats to himself: 'Don't over-control . . . easy does it . . . watch the attitude . . . watch the airspeed . . . recover from the stall . . . avoid a spin developing . . .' Tom positively manoeuvres the flying controls as he follows the stall recovery procedure. The navigator, meanwhile, braces himself in preparation for a possible bale-out. Tom's hands slickly move the throttles to the correct position. 'Hold it there . . . hold it . . .'

Tom experiences a rush of adrenalin when he realises that the engines are not reacting. He rechecks the engine instruments. They look wrong: their position is unusual, out of line. As he fights against rising angst he realises that he has a problem affecting not just one but both of the engines, he checks the engine instruments once again. The Beaufighter still shudders and wallows, but for Tom there is a further grave difficulty: during the violent manoeuvres, both of the engines have cut out. He is flying without power. His aircraft is now a glider.

Tom holds the Beaufighter's controls in the stall recovery position. He has to fly with finesse; rough movements could induce a spin. 'Steady . . . easy does it . . .' Gradually, as the nose of the machine begins to drop, the airspeed builds again and the airframe vibration subsides. Now he has to keep the nose lowered. He dives to pick up airspeed, and the flight instruments start to indicate a high rate of descent.

'Stand by.' Tom is uncharacteristically sharp when he speaks with his navigator. 'Both engines are out. Stand by for the emergency start drills.' As he continues to dive the Beaufighter, he then calls, 'Both throttles are closed. The ignitions are on. Feathering push-button – pressed. Releasing at eight hundred to a thousand rpm.' Tom is still diving the aircraft, pegging the airspeed as he monitors the flight instruments. At opportune moments he searches for the enemy machine, but sees no signs. His priority, though, is to regain control of the Beaufighter, his task not helped by the activities of adjacent searchlights. Conscious of the dangers of disorientation, and with the brightness of his cockpit lighting selected to maximum, he continues to focus on the readings of the flight instruments.

Gradually, with dreadful sluggishness, the engine instruments indicate a re-start. Tom watches them with caution, and when ready he advances the throttles. 'Easy does it. Don't move them too rapidly.' He moves the throttles anxiously as he tests the initial reaction. When this seems normal, he advances them some more.

By now, the Beaufighter has lost a considerable amount of height. However, as Tom advances the throttles, he's at last able to pull out of the dive. A sense of overwhelming relief floods through his body. The situation seemed protracted, almost an eternity, but in truth the whole incident lasted just minutes.

Now, as he returns to normal flight, Tom has to do several things as a matter of urgency. He rechecks the instruments: engine temperatures over 5°C . . . cylinder temperatures of 120°C . . . oil pressures above 60 psi. He tests the engine response with judicious throttle movements, and he verifies his position and height with his navigator. He tells the controller that visual contact with the enemy machine has been lost.

The two aircrew can now resume their search for the enemy aircraft. Tom turns the Beaufighter and adjusts his height. The controller, however, confirms that he no longer has the intruder on radar. 'And we can't see anything visually,' says Tom. Even so, the aircrew continue to search the surrounding area, convinced that the enemy machine has crashed. Confirmation by visual sighting remains their aim, but this proves impracticable. Eventually Tom speaks with the fighter controller again.

'We've still no visual contact with this bandit. Do you have further trade?'

'Nothing at the moment,' says the controller, 'no further trade at present. Stand by for further orders.'

The crew keep searching until the controller says, 'You're instructed to return to base now.'

'That's it, then, boss,' says the navigator. 'We'll be credited with a probable, but not confirmed.'

Tom turns his Beaufighter towards Tangmere airfield as he follows the wartime procedures for recovery to base. The searchlight activity in the area has quietened already; the enemy raids have disappeared, seemingly swallowed into the darkness.

The aircrew seem immersed in their own thoughts as they recover to Tangmere. It is wartime, and drastic situations are not so unusual. Nevertheless, Tom's navigator cannot avoid a growing sense of admiration for his pilot. 'The new CO's just survived the fieriest of baptisms,' he muses.

When Tom spots the dim paraffin lights that mark Tangmere's runway, he concentrates on precise flying as he makes the approach for landing. Airspeed and height control in particular have to be flown accurately, especially during the final stages before touchdown. The Beaufighter's characteristic awkwardness in the event of an engine failure during the landing run inevitably plays on the crew's minds.

At last, however, the aircrew feel the relief of terra firma as the aircraft lands without further mishap. Tom taxies the Beaufighter back to the dispersal area of 219 Squadron and parks the machine under the guidance of the ground crew. He then completes the shut-down checks before he and his navigator stiffly climb out of their cockpits. As they do so, they ruminate on the fact that had events worked out differently, the end of their flight would not have been so straightforward: their descent would have been by parachute or worse.

The two men leave their aircraft and walk to the 219 Squadron set-up to speak to the engineering staff, then to the squadron intelligence officer. The aircrew will file a combat report form 'F', classified secret, in the presence of the intelligence officer.

'Gentlemen, please sit down,' says the intelligence officer, standing up as he directs the CO and his navigator to chairs in the small office. 'Let's get started right away. I'll do the writing, if you could please try to remember as many details as possible. I'll note down the basics first. The date is the eleventh of March 1941. You're with B Flight of 219 Squadron, and the aircraft was Beaufighter R2083. Now, how many enemy aircraft did you engage?'

'Just one,' says Tom. 'We were controlled by Durrington – callsign Flintlock.'

'OK. Where and when was the engagement?'

'In the Guildford–Horsham area,' says the navigator, 'and we were airborne from Tangmere at 1910 hours. We were held for approximately one hour before we were vectored on to a target. The attack took place at 2030 hours.'

As the aircrew carry on with their debrief, the intelligence officer notes down the details in an impassive, routine way. Nevertheless, as the story unfolds, his increasing sense of esteem for the new CO becomes apparent. It was, after all, the CO's first operational sortie on the squadron, and the new boss had been with them just a matter of weeks.

There is a knock at the door.

'Come in,' calls the intelligence officer.

'Excuse me, sir,' says the flight sergeant from engineering.

'What have you got for us, Flight?'

'Just confirming that forty-one cannon rounds were fired, sir. No signs of weapon malfunction.'

'And the engines?' says Tom.

'We're still checking them out, sir. I gather you had a bit of bother.'

'You could put it that way,' says Tom. 'We had to take evasive action. The aircraft stalled during the manoeuvres, and both engines cut out.'

'As I say, we're still running checks, but the aircraft seems OK.'

'Thank you, Flight,' says the intelligence officer, and the flight sergeant leaves to return to his duties. 'Now, sir, can you confirm the range at which you opened fire, and the estimated length of burst?'

'I estimate the range was around one hundred to two hundred yards,' Tom replies, 'and judging by the number of rounds fired, the length of burst must have been about one second.'

The intelligence officer nods as he writes down these details. On one side of the office, a wall clock indicates 2145 hours. The aircrew remain quiet as they watch the intelligence officer complete combat report form 'F', and they overhear snatches of wartime repartee drifting through from the operations room: 'Bandits were at angels one five . . . Beau handed over by Beetle to Flintlock . . . pilot instructed to buster . . . he then called tally-ho . . . navigator flashed weapon when instructed . . .'

'We've just about finished, sir,' says the intelligence officer at length. 'But one more thing. What were the weather conditions like?'

'No problem. The weather was good, and the moon was behind us – we saw the machine clearly silhouetted. He held a steady heading, and we saw his shadow on clouds.'

'Sir?'

The intelligence officer gazes at the new CO, who seems about to say something else. The intelligence officer waits patiently. His new boss has been through an astonishing ordeal; he needs time to sort out his thoughts. It's only natural. At last, Tom breaks the uncomfortable silence in the room.

'Nothing else,' he says. 'That's it, I suppose. Nothing else to report.'

The intelligence officer continues to watch the new CO closely. A shrewd man, thrown into the war like so many others, the intelligence officer is doing a job far removed from his proposed vocation in civil life. In his wartime experiences so far, he has met a number of unlikely characters, quite different from the types he would expect to come across in his civilian occupation. But he is struck just now by the look on the new CO's face. It is such an uncommon look. The intelligence officer feels almost unnerved by a sense of sheer determination.

'Thank you, sir,' he says. 'That'll be all for now. I'll get this report typed up right away.'

And as he continues to gaze at the new CO, and as comprehension grows in his mind, the intelligence officer begins to understand just how exceptional is the nature of the man before him.

CHAPTER FIVE

Three Nights Later

'If you wouldn't mind, sir,' says the squadron adjutant, 'this'll be the last thing for you to sign this evening.'

'Let's hope it keeps Group HQ happy,' says Tom as he places his signature.

'They're being pressed by Fighter Command.'

'Fighter Command are no doubt being pressed by the Air Ministry. They're all looking for encouraging statistics. I know what it's like. The government is desperate for good news at the moment.'

'They might get some comfort from these figures. But squadron life must seem a bit humdrum for you after working in the Air Ministry?'

'I could say something about being brought down to earth with a bump. But perhaps that wouldn't be appropriate.'

The adjutant laughs, and says, 'Well, it's good to have you on the squadron, sir.'

Along with the rest of 219 Squadron, he has developed a telling respect for the new commanding officer. Just a few weeks ago, when squadron personnel showed their doubts about this ex-Air Ministry individual thrust upon them, the atmosphere was uncomfortable. Matters are different now.

'I must abandon the paperwork soon, though,' says Tom, 'and get ready for this evening's ops. Have you seen my DAGs anywhere?'

'Here they are, sir.' As the adjutant picks up the CO's dark adaptation goggles, he asks, 'Can I get you some tea before you start duty?'

'That's a kind thought, but my nav and I are about to go to the officers' mess for a night-flying supper.'

'Well, good luck, sir.'

'With the officers' mess or the night operations?'

'I suspect you may need it for both.'

'No doubt,' Tom says with a chuckle.

As the commanding officer leaves his office and makes for the crew room, he carries with him his flying gear. In the crew room, a number of aircrew sprawl in armchairs; some smoke nervously as they wait for a scramble order. It is just after sunset, and those on immediate standby wear dark adaptation goggles; others, programmed for later, perform secondary squadron duties. The wireless, as usual, is switched on, a constant source of contact with the outside world.

'Are you joining us for a night-flying supper, sir?' asks Tom's navigator, Flying Officer Duart.

'Definitely.'

'The bus leaves in five minutes.'

When the aircrew make their way outside, they head for a special aircrew coach, a converted Bedford van. As the group is driven to the mess by a WAAF driver, all are conscious of a subdued mood caused by the gloomy blackout conditions. Even so, there is still intermittent conversation and laughter during the short journey, though the crews have been briefed to resist the temptation, however enjoyable, to put off the WAAF driver. She has to struggle with the faint beams of light from the van's specially modified headlights. Few other vehicles are on the road, but she still faces hazards. When they reach the mess, the crews have to follow strict procedures to prevent stray light from breaching blackout rules.

Once safely inside the building, Tom and his navigator make for an anteroom where they read newspapers before the start of their night-flying meal. The newspapers, thin editions priced at one penny each, feature photographs of the Prime Minister inspecting bomb-damaged buildings. Readers are reminded of Churchill's remarks the previous year about the possible German occupation of London: 'If they come to London, I shall take a rifle – I'm not a bad shot – I will put myself in a pill-box at the bottom of Downing Street, and shoot until I have no more ammunition, and then they can damn well shoot me.' There are articles about yesterday's Italian offensive against Albania, personally directed by Mussolini. The editorials comment on the abortive Italian invasion of Greece in the autumn of 1940, and the columnists discuss last week's capture of an Italian stronghold by Haile Selassie's troops in Burye, Abyssinia. Advertisements encourage a patriotic population to put money into War Savings. Folk are urged to buy Hovis bread, Cuticura Powder and Bird's Custard. Brooke Bond Tea retailers are reminded that if they run out of permitted quantities they should apply to the local food office for supplementary permits. Customers should 'walk the Barratt way', and use the Scholl foot comfort service. For the height of wartime luxury, people are urged to buy Cadbury's chocolate. 'Assuming you can get hold of any,' mutters Tom's navigator.

'Shall we see what's on the night-flying menu?' says Tom.

'Spam stew, for a change?'

'Or Spam rissoles?'

'Spam dumplings, even.'

A cheerful atmosphere permeates the dining room, and outbursts of laughter reflect the typical humour of service folk. Tom and his navigator choose their seats, and are served by a mess steward.

'What can I get you gentlemen this evening?'

'What can you offer us?'

'We have lamb hot-pot, or Spam fritters.'

'Have you any fresh eggs?'

'A few, sir,' says the steward. 'But I'm afraid that supplies are very limited. The fresh eggs at the moment are restricted to those aircrew who've just completed operational flights.'

'Then I'm afraid we don't qualify yet.'

As the steward leaves, Tom chats with a squadron leader seated next to him.

'That was a good party last weekend,' says the squadron leader. 'These lunchtime drinks do's make a welcome respite. The ladies looked very elegant.'

'They do remarkably well.'

'My wife makes most of her own dresses these days.'

'So does mine.'

'Veg, sir?' A steward leans across after Tom has been served with a portion of lamb, and Tom watches as a pile of reconstituted potatoes is placed next to carrots and turnips. 'Tea or coffee, sir?'

'Tea for me, please,' says Tom. 'I can't stand that Camp coffee stuff.'

'Are you on duty tonight, sir?' asks the squadron leader.

'Later on, after supper,' says Tom.

'How soon do you have to put on the DAGs?'

'It takes about half an hour for the eyes to fully adjust to the dark. We normally put them on as soon as we get back to the squadron.'

'May I ask which was your first squadron?'

'Number fifty-six.'

'The squadron of Albert Ball VC?'

'Yes, that's right. A remarkable pilot, tragically killed in 1917. I joined the squadron eight years later, at the end of 1925, after my two years of training at Cranwell. Fifty-six Squadron flew Grebes when I joined them – rather elementary machines compared to those of today.'

'No night flying in those days, I suppose?'

'Not very much. It was basic stuff; we operated using techniques learnt from the first war.'

'I've been reading about that, and some of the flying escapades. It seems such a contrasting scene nowadays. Attitudes are very different.'

'Flying was a new art then, and the crews, friend or foe, seemed to operate at a more personal level.'

'On both sides they knew who was who. I've been reading about a brave chap called Bradley. His story illustrates this.'

'I don't think I've heard . . .'

'He was a navy man: Royal Naval Air Service. He was the CO of a squadron based in the Aegean, and his opposite number was the German ace Eschwege. One time the two were engaged in aerial combat when the German started to gain, and Bradley ended up in Eschwege's gun-sights. However, the German knew who he was fighting, so he held his fire. In a subsequent confrontation it was Commander Bradley who had Eschwege in his gun-sights, but again nothing happened. Some time later, Eschwege crashed over British lines. When he heard about this, Bradley organised a full military funeral, and even made arrangements to drop his opponent's belongings back to his own people.'

'There was honour and respect between foes then, but that seems to have evaporated nowadays.'

The two men continue to talk as they consume their meal. Tom's schedule, however, is strict. Time, as usual, is limited, and he is hardly surprised when Flying Officer Duart reminds him, 'The bus will be ready for us soon, sir. We should get going, I'm afraid.'

'Good luck with tonight's operations, sir,' says the squadron leader as Tom stands up to leave.

Back in the 219 Squadron building, the aircrew make directly for the crew room to join colleagues already on duty. With dark adaptation goggles fitted, reading is not practical; listening to the wireless is the main source of interest. The aircrew sit around, affected by a predictable mix of anxiety and boredom. There is intermittent chat, but generally the crews just listen to *Forces' Favourites*, *Cabaret Time*, and military bands. Now, during *Religious Reflection*, an army padre is speaking calmly about a ranting speech of Hitler's. 'Hitler should speak less, and listen more,' says the padre. 'He should appreciate the gifts granted by the good Lord in a less presumptive way. Hitler should remember this reality: we've been given two ears, but only one mouth.'

There's muffled laughter from the aircrew. 'You tell 'em, padre!'

'Cigarette, boss?' Flying Officer Duart offers a half-used pack.

'Thanks.'

'Waiting around like this can give you the spooks,' the navigator continues. He speaks in a confidential manner against the background music. 'There was a story on the wireless the other day about an air traffic control tower reckoned to be haunted.'

'These stories get around.'

'This one started when an aircraft was on its way back from a bombing raid. The pilot was told to overshoot, but despite his objections, saying that his machine was badly shot up, the controller insisted. As he was setting up for another approach, the pilot started to lose height on the downwind leg. Just before crashing, he vented his feelings to the controller.' The navigator slowly drags on his cigarette before continuing. 'There were no survivors, and shortly after the accident, bizarre happenings were reported by locals. Odd characters were seen to walk up to the control tower with parachutes tucked under their arms. One time, an airman working in the tower saw aircrew enter through the main door. When he challenged them, there was no reply; the aircrew merely walked straight through, stepped into an adjoining room, then disappeared. They had to post the airman to another unit. He was convinced he'd witnessed the restless souls of that bomber crew.'

Tom and his navigator are silent for a time as they ponder this. They reflect on other ghostly tales of wartime aviation. Even Dowding was rumoured to be in spiritual contact with some of his fighter pilots lost during the Battle of Britain.

At length, though, Tom says, 'We'd better not get too carried away with all this.' He adjusts his goggles. 'I think I'll make some tea. Would you like some?'

'Thanks, boss.'

Tom squints through his goggles as he copes with the makings. When he's finished, the two men remain silent, listening to the wireless and sipping their drinks. The minutes pass slowly, with erratic interludes of activity. Every so often the operations officer gives orders to a particular crew, and the scramble bell is rung. The nominated crew rush outside to calls of 'good luck', but the remaining aircrew soon return to their state of uneasy alert.

Inevitably, as the time approaches midnight, the aircrew grow more drowsy.

'Nearly 2330,' says Tom's navigator as he stifles another nervous yawn. 'Perhaps we won't be needed tonight after all.'

'Anything can still happen,' says Tom.

The crew fall silent again. The music of Geraldo lilts from the wireless; the melodies lull the crews away from reality. The steady beat is followed by a crewman's foot tapping against a table leg; another man hums discordantly. In the room next door, the operations staff chat: 'crew reported sharp evasive manoeuvres . . . bandits were headed for Liverpool . . . Bomber Command should co-ordinate with Kenley Control . . . bandits came out low after bomb release . . .'

When the background conversation is interrupted by the ring of a special telephone the operations officer lifts the receiver and the aircrew strain to overhear.

'219 Squadron ops,' he says. 'That's correct – still three crews on standby.'

His conversation is clipped, his tone matter-of-fact. The suspense rises and the aircrew remain quiet as he speaks. Tom and his navigator, however, are fully prepared for what happens next. They jump up from their seats when they hear the operations officer slam down the receiver and call, 'CO and Flying Officer Duart, Beaufighter number 2100 . . . scramble!' And as the operations officer shouts his instructions, his right-hand man rings the scramble bell with equal vigour.

CHAPTER SIX

Beware the
Ides of March

'Level at angels one five,' instructs the fighter controller, 'and take up an orbital pattern overhead base.'

Tom reduces the Beaufighter's climb attitude, and he eases back the machine's throttles to initiate the level-off. He has just completed the scramble procedures from Tangmere, and is judiciously monitoring the altimeter as he re-trims the aircraft at 15,000 feet.

'Orbiting overhead base at angels one five.' Tom is brisk when he confirms the controller's orders before asking the navigator, 'How's the radar behaving?'

'So far so good, boss.' The navigator works at his control panel to test the system.

'That's a relief,' says Tom. He continues to scan the altimeter and other instruments. 'What time were we airborne?'

The navigator refers to his log: '2340, boss.'

'We were quick after the scramble order, then.'

Tom glances outside, but he's relying on the flight instruments as he manoeuvres the aircraft to maintain patrol. As part of his orbital pattern he regularly overflies the town of Chichester. However, when he peers down at the darkened domain below, all he can spot is a coloured beacon placed next to a searchlight on standby mode. Other searchlights flare into life every so often, especially towards Kent and beyond Southampton; otherwise the blackout is unbroken.

After a while, the navigator says lightly, 'Perhaps we could tune in to Geraldo while we're waiting.'

'I don't want you to fall asleep up here.'

'Some hope.'

The weather, crisp and clear in that mid-March period, is similar to that for Tom's first operational sortie, just three nights ago. The airborne atmosphere, dominated by the glow of the moon, is frosty: a frown of disapproval spreads from the lunar face as if reproaching planet Earth and the disastrous global events taking place. As the Beaufighter flies along, the moon's ochre is mirrored by scattered clouds in the vicinity. The reflected light creates curious and exaggerated distortions; cumulus creatures emerge as sensational build-ups. On one occasion disfigured bears tyrannise the scene; on another giant sheep; then a gradual trans-figuration presents the weary aircrew with monstrous bison. While the figures transmute under the lunar glow, they creep through the area, as if determined to provoke the aircrew's strained imaginations: could the men be witnesses to spectral intervention?

Tom and his navigator chat from time to time, their discussions an expedient to bolster morale, though the pragmatically-minded aviators make no attempt to discuss spectral anxieties. On one occasion as the pair comment about the efficiency of the blackout system, the radar unit interrupts.

'Confirm the weather conditions are still good.'

'Affirmative,' says Tom without hesitation. 'There's some cumulus in the area, otherwise the weather's no problem.' He glances at his aircraft clock, and adds, 'Request time check, please.'

'Stand by,' says the controller. 'The time is exactly two minutes to midnight in . . . stand by . . . three seconds, two, one, now.'

The aircrew reset their timepieces, then Tom turns the Beaufighter to maintain patrol.

'We'll pass the bewitching hour soon,' says the navigator, as his pilot flies the turn.

Tom considers for a moment before saying, 'In two minutes' time the world should beware the Ides of March.'

'Of course,' says the navigator. 'It'll be the fifteenth.'

'The lessons of history,' says Tom. 'When Caesar was murdered, I wonder . . .' He glances at the lunar face. 'Perhaps there was a full moon then as well.'

The navigator thinks for a second or two and says, 'Then perhaps Adolf Hitler will sleep uneasily this evening.'

'I suspect some of his bomber crews will sleep uneasily this evening,' says Tom.

He rolls the Beaufighter out of the turn and rechecks his altimeter to maintain 15,000 feet.

'It seems as if this war's been going on for ever,' says the navigator, scanning the horizon as he observes distant searchlights continuing to pierce the blackout from time to time. 'After a while, you forget what it was like in peacetime.'

'There's still peace on the other side of the Atlantic. It's OK for them at present, I suppose, but I wonder if they'll ever enter the war.'

'Roosevelt's just announced Lend-Lease, but I guess he'll delay as long as possible before becoming directly involved. Perhaps,' says Tom with prophetic accuracy, 'some momentous event will force his hand.'

He checks the aircraft clock again and peers down to confirm his position in relation to the coloured beacon. He shivers as he glances at the moon. His eyes then focus on the galactic infinity, and he cries out, 'Look at that – beyond the moon.'

'I caught a glimpse,' says the navigator. 'A shooting-star.' An appendage of mist follows the meteoric blur, but the sight vanishes within seconds. 'It's a good job I'm not superstitious. That happened pretty much on the stroke of midnight.'

'So it's now the fifteenth of the month.'

'The Ides of March are upon us.'

Tom checks the coloured beacon once more and applies bank to initiate another turn. The aircrew note that the searchlight activity towards Southampton has become more pronounced. The men are just commenting on this when the controller interrupts again.

'Confirm still at angels one five.'

'Affirmative. And we're still overhead base, maintaining patrol.'

'OK,' says the controller. 'It looks as if we may have trade for you shortly.'

Tom rolls the Beaufighter's wings level and runs through the pre-combat checks: confirm cannons . . . gun button selection . . . ring-sight.

He will repeat the checks later when closer to the target. He glances around to confirm the layout of the clouds, anticipating how to use them to best advantage to conceal his position in the moonlight. At this point, though, the aircrew maintain sentinel as they continue to fly the assigned orbital pattern.

'Did you see that?' cries the navigator. 'Among the searchlights? I think that's flak.'

The two aircrew stare at the increasingly agitated searchlight movements now supplemented with distinctive bursts of brilliance. The next radio call makes them jump.

'Change to Channel Charlie,' the controller's voice pounces at them. 'Call Durrington control.'

Tom feels for the channel selector, then briefly looks down at the radio box to confirm the correct frequency before saying, 'Good evening, Durrington.'

'This is Durrington. Stand by.' The new controller, it seems, has no time for niceties. 'Head south – *head south*,' he says urgently. 'Make your vector one eight zero degrees – BUSTER.'

Tom pushes the Beaufighter's twin throttles to full power. He applies a high angle of bank, and the aircrew feel a spontaneous rush of adrenalin.

'We're on a southerly vector now,' Tom says to the controller.

'OK. Maintain that vector. Stand by to flash weapon.'

'To order that so soon,' the navigator observes, 'a target must have appeared from nowhere.'

The Beaufighter's airspeed increases rapidly. As the machine passes Bognor Regis towards Selsey Bill, the aircrew see occasional searchlights in the area directly beneath them. Soon, however, the aircraft passes above Selsey Bill, and the searchlights cease as land changes to sea. The Beaufighter's airspeed is in excess of 300 knots when the controller calls, 'Flash weapon now.'

The navigator peers intently at the twin scopes of his radar indicator, and when the picture clears he suddenly exclaims, 'Contact!' He sees a return rushing across his scopes. 'Turn hard left – quickly!' Tom slams the flight controls to the left. 'Roll out there,' the navigator continues. He works at the radar system, but after some moments says, 'Contact lost . . . stand by.' Then he remains silent for a period. He is still operating the radar controls, but sounds deflated when he eventually comments, 'I think that initial pick-up was just a stroke of good luck.'

'Durrington,' says Tom hastily, 'we've lost radar contact. Request vectors on to bandit.'

'Suggest you turn left twenty degrees,' says the controller, 'and descend to angels one three.'

Tom flies with uncharacteristic harshness as he again applies bank to the left, and lowers the aircraft nose. He glances at the airspeed indicator as an eerie whistle resonates through the airframe (the noise later to be nicknamed 'whispering death' by the Japanese).

'You're trailing the bandit by six miles,' says the controller. 'He's flying fast on a homeward heading.'

Tom checks the engine settings: 2,400 revolutions, cylinder temperature not above 290°C, oil not above 80°C. Should he set the engines for combat performance? No, not yet. With a combat performance limit of just five minutes, he must keep this in reserve. He's aware, as his left hand anxiously clasps the throttles, that the pursuit will be won by the fastest machine.

The Beaufighter's whistle is beginning to unnerve the aircrew, but there's relief when the controller eventually says, 'Your range is slowly reducing: he's now five miles ahead.' The navigator, however, still sees no blip on his radar scopes and Tom sees no visual signs, despite the good weather conditions. In the sea-going environment the aircrew note a few cumulus build-ups but in general the sky is less cloudy than in the vicinity of Tangmere. 'He's four miles ahead now,' says the controller. Tom monitors his airspeed indicator and he accurately flies the demanded height and heading, though from time to time he manoeuvres the Beaufighter as he searches. But the enemy is well camouflaged and is flying with lights turned off. By three miles there's still no sighting. The controller continues to count down the ranges, but he sounds anxious when he says, 'Just over two miles ahead.'

'Still no contact,' says the navigator, his task not helped by spurious returns on the indicator. 'No contact . . . no contact,' he repeats.

The controller's voice begins to sound tenser now. Proficient co-ordination becomes more difficult at these dangerously close ranges, as well as more crucial. But as he calls, 'Less than two miles ahead,' the navigator suddenly exclaims, 'Contact regained!'

'That's understood,' says the controller, relief in his voice. 'I confirm that you're cleared to smack.'

Tom repeats the pre-combat checks and stares ahead as he tries to pick up the machine visually. He fails to do so at this range but nevertheless calls, 'Tally-ho!' Further ground radar assistance is not needed, and the navigator takes up the commentary.

'Maintain this heading. He's dead ahead. We're closing slowly.'

But the moon's glow is weak and Tom still can't see the bandit.

Before long the navigator calls, 'He's approaching one mile. Your heading and rate of closure are good.'

Despite this close range the enemy machine makes no attempt to evade, the crew evidently oblivious of the Beaufighter's presence. Perhaps, on their home-bound course, their duty done, they feel secure over the Channel. A lone machine in an obscure spot – who could possibly find them there?

'He's at eight hundred yards, dead ahead,' says the navigator.

'I can't see him yet.'

'We're catching him slowly. Hold this height and heading. He's now seven hundred yards ahead.'

'Still no sign.'

'OK. This height and heading look good. Keep closing. He's approaching six hundred yards ahead.'

'Stand by,' says Tom.

As he stares out, he thinks he can just discern the outline of an aircraft. The pursuit has now been under the navigator's control for over five minutes. The crew have been dependent on the Beaufighter's radar during that period; it seems that this war is being fought with more and more reliance on technical innovation.

'Contact!' cries Tom, at last confident of his visual sighting.

Even so, the navigator continues to call out radar ranges as the Beaufighter creeps closer to its target. 'He's now at five hundred yards. Hold this heading as you close.'

As the Beaufighter draws nearer to the enemy machine, still on a constant heading, Tom gazes at the silhouette. He makes another nervous check that the gun button is set to 'fire'. Gradually, the intruder becomes more conspicuous in the insipid light.

'Maintain this heading and rate of closure.' As if wary of being over-heard, the navigator now speaks in a half-whisper. 'Four hundred yards now.'

Tom begins to feel a new kind of misgiving: he is fully aware of the need not to fail at this late stage. His eyes narrow as he focuses on the intruder, determined not to lose sight of it.

'Three hundred yards.'

Tom softly strokes the gun button with his thumb. His gaze remains fixed on the outline ahead, now within the cannon's firing parameters. The enemy still has made no attempt to evade. This causes Tom to feel doubtful: is this honourable? The machine is flown by living souls, aircrew like himself and his navigator – comrades under different circum-stances; individuals with wives, children, fathers. What would they all make of this? How are their lives about to be devastated? This sneaking up from behind seems so sly. A line of perspiration moistens his top lip; he feels an uncanny chill; he's tempted to cry, 'Watch out, my friend!'

As he stares through the Beaufighter's ring-sight, Tom remembers the havoc created by these German bombers. He notes how the intruder maintains its steady course. Perhaps the crew are thinking about their welcome back at base; their comfortable mess with its log fire; their keenness to report on the night's events. He wonders what bedlam this machine, this idol of the hated Hun has caused, what trail of deadly chaos it has left behind.

The bomber is now clearly revealed by the moonlight. Tom experi-ences a feeling of detachment when his thumb stops stroking the gun button. Still the bomber keeps a steady course as Tom rechecks his aim, squinting through the ring-sight. He applies firmer pressure to the gun button and the navigator hears him cry, 'Here we go!' followed by, 'Counting. Thousand and one, thousand and two, thousand and three, thousand and four, thousand and five.'

There's a startling transformation: night is turned into day. Tom experiences a sense of disbelief. He is at once elated and dismayed, his sentiments in turmoil as he watches the destruction caused by the Beaufighter's pernicious combination of cannon and machine-gun.

'Direct hit – direct hit!' cries the navigator.

Tom has now released the gun button, which he has kept down for a full five seconds. However, he still holds the target in his ring-sight, and his eyes blink as his vision struggles with the sudden brilliance. He recalls the lessons learnt from three nights ago: he eases back and to one side of the intruder as he attempts to hold a safe position to observe.

Two fires appear almost instantaneously, one in the cockpit area, the other in the starboard engine. The fires are supplemented from time to time with erratic flashes and sparks; these flick out in patterns, illuminating a pall of black smoke. As Tom watches he sees the machine bank away from its steady course, slowly at first, but with the angle of bank gradually increasing. Before long a downward spiral towards the sea develops. The Beaufighter's crazy whistle shrieks even louder as Tom tries to follow the flight-path.

As the enemy machine plummets, Tom's navigator calls out the altitude. 'Passing twelve thousand feet, eleven thousand feet, ten thousand feet . . .'

Eventually when he gets to five thousand feet, Tom says, 'There's a haze layer coming up. I'll have to ease up.'

But the crippled bomber continues its descent. The machine, still with clouds of black smoke following behind, begins to disappear within the haze layer as if falling into an abyss. Tom levels at 4,000 feet, and takes up an orbit over the spot. He tries to see what is happening below, whether or not the crew bale out, but he's interrupted by the navigator.

'We've got a fuel leak, boss. I think I can see something coming out of our port tank.'

Tom eases back on the stick to initiate a climb, and to reduce airspeed. He turns towards the coast, and advances the throttles. The 'Beaufighter whistle' peters out as the machine's airspeed is reduced. While he climbs to a prudent height, Tom asks his navigator for a position check.

'Stand by,' the navigator replies as he makes calculations. 'I estimate we're thirty-five miles due south of Beachy Head. Make your heading three four zero for Tangmere.'

'Can you still see fuel leaking out?'

The navigator reaches for his night flying torch and aims a beam of light at the port wing. 'I can't make it out very clearly,' he says. 'It could be fuel, but it could be just loose material.'

'OK,' says Tom. 'We'll head back towards base now.' He assumes a north-westerly heading, and asks, 'Can you still see the bandit?'

'I've lost him,' says the navigator. They scour the area to the south, but soon the navigator says, 'No sign at all, boss. We can't make out much below this haze layer. I guess he must have crashed into the sea by now.'

The crew inform the controller of their intentions but fall silent as they consider their dilemma: satisfaction at duty done, regret that they observed no one bale out. The excitement of the chase has taken on a new perspective and the men experience a sense of anti-climax. They feel the need to land as quickly as possible, to return to their squadron environment so they can talk through what has happened.

'We're levelling at angels one five,' says Tom, as he passes routine information to the controller.

'Understood,' says the controller. 'Have you still got a fuel leak?'

'We think it's just packing in the vicinity of the tank.'

'OK. In that case, head for Selsey Bill and take up patrol. Is the weather still good?'

'No problem,' says Tom. 'We have a full moon.'

'That's a point,' says the navigator to his pilot.

'Meaning?' says Tom.

'Just that.' The navigator hesitates, then says, 'I was thinking again about the Ides of March.'

Tom ponders this remark but he doesn't reply. He realises that his own sense of guilt, however unjustified, is shared by both. The crew are still keen to end their flight but they have no choice when the controller orders them to patrol above Selsey Bill for a further thirty minutes. In typical wartime fashion, they just 'have to get on with it'.

As they orbit over Selsey Bill the crew realise that their need to talk things through on the ground is matched, just now, by a disinclination for airborne conversation. They spend the next thirty minutes in silence, broken only when Tom says to the controller, 'We're approaching our recovery fuel limit.'

'Understood,' says the controller. 'You're cleared to return to base now.'

Tom turns towards Tangmere, and at one hour and forty minutes past midnight on 15 March 1941, Beaufighter number R2100 touches down at the airfield.

After landing, the crew go through the required post-operations routine. Details of the flight are taken by the intelligence officer and on combat report form 'F' the crew claim the enemy aircraft as 'destroyed'.

When the debrief has been completed, Tom and his navigator feel exhausted, though the agitation of their thoughts conflicts with their need for sleep. Both men still have an overriding desire to talk things through together and with other squadron members. Tom also yearns to speak with his wife and to see his children, though his family live in

Bedford and he will not be able to visit them for weeks.

As Tom and his navigator move towards the crew room, the pair now deep in discussion, they see that the room is deserted. Even the wireless has been turned off. They collapse into armchairs and then become subdued, disappointed that no one else is around to hear about their experience. They will be driven to the mess shortly, but for now they are content to sit in the crew room, glad at least of their own companionship for a while longer. The solitary rooms in the mess seem incongruous; there's something comforting about the work-a-day atmosphere of the crew room. Anyway, Tom realises that his navigator has already started to fall asleep in his armchair.

Tom, too, begins to drift off. He's so weary, his sentiments still confused. As his eyelids droop, he slips into a dream. Vivid, insane events swim before his eyes. Tom is falling. He's in an aircraft of some kind but he's not sure which type. He sees how the moon glares at him. But his gun button is jammed. The moon's glare is persistent and obnoxious. Tom tries to move the throttles, but the throttles are stuck, hopelessly stuck, and the moon seems to become . . . he's not sure. Derisive, he thinks. Then the clouds begin slowly to transfigure: giant ogres, heinous and depraved, start to cackle in cruel laughter as Tom falls towards a hazy abyss. The moon has begun to . . . to move. The moon wants to tell him something . . . tell him something . . . tell him something . . . *Hitler's bomber crews will sleep uneasily . . . the Ides of March . . . watch out*. Flintlock, too, has started to shout. Tom begins to shout back. 'Althea,' he yells. 'Althea . . .'

Tom's eyelids flick open. He stares with distaste at his trembling fingers, then he slowly looks up to assimilate the surrounding scene. His navigator is sitting in an armchair nodding in uneasy slumber. The operations officer is quiet; the other duty staff are quiet; even Geraldo has been silenced. It's still the middle of the night; everywhere is darkened. He hears the beat of the operations room clock. He tries to check the time but he can't quite see the clock.

The moon . . . the throttles . . . Flintlock . . . Tom shudders. He thinks of the Beaufighter's ability to transform night into day. He thinks of the condemned aircrew. He thinks of his sense of loneliness. 'Althea,' he sighs to himself.

But he's glad of the darkened conditions and the empty crew room. He's relieved that Geraldo has been silenced and that the operations officer is quiet, because Tom feels embarrassed about his eyes and the way they have started to brim.

CHAPTER SEVEN

A Break in the Country

Beyond Ampthill, the flat terrain of Bedfordshire looks bleak as Tom stares out of the carriage window. His view is hampered by a layer of gauze pasted inside the window to minimise glass splinters in case the train is caught in an air-raid. Nevertheless, as the train makes steady progress, Tom manages to glimpse the moving outline of the carriage which is reflected by the shadows on the ground. He gazes towards the area of Houghton House and shifts uncomfortably in his seat. As the train proceeds northwards, he thinks about his protracted journey.

From Bognor Regis he caught a train to London's Victoria station. During the train ride from Sussex he entered into conversation with an army officer. The officer worked with an anti-aircraft artillery unit based in the outskirts of London. Both men were cagey at first, worried about the prying eyes and ears of enemy eavesdroppers. They spoke in broad terms, however, and each man soon recognised the authentic nature of the other.

'It was amazing one night,' the army officer said. 'A local boarding school was hit by a string of incendiary bombs. By the time we got there to sort it out the headmaster had organised his pupils with shovels and they were all dashing about trying to smother the fires with earth.'

'A case of "all hands", I suppose,' said Tom with a chuckle. 'We've had problems of our own,' he continued. 'Our officers' mess was damaged when it was hit by a bomb recently, although we were lucky not to have more casualties.'

The two men went on to compare notes in a general sense. Each found it fascinating to hear the other's viewpoint – anti-aircraft operations from the airborne and from the ground perspective.

Their discussions were interrupted when they reached outer London and the army officer disembarked before the train went on to central

London. When the train eventually arrived at Victoria station Tom encountered large crowds of people pressing through the area. The station still bore the scars of the spectacular crash of a German Dornier bomber the previous year, at the height of the Battle of Britain. Tom looked gloomily at the damaged sections as he walked through the station.

Eventually, he hailed a taxi to take him across London to St Pancras station. 'We make do,' the taxi driver told him. 'It's sometimes hard to find petrol, and after a raid we can't get around easily. But everyone does their bit; it's amazing how quickly we seem to bounce back.'

As they drove along, Tom gazed at some of the devastation caused by the bombers. At intervals, collapsed walls could be seen next to surviving chimney stacks, twisted doors and distorted window frames. Sometimes entire structures were heaped in concentrated ruin, a pathetic abuse of bricks, tiles, glass and once-solid woodwork. The sad scenes gave Tom an eerie reminder of his time at the Air Ministry the previous year.

When the taxi reached St Pancras, Tom coped with agitated people as they thronged around the station precinct. Most seemed to wear military or other uniforms, and folk rushed about, caught up in their individual problems. Around the station, advertisements reminded people about the dangers of loose talk: 'Careless talk costs lives'. Everyone was encouraged to be suspicious; spies were a constant worry. Tom found that the station's hectic atmosphere made him feel claustrophobic.

When it was time to embark, Tom's rail warrant entitled him as a senior officer, to a seat in the first-class section. He settled himself in and as the train proceeded slowly out of London he noted how the passengers glared with a mixture of indignation and concern at the surrounding bomb devastation. In one place, where rolling stock had been hit, gangs were working to clear up piles of rubble. In time, though, once the train had progressed beyond the suburbs of London, the countryside revealed fewer signs of bomb damage. In these parts, promising signs of springtime defied the wartime hazards.

Now beyond Ampthill, the train starts to slow down for the approach to Bedford. Tom begins to feel a surge of different emotions, a turmoil of excitement and apprehension. He continues to stare out of the window as the train gradually draws to a halt at Bedford station.

Tom picks up his suitcase, and he looks around when he steps onto the platform. As in London, people are agitated as they dash about. Tom thinks the station has a run-down air, lacking care and maintenance. Folk push past as he tries to search for his family. Military uniforms are still prevalent; raised voices punctuate the general hubbub.

'Daddy!'

Tom swings round as he feels the tug at his elbow, and he hurriedly puts down his suitcase. He grins as he leans forward to pick up Caryl. He hugs his young daughter, then catches sight of Althea struggling through the crowds as she carries Annie. Tom moves towards his wife. Both feel anguished by the people barging by. When the couple draw close, Tom spots his wife's special dress, and he notices that the children, too, are smartly clothed.

'I see you've got your party frock on already,' he says to Caryl.

Tom gazes at his wife. She looks thin, her face drawn. Her eyes start to fill, though she had been determined not to let that happen. People still push past as the couple hug. At last they are together for a spell. Tom picks up both the children but he's surprised by their hesitant smiles. As the family move away from the station there seems an air of distance between them, a sense of confusion. So much has happened since they were last together.

'How was the journey?'

The question sounds formal, an obvious palliative. They have to make efforts to ease the atmosphere, but as they move further from the station, the family start to relax. And when their familiar bond returns, a sense of normality, they chatter happily as they walk through the streets of Bedford. Tom tries not to mention details about his flying; these are best discussed later. Althea, well aware of the perils faced by her husband, avoids the subject too.

'How much leave have you got?' she asks.

'I'll return to Tangmere the day after tomorrow. The group captain was feeling generous: he's allowed me two nights away.'

'You'll be here for my birthday party, Daddy,' says Caryl, who is pushing her sister in a pram beside her parents, who walk arm in arm.

'That was the plan, scallywag.'

'The party's tomorrow,' says Caryl. 'We've been getting ready.'

'I'm glad to hear that. I haven't been to a decent party for ages.'

'How long?' says Caryl.

'At least three weeks. No, make that three months. Maybe even longer.'

'Three years?' says Althea.

'We've got some special food,' Caryl continues. 'Do you have rationing where you work?'

'There's rationing everywhere,' Tom replies.

'We know all about that,' says Althea.

'We don't get very nice meat,' says Caryl.

'I thought you liked Spam?'

'Sort of. But we're not having any at my party.'

'We've got other treats,' says Althea.

'We normally have lots of Spam,' Caryl points out.

'We don't have much choice in the matter,' says her mother.

'Why?' asks Caryl.

'Because we're not allowed very much fresh meat. They reduced our ration at the beginning of the year.'

'What allowance do you get now?' asks Tom.

'It used to be two shillings and tuppence, now it's half that amount – not much when you have to feed young children.'

'You cope remarkably well,' says Tom.

'I suppose we survive. And your mother helps us a lot.'

'I'll remember to thank her when I see her tomorrow. How is she?'

'Worried about her sons. Perhaps you should go ahead of us tomorrow. It'll give you some time together.'

'That's thoughtful. Time is always short.'

'Everything will be better when the war's over.'

'Let's look forward to that,' Tom agrees. 'Just as I'm sure you look forward to school,' he adds to Caryl. He's surprised, though, when Althea touches her daughter's head in a gesture of encouragement. 'Is there a problem?' he asks.

'Some of the other children aren't very kind to me,' says Caryl with a gloomy expression.

'Have you had a word with the headmistress?' Tom asks his wife.

'The headmistress says she's trying to sort it out. But dealing with bullies seems low on their list of priorities at the moment.'

'We'll see about that,' says Tom.

'The school have got so much to cope with just now. Some of the pupils have lost their fathers in the war recently. The school's short of staff and the rationing causes difficulties. I feel sorry for the headmistress.'

'Look!' Caryl exclaims, brightening. 'Our house is round the next corner.'

'That's good,' says Tom. 'It seems a long way from the station and this suitcase is heavy. Even heavier, I think, than your sister. Look how she's grown!'

'She's getting big and strong despite the rationing,' says Althea.

'Come and look at this, Daddy,' says Caryl, abandoning her sister's pram as she pulls on her father's hand. As the two run ahead, Caryl cries out, 'Aren't they pretty?' Tom leans forward to inspect the spring daffodils, the flowers' spindly appeal reminding him that even a wartime world is not wholly devoid of grace. 'This is my bit of garden,' says Caryl with pride.

'You're a clever gardener.'

'Come and look inside the house.' Caryl tugs his hand again and as they enter the kitchen, she says, 'Do you like my painting?'

'You're a clever artist as well as a good gardener,' says Tom as he studies his daughter's handiwork placed on the walls. 'I don't know why they should bully you at school,' he says, ruffling her hair as her expression clouds.

'I don't know either,' she says. 'Some of them aren't very nice children.'

'Some of them have lost their fathers because of the war.'

'But that's not my fault, is it?'

'No,' Tom reassures his daughter, 'it's not.' He smiles. 'But we must cheer up. I'm going to think about it and see what can be done. It's your birthday tomorrow – your last birthday in single figures. We must be happy.'

'Tomorrow's going to be fun,' says Caryl. 'I've asked some children who *are* nice to come to my party. And we're going to have it at Granny's house – she says there'll be more room.'

'Granny and I have saved up coupons to make you a special cake,' says Althea as she enters the kitchen.

'Perhaps we should try the cake now?' says Tom.

'You mustn't do that,' says Caryl.

'Shouldn't we make sure that it's safe?'

Caryl glances at her parents doubtfully.

'Definitely not,' says her mother. 'You'll just have to wait until tomorrow. It'll give you something to look forward to.'

Caryl giggles as her father pulls a face.

'About three weeks' worth of coupons have gone into that cake,' Althea adds.

Later that evening, when Tom and Althea have time to themselves, they sit together and talk. They have so much to discuss but Tom feels restricted: he mustn't cause his wife unnecessary alarm and he has to think, too, about the constraints of operational confidentiality. Since his first sorties the previous month he has been involved in more such flights, and he's eager to talk through his thoughts and his misgivings. He speaks quietly when he broaches the subject.

'The squadron's beginning to shape up better now, after a fairly poor start.'

'You said they were suspicious about getting a new CO direct from the Air Ministry.'

'You could understand their point of view, but it didn't make life any easier for the new CO himself.'

'The new CO's a strong character. I'm sure he could cope. Have you had much operational flying?'

'Quite a bit. We're gathering one or two war trophies. In one corner of the crew room there's a clock from the cockpit of a Heinkel.'

'What happened?'

'We intercepted some bombers heading for Coventry recently. The following day clear-up crews came across the clock and they made arrangements to hand it over to the squadron.'

'Who shot down the bomber?'

Tom turns his face towards the fire, and he stares at the glow of the coals. He spreads his fingers wider on his knees, then says in a quiet voice, 'I did.'

'You were doing your duty.'

'I keep telling myself that.'

'Do you not enjoy the flying?'

'It's exciting and our task is vital. It's just that when an aircraft has been shot down, you get this mixture of feelings: one minute elated, then a sense of anti-climax.'

'I can understand that.'

'You remember what the Prime Minister said last year? "Our aim is .. . victory at all costs, victory in spite of all terror, victory however long and hard the road may be; for without victory, there is no survival." I don't think any of us realised at the time the implications of what he was telling us.'

'We gained victory in the Battle of Britain.'

'At the cost of five hundred pilots. And the war still goes on.'

They stare at the fire, at the sparkle of the flames slowly petering out. Their spirits seem to sink in sympathy.

'Hitler's a madman,' says Althea bitterly.

'Perhaps that may be our salvation in the end.'

'How do you mean?'

'Well, suppose Hitler tries to push out his horizons. There's this speculation that he'll open another front by attacking Russia. It would mean an unbearable burden for Germany, but from our point of view it would ease the pressure and ultimately I'm sure it would lead to Germany's downfall.'

The couple fall silent as they consider this, then Althea looks at her husband and says, 'By the way, you were going to tell me something about the bombing of the officers' mess at Tangmere.'

'There was quite a bit of damage I'm afraid,' says Tom in a noncommittal way. He leans forward and picks up the poker to rekindle the fire.

'Where were you during the raid?'

'I was at the squadron, but the buildings there weren't badly hit.'

'Only the mess was damaged?'

'Only one wing of the mess.'

'Did it affect your room?'

Tom hesitates. 'My room was destroyed.' He glances at Althea. 'I'm afraid to say I lost everything: log books, bank books, insurance policies, passport, family papers.'

Althea gasps, and says, 'Thank God you were on duty then.'

'I should have been off duty,' says Tom, gazing nervously at his wife. 'But I had to stand in for another pilot who was sick.' He pauses, then says, 'I'm sorry. I wasn't going to tell you all the details.'

'You did the right thing to tell me. It's wrong for you to bottle things up.'

'It's hard to find the right balance.'

'You must tell me these things. It's only right.'

'Some things I'm not allowed to tell you, but when I can, it is helpful to talk things through.'

'Of course it is.'

'Anyway,' says Tom, 'we've got to be cheerful for Caryl's birthday tomorrow. She's got her own problems and we must try to keep her spirits up.'

'Yes, we must. We must keep her spirits up.' Althea clasps her husband's arm as she stares at the fire. 'We must keep all of our spirits up. At all costs, we must keep going.'

CHAPTER EIGHT

At Peace with the Family

Bee holds on to Tom's arms for a moment and gazes at her son. She sees him so infrequently and she longs to ask him about his life and about his work.

'I'm the advance party,' says Tom. 'The others will join us later. You and I will have a chance to talk.'

'That'll be wonderful. We don't get much time together these days.'

'It's difficult and I see little enough of Althea and the children.'

'How are they today?'

'I think Althea looks pale, but the children seem well, apart from this business at Caryl's school.'

'She's not alone with that problem. With their fathers away fighting the war, and with their mothers often involved in war work, a lot of children are having problems.'

'Another form of war damage, I suppose.'

'But you must tell me about yourself and what you've been doing. There's so much I want to ask you, although I expect you're restricted by confidentiality. Your work must be very hush-hush.'

'I can talk generally,' says Tom. 'And it's good to talk things through.'

'Can you talk about your flying?'

'In general terms, yes.'

'The pilot shortage must be such a worry.'

'Things are gradually getting better after the Battle of Britain. We're training new pilots all the time.'

'Over five hundred pilots lost,' says Bee, shaking her head, 'and over eight hundred aircraft, so we hear. At one point they seemed to use mere boys to fly the Spitfires.'

'At the height of the battle there was no time to train them properly. Pilots reporting to new units had to be used right away.'

'There were some extraordinary stories.'

'There was one about two young pilots who were just parking their cars.'

'What happened to them?'

'These two had completed their conversion training and were posted together to a squadron. They were parking their cars, their pride and joy, outside the mess when someone from the squadron ran up to them. They were needed immediately: a scramble order had been received, and there weren't enough pilots. The two of them sprinted at once to the operations set-up, but the CO and the other pilots were all airborne. Nobody was around to meet them, let alone brief them. The operations officer told them he had no choice: they'd have to get airborne and just do their best. Their first sortie, thrown into the thick of air combat.'

'Did they cope?'

'I'm afraid that both were killed.'

'What desperate times,' says Bee.

'Desperate times have led to desperate decisions. The government have faced such dilemmas. They even tried advertising abroad for pilots.'

'In Commonwealth countries, I assume?'

'Well, not exactly in Germany.'

'Did they have any success?'

'There was a fairly mixed response. I've talked with a young man, for instance, who was a law student in Delhi before he joined the Royal Air Force. He was an amateur flier and when he spotted the newspaper advertisement urging pilots to join the RAF, he decided to volunteer. He was posted to Uxbridge aerodrome last year, just in time for the Battle of Britain. He was a Sikh, so he proudly wore the Royal Air Force badge on his turban.'

'Was he a good pilot? How did he get on?'

'He flew Hurricanes and Spitfires, and he was shot down twice.'

'Twice? Did he survive the second time?'

'Only just. Enemy bullets brushed against his flying jacket, smashed through his instrument panel and ended up buried in the engine, which consequently cut out. As he was over water, he had to glide across the Channel to reach the first available piece of dry land. He told me he had good reason not to bale out: he couldn't swim! However, he just made it. His aircraft burst into flames when he lowered the undercarriage, and he crash-landed in a field where he was rescued by farm workers. But he flew again virtually the next day.'

'It's easy to forget just how many people from that part of the world are fighting for us. It was the same in the last war.'

'Many thousands, in fact millions, have been involved, and some have been awarded Victoria Crosses and George Crosses.'

'We stand in their debt. How many different nationalities fought for us during the Battle of Britain?'

'An amazing number: fourteen. There were Poles, Czechs, Norwegians, Americans, as well as pilots from of the Commonwealth.'

'Their efforts were outstanding. Churchill's comments about "the few" were so apposite.'

'They were, but we couldn't afford to lose as many as we did. On top of that, we had the problem of dealing with large numbers of injuries.'

'We have to be grateful for Doctor McIndoe and his team of surgeons.'

'He was a godsend.'

'We haven't been told the full story yet,' says Bee, 'but I believe that it was touch and go. Rumour has it that we very nearly lost the Battle of Britain.'

'Bad judgement by the opposition and good leadership on our side were crucial factors.'

'Thank goodness we had Winston Churchill. Although he sometimes worries me.'

'In what way?'

'His age, for one thing. People seem to forget that he's fifteen years older than Hitler. Churchill was eligible to draw an old-age pension even before he became Prime Minister.'

'He was a tonic after the feeble leadership we had before.'

Bee then asks her son about his own flying experiences. Tom is guarded about points of detail, but he's anxious to discuss some of his inner feelings and personal doubts with his pragmatically-minded mother. Bee is a source of strength to him. As they talk, though, he begins to feel troubled about his mother. Tom hardly knew his father, and when Bee was widowed at such a young age she faced severe difficulties as she struggled to bring up three boys on her own. Then her eldest son, Roy, died of pneumonia, afflicting her with another grim burden. Now, with both her remaining sons involved in fighting the war, she faces more uncertainty.

'Is it not unnerving having to do all your flying at night?' she asks at one point.

'It's a matter of practice. We do a lot of training flights; you soon acclimatise to night flying and to the night environment.'

'Can you tell me how you practise your interception techniques?'

'The broad principle is no secret and there's nothing magical about it. Two aircraft take off within minutes of each other and take it in turns to act as the target. A ground controller guides the fighter pilot, then the navigator takes over the commentary. We practise for the worst case, in what's sometimes called "popeye" conditions: in cloud, and with nil visibility.'

'How far from the enemy machine do you pick him up?'

'Now that, I'm afraid, *is* a secret.'

'But presumably it's near enough to fire your weapons successfully?'

'We have no problem destroying the enemy machines.'

'It must be a strange feeling, acting as if you were God.'

'There's no time to worry about things like that during the interception. And you know that if events work out badly, you'll end up as the victim yourself. However, when the chase is over, and when your enemy has been shot down, your initial sense of elation quickly evaporates. You get a feeling of flatness, especially when you know there have been fatalities. It's hard to describe, but it is, shall we say, very unsettling to be involved in calculated murder.'

'What does Althea make of it?'

'That's another problem. Because I see so little of her, there's hardly any opportunity to discuss these things.'

'It must be a lonely feeling.'

'We talk things through among ourselves on the squadron, and as CO I have to give advice to the other pilots, especially to the younger ones. But the CO himself needs to unburden from time to time.'

'So where does he turn? Who does he speak to?'

'He speaks with his family.'

'I'm sorry we're so far away.'

'We have to learn to cope, I'm afraid. For those serving overseas it's even worse.'

'For Bill, for instance?'

'Have you heard from him lately?' Tom puts the question about his brother gently.

'As you say, it's hard to keep in touch, but he does his best. I receive letters from time to time.'

'So do I. He's doing well in the army.' Tom falters. 'We miss Roy,' he adds quietly, knowing it is helpful for Bee to discuss her late son occasionally.

'The country could use his scientific brain at the moment,' she says. 'I can't recall – did Althea ever meet Roy?'

'It was sad, really,' says Tom. 'Shortly after I met Althea, we were driving through Bedford in my car. I remember feeling especially proud: we had the hood down, and we spotted Roy as he walked along. We waved, but there was too much traffic and we couldn't stop. Just a few days later, Roy left for California, and that was that. The brief wave from the car was the only time they "met".'

Bee stands up then, and says, 'Let me show you my garden.' She's keen not to dwell too much on the past. 'You'll have to admire my vegetable plot. I do my bit for the "Dig for Victory" campaign. It's hard work, but productive, and I can share the benefit with Althea and the children. It's also helpful when it comes to bartering.'

'Bartering? At your time of life?'

'And why not?'

Tom admires his mother's handiwork, but he looks up when he hears a knock at the front door. He and his mother hurry through the house to let in Caryl, who has run ahead of her mother and sister. Althea soon catches up, and as she reaches the house and greets the others, she hands over a special container.

'Mind this treasured cake,' she says to her husband. 'Have any of the children arrived yet?'

'Not yet,' says Tom. 'Shall we have the party outside? The weather's good enough.'

'That's a good idea. Let's do that.'

As the family set about organising the birthday party, Annie rushes around excitedly. Tables and chairs are taken outside, rugs are placed on the grass, paper and pencils are made ready for party games, and a picnic-style tea is arranged.

When the young guests arrive, they start with a drawing skills contest before moving on to blind man's buff and pin-the-tail-on-the-donkey. Squeals of delight accompany several rounds of musical bumps, performed to the tunes of '78' records that sing out from a wind-up gramophone.

In spite of wartime constraints, Althea and Bee provide a lavish birthday tea with sandwiches (Spamless), jellies, buns and home-made squash, giving the children a feeling of plenty for once. When the cake's candles are lit, everyone sings 'Happy Birthday', and Caryl is at last allowed to cut her cake.

At the due time, parents arrive to take their children home. Tom is amused by Caryl's quizzical expression when he says, 'I suppose your next party will have to be a rather grown-up affair, young lady. You'll be in double figures by then.'

When the time comes to bid farewell to Bee, Tom has an inevitable feeling of awkwardness. 'I'm not sure when I'll be able to see you again,' he says quietly.

Bee gazes up at her son, but she does not like sentimental goodbyes. 'Let's just hope it's soon,' she says. As she stands at the door, the family wave back as they walk from her house.

'I try to visit Bee as often as possible,' says Althea. 'But it worries me that she's lonely, and that she spends so much time on her own.'

'She's a very resilient type.'

'She's had to be.'

As her parents talk, Caryl skips along happily and thanks them for her party, but her expression clouds when she asks her father, 'When do you have to leave us, Daddy?'

'Tomorrow morning, I'm afraid.'

For the rest of the day, the family make determined efforts to enjoy being together, and Althea uses carefully saved-up coupons to make a special meal. Their attempts to be cheerful, though, are affected by their awareness of limited time. Tom's departure is never far from their thoughts.

'Shall we see you off at the station tomorrow?' asks Althea that evening.

'It'll mean an early start, I'm afraid.'

'At least we'll all be together for a bit longer.'

The next day, as they walk to the station, the family fail to appreciate the offerings of the spring morning. The triumphs of narcissi, daffodils and crocuses in local gardens, of the air alive with birds, of the trees welcoming them, all fail to dispel the family's sense of gloominess. The heady atmosphere around them is lost.

'I don't want you to go, Daddy,' says Caryl, attempting to dawdle.

'I'll come back again as soon as I can.'

'When will that be?'

'I'm not sure yet. But I'll try not to make it too long, I promise.'

'I hope it won't be long,' says Caryl tearfully. 'We miss you when you're away.'

The crowded station makes matters even harder. As the family walk along the platform, jostled by busy people, the noise and disorder depress their spirits further. When the train for London draws up, and when there's a scramble as passengers disembark, the departing passengers begin to make their emotional farewells. Tom turns to hug his children goodbye, and he feels in turmoil as he looks at his wife. He embraces her before hurriedly turning away, reluctant to linger.

He lifts his suitcase onto the train and climbs the carriage steps. He tries to stay by the door to wave goodbye, but it's difficult: even the first-class carriages are crowded, and other folk press around him to deliver their own goodbyes. He hears the shrill tone of the guard's whistle; there's a further surge of passengers. Carriage doors are slammed. The guard blows his whistle again, and the train starts to jerk forward.

Tom sees shafts of sunlight flicker through the carriage as the train picks up speed. He cranes his neck, anxious to keep his family in sight, but he experiences an odd sense of detachment as he sees their silhouettes shrink. Even so, by the time they stop waving, and although he can only just make them out, he still stares in their direction. By now he's aware that his vision has become blurred.

Absorbed within his own thoughts, Tom no longer seems bothered by the throng of passengers around him. As he continues to stare outside, he observes unusual patterns on the carriage glass. Little by little, as the train accelerates, drops of spring dew spread along the grimy surface of the window. Sad tears trickle across the glass, their smears adding to the distortion of the anti-air-raid gauze. As he stares out, Tom is barely conscious of the train's progression, or of the bleak Bedfordshire countryside. He focuses instead on the work of liquid craft forming in front of his eyes. He sees a nebulous shape stencilled by nature's artist, a loose depiction of a child's face. The young face, soft and innocent, seems so much in need of protection. He glances back now, but he can no longer see his family.

Tom looks again at the invisible limner's sketches. He notices erratic changes of expression – fierce with accusation, then smiling – and as he observes, his subconscious mind begins to pick up terrifying glimpses of what lies ahead. He stares at nature's creation with a growing sense of paradox. He knows he will be programmed to fly later on this evening. His two-night break will become a distant dream – is becoming so now, because, locked within the shadows of his memory, already he can see images of the violent activities it is his duty to confront.

CHAPTER NINE

Tangmere, 16 April, 1941

Tom is sitting at his desk, studying reports, when there is a knock at his office door. He looks up and sees a dark-haired young man of stocky build standing in the doorway.

'Come in, Sergeant Clark,' says Tom in a friendly way, and the young navigator starts to look more relaxed. 'I've just heard from the ops officer. He's confirmed that we're crewed together this evening.'

'That's right, sir,' says the navigator. He's well aware of the CO's reputation as an austere man, but he's mindful, too, of the wing commander's renown for being highly effective, and of his surprisingly light touch when dealing with personnel of all ranks.

Tom stands up and moves across to sit on a bench in one corner of his office. 'Come in, and let's have a chat. You've been doing well recently; that practice flight we flew earlier was a good one. It seems you're one of the squadron's best when it comes to operating the radar.'

'Thank you, sir.' The navigator steps into the CO's office, and glances around. He notices pictures of German bombers – Junkers 88s, Heinkel 111s and Dorniers – on one of the walls, near a row of rifles. The navigator coughs lightly. 'Do you mind if I smoke, sir?' he asks as he produces a pipe.

'No, I don't mind. Light up if you'd like to.' Tom reaches for a packet of cigarettes. 'Do you use these things?'

'I'll stick to the pipe, sir, thank you.'

As the navigator strikes a match and takes it to his pipe, Tom says, 'Yes, your performance on that practice flight bodes well if we see action tonight.'

'Thanks, sir. We've intercepted some heavy raids lately. I suspect we'll be busy tonight.'

'The enemy are focused on London and the south-east just now.'

'It seems to be Goering's plan.'

'There've been some bad shows.'

'Like that London dance hall? The papers were full of it.'

'A five-hundred-pounder,' says Tom. 'And a crowd of young people inside: munitions workers, soldiers on leave and girls in party frocks. It was a bad night; too many got through the defences.'

The navigator sucks at his pipe. He pauses, then says, 'And what about Jerry's attempt to destroy Buckingham Palace? Flares, incendiary devices, low-level bombing runs – it was surely a miracle that the palace escaped a direct hit.'

'We made some interceptions that night, but I'm afraid we're not going to catch them all.'

'Londoners have become a pretty resilient lot.'

'After nearly nine months of blitz, it's incredible what they've learnt to put up with.'

'I don't know how they cope. This war just seems to go on and on.'

'Churchill said it might take ten years to defeat the Nazis.'

'Ten years! When it all started, I hoped it would be over and done with in a matter of months.'

'I don't think any of us realised what a long haul was involved. Now we're nearly two years on already, and still carrying a heavy burden on our own.'

'What about help from across the Atlantic? What about Lend-Lease?'

'We should get more help soon.'

'What do you reckon are the implications, sir?'

'I think they're pretty far-reaching. Roosevelt was empowered by Congress to give us virtually anything we needed, and the President himself can decide the terms. The PM said, 'Give us the tools and we'll finish the job", and I suppose Lend-Lease was the result. There are some powerful lobbies of isolationists in the US, so it's an important step.'

'Let's hope it works,' says the navigator. 'Some of the other measures seem draconian.'

'Raising income tax to fifty per cent?'

'Unbelievable!'

'And using women in the factories?'

'Even worse. They're looking for a hundred thousand young women. Mr Bevin made that personal appeal.'

'Some of the women are glad to do war work. At least they get paid, and they get a measure of independence.'

'Tell that to my girlfriend.'

'She's been "volunteered"?'

'It's looking that way. She'll have to leave home, and move to an industrial centre.'

'I suppose the women have to take over the jobs to free men for active service. However, if there's anything I can do to help . . .'

'Thanks, sir, but I reckon she's slowly coming round to the idea. As you say, she'll be paid, and I think she wants to do her bit for the war effort.'

'Good luck to her,' Tom says. 'I feel sorry for these girls. It won't be at all easy for any of them. Anyway, let me know how she gets on.'

'Thanks again, sir.'

'I'll have to get on with some paperwork now,' Tom says, drawing the meeting to a close. 'I seem to be snowed under these days.'

'Group HQ churning it out?'

'Not to mention Fighter Command. But it's been good to have a chat.'

'Yes, sir.'

'I'll see you in the crew room later.'

'OK, sir,' says the navigator. 'By the way,' he adds, 'we've had a delivery of cocoa today. I could make you a drink when you're ready.'

'Thanks. I'll look forward to that.'

Later that evening, Tom is sitting at readiness with other members of the squadron in the crew room. They have their dark adaptation goggles fitted, and, as usual, wireless programmes provide background entertainment.

'Shall we see what Haw-Haw's got to say for himself?' asks a member of aircrew after a while.

'Anything for a laugh.'

A volunteer stands up, and the room is filled with distinctive squeals and crackles as he turns the bulky tuning knob. The airwaves begin to modulate, and before long the wavering din of Nazi military music is picked up.

'Here we are. This is it.'

The aircrew shift in their chairs in anticipation until, when the music ceases, there's a silence for some seconds, followed by a series of special tones. The aircrew stop fidgeting as an expectant hush permeates the room.

'Germany calling, Germany calling. This is the Reichssender broadcast . . .'

The wireless reception continues to fluctuate, in an echoing way, as the well-known voice ranges through the room.

'Tonight I wish to tell you about the successes of our U-boats,' says the voice. 'The German Navy has stepped up activity against your shipping convoys with considerable success. Day and night, your merchant ships are being attacked; your sailors are being sent to watery graves. Our U-boat successes will make life in Britain even more uncomfortable than it is already. You will become shorter of basic supplies; even the bare essentials will become unavailable. Ask yourselves: are the sacrifices really worthwhile?' The deliberate, arrogant tone of the voice pauses, then goes on. 'Just think: the foolish Lend-Lease arrangement with America will have little impact compared with the might of the German Navy, the effectiveness of our U-boats . . .'

The aircrew listen warily as the traitor, thirty-five-year-old William Joyce, delivers his message. Occasionally, when some outrageously exaggerated claim is announced, peals of laughter resound through the room, but eventually the hated voice of Lord Haw-Haw begins to grow wearisome. 'Let's go back to good old Geraldo and his good old Savoy orchestra,' becomes the unanimous cry. Tom and his navigator nod in approval.

'That Haw-Haw fellow's heading for the gallows,' says Tom's navigator.

'Public enemy of the first order, after Adolf himself,' says another navigator, 'although we'll miss the free entertainment.'

When the Savoy orchestra's music once more serenades listeners, the aircrew start to relax again. But their peace is shattered when the scramble bell is sounded and the names of the next-in-line crew are shouted out by the operations officer. The nominated crew immediately jump up and move towards the door.

'Good luck, chaps!' yell out the other aircrew.

When the called-out crew have left, those who remain start to settle down again, although Tom fiddles anxiously with his goggles, and he is restless in his chair.

'How about that mug of cocoa?' he asks his navigator.

'I hope there's still some left.'

'I thought you made a promise.'

Tom is used to the crew room's atmosphere by now. The uneasy air, the sense of apprehension produces a feeling akin, he thinks, to the butterflies-in-the-tummy sensation of a new student at the beginning of term. At least when airborne the crews are occupied and absorbed, but the waiting around in the crew room, the sense of uncertainty, creates an almost unbearable strain on the nerves.

'Here you are, sir.' Tom's navigator hands him a mug of cocoa. 'It's hard to read properly,' he adds, touching his goggles, 'but I think there's something about "Fry's cocoa – rich in nerve food".'

'Thanks,' says Tom, taking hold of the mug. 'Let's hope Mr Fry and company are right.' He frowns as he adjusts the position of his goggles again.

'Have you seen the latest Bob Hope film?' asks the navigator, attempting to lighten the atmosphere.

'I don't think so,' says Tom. 'What's it called?'

'*The Road to Zanzibar*. There's something about it in the papers today. It was released a week ago and stars Bing Crosby and Dorothy Lamour alongside Bob Hope – a pretty good line-up. I'm going to take my girl-friend when we get a chance.'

'I like Bob Hope's brand of humour.' Tom sips his drink, and crosses his legs in a nervous movement. Then he sighs and stands up. 'I'm just going to check our Luftwaffe clock,' he says as he walks towards one corner of the room.

Tom picks up the timepiece, and squints through his goggles. 'I can't see properly with these bloody things on. What's the time?'

'The midnight time signal sounded a few minutes ago, boss.'

'Well, in that case—' But Tom stops talking, aware of a flurry of move-ment in the operations room.

'CO and Sergeant Clark, aircraft 2253 – scramble, scramble, scramble!'

Tom hastily puts down the Luftwaffe clock and fumbles as he tightens the straps of his parachute pack and Mae West lifejacket. In company with his navigator he dashes towards the door. The scramble bell sounds, and the two men hear calls of 'good luck' as they hurry across the room. Tom and his navigator tear off their goggles as they run to Beaufighter R2253 and their respective entrance hatches. They climb the steps, ease head-first through the hatches and pull themselves up into the belly of the aircraft. When inside the machine, they make for their separate cock-pits and their individual seats. As Tom sits down, he feels for the seat collapsing lever by his right hand, the lever which, if operated, will facil-itate escape from the cockpit. He's used to the routine by now, and in the dark his hand automatically reaches down to check the lever. When strapped in, he dons his flying head gear and oxygen mask, carefully placed beforehand on the top part of the cockpit coaming.

As Tom goes through the pre-start preliminaries and the engine start procedures, he realises how glad he is to be active at last. 'The sitting around can drive you mad,' he muses. 'And it's such a relief to remove those goggles.'

When the Beaufighter's start-up process has been completed, the ground crew hand the undercarriage safety locking pins to the navi-gator who stows them in a special bag. The ground crew run from under the aircraft and signal to Tom that he's clear to taxi out. Tom feels for the parking brake catch on the aileron control hand wheel, at the top part of the stick, which he then releases. As the aircraft moves forward, he squeezes the brake control lever, and simultaneously operates the rudder pedals left and right to achieve differential braking. As he moves away from the parking area, Tom notes that, as usual, everywhere is in blackout, and he manoeuvres the aircraft cautiously as he heads towards the in-use runway. When he receives a green signal from the Aldis lamp in the control tower, he continues to move as rapidly as possible onto the runway.

As he lines up the Beaufighter, Tom makes sure the tailwheel is straight before he reapplies the brakes. He grips the throttles with his left hand while he goes through the engine response checks, then he advances the throttles and monitors the cockpit dials. When satisfied, he brings the throttles back again and speaks with his navigator. Then he releases the Beaufighter's brakes and starts to ease the throttles fully forward.

Tom cannot know at this point, of course, that his activities over the next two hours and forty minutes will clinch the decision to award him a Distinguished Flying Cross.

An increasing clamour from the engines marks the start of the Beaufighter's take-off run. The navigator braces himself while the machine accelerates and Tom monitors the airspeed as he gradually applies forward pressure to the control stick. Soon, the tailwheel comes up, and he uses the rudders firmly to control the Beaufighter's tendency to swing. He eases back on the stick to lift the main wheels clear of the runway at ninety knots.

When the machine becomes airborne, Tom concentrates on accurate flying. He raises the undercarriage at a safe height and at 300 feet he raises the flaps before setting the hydraulic power lever off. He goes through other after-take-off checks, and as the Beaufighter climbs up steeply he monitors the flight instruments to maintain a climb speed of 150 knots. When the aircraft nears the required level-off height, he changes radio frequency to speak to the fighter controller.

'Flintlock, good evening.'

'Stand by,' says the radar controller, sounding harassed. 'Make your vector three six zero . . . stand by.'

Tom reacts by applying a high angle of bank to turn the Beaufighter on to the northerly heading required, and he advances the throttles to check any height loss during the turn.

'Rolling out on three six zero.'

'Maintain that vector,' says the controller. After a few seconds, he continues, 'Flash weapon immediately.' He falters, then says, 'There's a bandit ahead of you; he seems to be headed towards the London area. Any contact?'

Tom peers ahead while his navigator operates the radar controls. The weather is fine, with some upper cloud, but there's no moon yet, and the conditions are too dark for a visual sighting.

'Any joy?' says Tom to his navigator, who continues to work at the radar controls.

'Nothing seen.'

'No contact,' says Tom to the controller. 'Can you give us further vectors?'

'Stand by. The target's faded from my screen. Confirm still no contact.'

'Still no contact.'

'Stand by,' says the controller as he gazes at his radar screen.

'We're still looking.'

'OK,' says the controller. 'I've just been informed that the bandit will be pursued by another squadron. Stand by for further instructions.'

Tom eases back the Beaufighter's throttles to the cruising gates and adjusts the engines to achieve 2,400 revolutions for a fuel-efficient cruising speed. He maintains the aircraft heading for the moment and notes the appearance of sporadic searchlights some distance ahead, beyond Guildford. He discusses this with his navigator but he is cut short by the controller, whose voice sounds excited.

'Turn on to reciprocal heading. Vector one eight zero. Head for the coast. I think there'll be another target for you there.'

Tom turns the Beaufighter as ordered, but he decides to maintain cruising speed for now as he takes the machine back towards Tangmere. He plans to go beyond the airfield, towards Bognor Regis, and as they fly along the aircrew see further searchlight activity, this time in the far distance towards Kent.

'Bandits to the east of us, bandits to the south of us,' mutters the navigator.

'Confirm you're on a southerly heading now,' says the controller.

'Affirmative. As instructed.'

'OK, stand by.'

The controller continues to stare at the picture developing on his radar screen, which portrays the ground radar equipment's rotational sweep. A bright spot will denote the presence of an aircraft, often displayed faintly on first pick-up. As he studies his screen, a specific return gradually becomes stronger with each new sweep. He follows a particular blip, and his colleagues eventually hear him say quietly, as if to himself, 'Another one's just beginning to paint . . .' The fighter controller hesitates for a few more seconds. He has to verify the blip before giving further orders. He uses the new IFF (identification friend or foe) system, a signal produced from a black box fitted to friendly aircraft, and he directs the radar aerial to a particular part of the sky. He instructs the 'binders' – two airmen pedalling a device to turn the aerial – to stop or reverse the sweep.

'Stand by,' he says once more, still absorbed by the picture on his screen.

The suspense in the Beaufighter's cockpits builds.

When the controller is satisfied, he says in a calm but imperative tone, 'Reverse your turn again. Make your vector zero three zero. I have another target for you.'

CHAPTER TEN

Night-time Dogfight

'OK,' says the fighter controller anxiously, 'you'd better flash up your weapon again.'

'We'll do that,' says Tom. 'Stand by.'

The controller frowns, and taps the table-top as he concentrates on the picture on his radar screen. He passes instructions to the binders, and there's an air of tension in the darkened control room, although his voice sounds calm and impassive.

'Confirm on heading now,' he says.

'Affirmative. Rolling out on zero three zero.'

'The bandit's at angels one seven, I say again, one seven. He's on a northerly vector, and he'll be on your starboard side, crossing from right to left.'

Tom scans the flight instruments, in particular the artificial horizon and the direction indicator – it's crucial that he maintains an accurate heading.

'We're holding zero three zero,' he says to the controller.

'He's still on your starboard.'

'Any signs on radar?' Tom asks his navigator.

'Nothing yet.'

'No contact,' says Tom to the controller.

'Turn right ten degrees,' says the controller. 'Make it zero four zero.'

'Still no contact,' says the navigator.

'Steady on zero four zero,' says Tom.

'Hold that for now,' says the controller. 'That's a good intercept angle.'

'Stand by,' says the navigator to his pilot. 'I think I can see something now.'

'Well?'

'I just need to confirm . . .' The navigator falters. 'There's definitely something . . .' He hesitates again before exclaiming, 'Contact!'

'We have contact,' Tom says to the controller.

'Can you identify the type?'

'Negative,' says Tom. 'It's too dark to see anything visually yet.'

'Turn right another ten degrees,' says the navigator. 'Make it zero five zero. But hold this height; your height looks good.'

'Are you happy for the tally-ho call?' Tom asks his navigator.

'Go ahead,' says the navigator.

Tom passes this on to the controller, but as he does so he jumps with alarm when the navigator cries, 'He's turning! The bandit's taking evasive action!' Tom keeps a steady heading for a few more seconds, but he turns sharply when the navigator demands, 'Go hard left!' Tom turns the Beaufighter aggressively, and the pitch of the engine note soars as he advances both throttles. The navigator calls a steady flow of instructions: 'Keep turning . . . *keep turning*. Increase your angle of bank. Hold it like that . . . hold it . . . hold it. He's still evading hard to the left. Keep up the turn . . . *keep turning*.' He falters. 'Stand by, he's rolling out here.' Tom eases the angle of bank.

'We're on a westerly vector now,' says Tom. 'Confirm you've still got good radar contact.'

'Affirmative: good contact.'

'Well done. But I still can't see him visually.' Although the weather conditions remain fair, there's no sign of the moon yet.

As Tom holds a westerly heading, he notes the flash of searchlights in the vicinity. He wonders if the target is about to be revealed by them, and ponders the dilemma of searchlights: the danger of exposing the fighter as well as the intruder, and the problem of interference with night vision. He has to rely implicitly on his flight instruments for orientation, and his experience as a pilot pays dividends as he concentrates on accurate flying: poor techniques could soon lead to loss of radar contact.

'That last turn took us through one hundred and forty degrees,' he says to his navigator.

'Understood,' says the navigator. While he concentrates on his radar scopes, he makes adjustments to achieve a clearer picture. When he detects further blip movement, he says, 'Confirm we're still on a steady vector.'

'Holding two seven zero.'

'OK. I think he's turning the other way now.' He pauses, then calls, 'Turn hard right!' Tom immediately applies control inputs. 'Hold that angle of bank,' continues the navigator. 'Keep turning . . . *keep turning*.

He's moving off to our right now; increase that angle of bank. That's looking better. Keep up the turn. Hold that bank; the rate of turn is good. Stand by. It looks as if he's rolling out. Start to ease your angle of bank now.'

'Confirm our range.'

'Seven hundred yards, closing slowly,' says the navigator. 'Your speed and height are OK; we're about two hundred feet below him.'

'Can you maintain radar contact?' says Tom, mindful of the demands these hard manoeuvres place on the navigator.

'So far so good, boss.'

'Well done,' says Tom, in an encouraging tone. 'Good man. But I still can't see him visually.'

'OK, but I've got a reliable radar contact,' says the navigator. 'Stand by! I think he's evading again. Stand by . . . *turn hard left*!' Tom reacts at once. 'Keep turning . . . *keep turning*. He's evading hard now. Keep going left.' Tom vigorously follows the directions, but eases the angle of bank when the navigator says, 'He's beginning to roll out.'

'Confirm we've still got sufficient height separation.'

'He's about a hundred feet above us now. And his range has reduced: he's just six hundred yards ahead.'

'OK,' says Tom. 'But it's still very dark – I can't see him.' He stares out in front, desperate to catch a visual glimpse. 'No, nothing yet.'

'He's at five hundred yards now.'

'Five hundred yards,' says Tom, still anxiously gazing ahead. Then he suddenly cries out, 'Got him! I can barely make it out, but I think I've got contact. I think I can see his exhaust flames. Keep up your commentary – keep calling the ranges.'

'We're closing up slowly. We're at four hundred yards, and he's on a constant heading at present. No signs of further evasion yet.'

'His silhouette is very faint, but I can definitely see his exhaust flames now. I'll continue to close.'

'He's still on a steady heading.'

'What's our range now?'

'Three fifty yards.'

'I can see his exhaust plumes more distinctly as we close.'

'Still no signs of evasion, and my radar picture remains sound. Hold this speed; we're slowly catching up. Range now three hundred yards.'

'Let's close up to two hundred yards.'

'Maintain this heading, then. We're just over two hundred and fifty yards.'

'Two hundred and fifty,' says Tom.

He double-checks that the gun button is selected to fire, and ensures that his thumb lightly covers the gun button itself. He adjusts his hand position on the aileron wheel. His thumb rests on the surface of the button, protected by a special guard; a gentle squeeze is all that is needed. He turns the brilliance of the Beaufighter's ring-sight fully to dim as he watches the faint glow from the twin exhausts ahead. Without ambient moonlight, the tenuous glimmer from the exhausts provides his main source of visual contact.

'He's starting another turn,' says the navigator.

'Confirm his range.'

'Just two hundred yards now.'

'Exactly two hundred?'

'Yes.'

Tom fractionally increases the pressure of his thumb on the gun button. As he looks through the ring-sight, taking aim, he notices the twin plumes start to move.

'Watch out!' exclaims the navigator.

Tom feels a chilling mood of hostility. He has no time to lose. He stares at the twin exhausts, but he's not yet satisfied with his aim. He turns the Beaufighter to duplicate the other's angle of bank, and continues to scan his flight instruments, but at this close range he has to operate head-up as well. In these darkened conditions it will be easy for him to become disorientated, and to lose sight of the target. Alignment within the ring-sight will soon become unreliable; he has just a few seconds to confirm his aim. He squints through the ring-sight. The line-up still isn't right . . . pull up a bit . . . increase the turn . . . watch the deflection. That's better; just check again. That's it; that should do the trick.

Tom applies positive pressure to the gun button, shouting 'Opening fire!' There's a burst of flame, abrupt brilliance, a smell of cordite. He holds down the gun button for just one second, then there's sudden silence.

Tom's aim has been good. He hears his navigator yell, 'We've got him!' and they see the bomber start to turn steeply. Tom manoeuvres to keep clear of falling debris, and as the intruder's angle of bank steepens, he follows the machine. He notes spontaneous fires begin to highlight swirls of black smoke.

'We've hit him all right!' says the navigator.

The bomber's angle of bank increases towards ninety degrees, and the machine begins a downward spiral as smoke and flames spill out from the wings and the fuselage. Tom's navigator starts to call out heights as they descend: 'Passing sixteen thousand feet . . . passing fifteen thousand feet . . . our rate of descent is increasing . . .' They shield their eyes as they see explosions erupt from the bomber, which they assume is ammunition being set off.

'He's going down fast,' says the navigator.

'We'll follow him down.'

'We're below ten thousand feet now,' says the navigator, but it's difficult for Tom to match the high rate of descent. 'Beaufighter whistle' starts to shriek through the airframe.

'His rate of descent is increasing.'

They watch the bomber accelerate away, a red-hot trail following behind as the machine enters a vertical dive. The navigator cries out, 'He's about to hit the deck!' They watch for a few more seconds, then they see a violent explosion at ground level. Tom pulls out of the dive, levels the Beaufighter at 2,000 feet, then turns in an orbital pattern so that he and his navigator can observe. They watch flames violate the blackout as a ball of fire billows upwards; they see further bursts as, one by one, incendiary bombs explode; they see streams of black smoke illuminated by the flames.

They speak little during this, but the cockpit silence is interrupted by the controller. 'This is Flintlock. Anything to report?'

'That's affirmative,' says Tom. 'DCO – duty carried out. The bandit's crashed in the Guildford area. Stand by for an accurate position report.'

'Are there any survivors?'

'No signs of parachutes.'

'OK. Confirm your position, then climb up to angels one five to hold in the Guildford area. There might be more trade. We're checking.'

The crew calculate the position of the crash site, then Tom advances the Beaufighter's throttles to initiate a climb. The controller watches his radar screen and begins to pick up the radar return as the Beaufighter climbs.

'I have you back in radar contact now,' he says.

'OK. Shortly levelling at angels one five.'

'Maintain that,' says the controller.

As Tom eases back the throttles, and as he trims the aircraft for cruising speed at 15,000 feet, the controller says, 'We've just heard from Tangmere. There's a problem with the weather: it's closing in – there are reports of fog. We have no further trade at present, so you can return to base now. Call Tangmere control on Channel Delta.'

'Channel Delta,' says Tom as he glances down at the radio box. He finds the selector box and slickly changes frequency. He makes a nervous adjustment to his oxygen mask, then stretches his fingers stiffly. 'Tangmere, we've been handed over by Flintlock. They've no more trade, and we've heard about your weather report.'

'The weather's OK at the airfield at present,' says the Tangmere controller, 'but there are signs of patchy fog developing to the south. It's drifting this way. If necessary, you'll have to divert to Middle Wallop.'

'Keep me updated on that, please. We'll attempt an approach to Tangmere.'

'Just now, I think you should get in all right. Vector two zero five for Tangmere.'

As Tom turns the Beaufighter, he notes the lack of moonlight and makes a minor adjustment to the brilliance of his cockpit lighting.

'Rolling out on two zero five,' he says to the controller.

'Maintain that for the present.'

As the Beaufighter progresses towards Tangmere, the aircrew carry out routine duties. Tom checks his fuel gauges and mentally calculates the reserves needed in case of diversion to Middle Wallop. The navigator makes other calculations, and as they proceed he scans his limited instrument display, with its altimeter and airspeed indicator.

Absorption in such procedures may assuage recent images, but the crew have pragmatic feelings too: a sense of satisfaction at duty done against a difficult target. They muse that this interception revealed the Luftwaffe's new tactics. But were the enemy crew aware of the fighter's presence through some form of tail radar, or were those manoeuvres flown as a matter of routine? In either case, this interception had an unusual slant – the night-time equivalent of a dog fight. Matters progressed rapidly once they were in firing range, and when the gun button was pressed the burst was uncannily short – just one second. What power, what deadly punch, must be delivered by those Hispano cannon and those Browning machine-guns?

'This vector looks good,' says the navigator. 'Tangmere should be directly ahead.'

'What's our range now?' asks Tom.

The navigator refers to his chart. 'On this heading we—'

'Did you see that?' exclaims Tom.

'What the hell . . .'

The crew's attention is drawn away from instrument flying as they observe a series of detonations at ground level.

'Bombs!' cries the navigator as they stare at the explosions.

'Two of them.'

'No, three. Another one's just going off.'

'The bomber must be in the vicinity still. Quickly, man, you'd better flash the radar up again.'

The Beaufighter's radar, as usual, is turned off until needed operationally. As the navigator works the switches on his control panel, he studies his indicator anxiously. 'Searching, searching . . .' He scans the twin screens on the indicator, one to display a target's elevation, the other for range and azimuth. The picture is often cluttered and confused when the system is first brought into use.

'Any joy yet?'

'We're nearly there.' The navigator speaks hesitantly, but within moments his voice is more confident. 'I've got something. I have a contact.'

CHAPTER ELEVEN

Chance Encounter

With urgency in his voice, Tom asks his navigator, 'What range is the contact?'

'The radar's just warmed up,' says the navigator. 'The controls are . . .' He pauses as he gazes at his indicator. 'It looks like he's fifteen hundred yards ahead.'

'Fifteen hundred yards?' gasps Tom. 'Are you sure?'

'Affirmative. It was sheer providence . . . we just happened to be here when the bombs went off.'

'You can say that again. Have you still got good contact?'

'I'm trying to confirm the target's height and heading.'

'I'll have a word with Tangmere while you're doing that,' says Tom.

In reply to his message, the controller says, 'I'll check with Flintlock about that contact.'

'And have you any known friendly air traffic in the vicinity?'

'There's Black Hat Two Five,' says the controller, who then calls: 'Black Hat Two Five, this is Tangmere, do you read?' He receives no reply. 'Black Hat Two Five. Black Hat Two Five. This is Tangmere. Do you read, over?'

'Can you confirm this target's height and heading now?' Tom asks his navigator.

'He's on a southerly heading, slightly above us. Turn left ten; make it one nine five.'

Tom applies the heading correction. 'I can't see anything visually yet – it's still too dark.'

'That's understood. I've got a good radar return now; we're holding good contact. The target remains on the nose, still at a range of fifteen hundred yards.'

'Well done. Let's keep him at that until we get confirmation whether he's friendly or hostile.' Tom hesitates. 'What's his height? Are we OK at fifteen thousand feet?'

'This height's OK, boss. We're slightly below the target. His radar return is clear.'

'Black Hat Two Five. Black Hat Two Five. This is Tangmere control. Do you read, over?'

'Why doesn't the fellow answer?' says the navigator.

'I trust he hasn't fallen asleep,' says Tom lightly. 'After all, it is two o'clock in the morning.'

'Black Hat Two Five. Black Hat Two Five. This is Tangmere.'

'Tangmere, this is Black Hat Two Five. Hello. Are you trying to call me? Over.' The voice sounds quite nonchalant.

'I've been calling you several times, Black Hat Two Five,' says the controller, whose own voice reflects a combination of annoyance and relief. 'Confirm your present position.'

'I'm at twenty-two miles from the airfield, bearing three one five.'

'And your height?'

'Ten thousand feet.'

'Black Hat Two Five, there's a possible bandit in your area. Descend to low level and return to base immediately. I say again: return to base immediately. Acknowledge, over.'

'That's copied, Tangmere,' says Black Hat Two Five, now sounding flustered. After some minutes he makes another transmission: 'Black Hat Two Five's at low level, heading for the airfield.'

'Our target's hardly moved,' says Tom's navigator as he presses his head against the visor covering his radar indicator. 'He's still on a steady vector, just left of the nose. Shall we close up now to identify?'

'Stand by,' replies Tom, who speaks again with the controller.

'I'm still checking with Flintlock,' says the controller, but within moments he adds excitedly, 'That target has been confirmed as hostile. Repeat, hostile. You have clearance to smack.'

'Acknowledged as hostile,' says Tom.

'Turn left another ten degrees,' says the navigator. 'Make your heading one eight five degrees. We're still at fifteen hundred yards; you can increase speed.'

Tom's hand grip tightens. He advances both throttles; the Beaufighter's engine note rises and he monitors the airspeed indicator as the distance starts to reduce. He notices the moon just beginning to appear on the horizon, and says quietly, 'That'll be useful.'

'Say again, boss?'

'Can you see the moon?'

'I see it now,' says the navigator, glancing up from his radar indicator.

'It should be a nearly-full moon tonight.'

The navigator returns to his radar picture, and after some moments exclaims, 'The bandit's started to evade! We've got another one! Stand by to turn.' He pauses for a few seconds. 'He's going left. Turn left now . . . *turn left* . . . not too steeply; ease that angle of bank. Easy does it. He's evading gently. Steady does it . . . *steady*. Ease the bank a bit more. Hold it like that . . . *hold it*. Stand by. Start your roll out here.'

Tom moves the flight controls judiciously as he follows these commands. He glances at the direction indicator and says, 'We've rolled out on one zero five.'

'Hold it there for now. He's on a steady vector at the moment.'

'Confirm his range.'

'One thousand yards.'

'This rate of closure seems about right. I'll maintain this airspeed.'

'Stand by to turn again,' says the navigator. 'He's going starboard; begin a turn to starboard, but not too steep. He's still evading quite gently.' Tom receives more instructions, and eases his angle of bank when the navigator says, 'He's rolling out here.'

'What's his range now?' asks Tom.

'Eight hundred yards, dead ahead. This rate of closure still looks good.'

'Understood.'

'He's just weaving methodically,' says the navigator. 'Don't overdo the bank, but start going left now. He's turning gently to port. Hold it like that; keep that angle of bank. He's still in a left turn.' Tom monitors his artificial horizon, but occasionally he glances up as he tries to spot the intruder visually. He is focusing on his flight instruments again when the navigator says, 'Begin to ease the bank – he's rolling out slowly. He's at six hundred yards now. Any joy?'

'He was silhouetted against the moon,' says Tom, 'but only fleetingly. I couldn't make out the type.'

'We're closing steadily.'

'Keep calling the ranges.'

'Just approaching five hundred yards.'

Tom peers in front of him. 'I think I've got his exhaust flames,' he says. His grip on the throttles tightens as he strains to see the faint glow ahead. He glances at the airspeed indicator as he slows his rate of closure. He must not be tempted to rush; his approach has to be one of stealth.

'He's evading again!' cries the navigator. 'He's going starboard this time. Turn right now.'

When Tom complies, he uses positive and precise control inputs to match the target's weaving technique.

'He's at three hundred yards now,' says the navigator.

'Three hundred yards?'

'Confirmed.'

'I can still see his exhaust flames, but not very clearly.'

'Is it the same type as before?'

'It's a different type, but I can't positively identify it yet.'

Tom is now peering through the ring-sight. His thumb rests against the gun button, and he ensures, slickly and by feel, that the gun button is set to 'fire'. The navigator feels a series of jerks as Tom makes continual small movements to the flight controls as he adjusts his aim. He sees the intruder start another turn and hears his navigator's warning cry: 'He's going left!' But this time Tom will use delay to his advantage: the intruder is turning back towards the globe of the moon.

'His silhouette should be clear against the moon shortly,' he says to the navigator.

'He's at two hundred and fifty yards, and he's still turning slowly. Your present angle of bank looks OK.'

With these gentle turns, Tom isn't worried about deflection problems. But his timing will be crucial as the enemy machine approaches the moon. Tom squints through the ring-sight, although he is still monitoring the flight instruments: the airspeed indicator to the left, the rate of climb and descent indicator to the right, the altimeter, in a design of ergonomic eccentricity, half hidden just below that, and the artificial horizon in the centre of the panel. He still makes regular small manoeuvres to maximise the advantage of the moon's sphere. The twin exhaust flames he can see faintly, but the rest of the machine is barely visible. 'Hold it, we're nearly there,' he thinks to himself, 'but not quite yet.'

Tom keeps his right thumb poised above the gun button; his left hand still grasps the throttles. He makes more positional adjustments; he checks and rechecks his alignment. The bandit's profile will touch the edge of the lunar globe at any moment. But impatience could spoil his advantage; he'll delay until the silhouette is more fully revealed.

He sees the first part of the machine highlighted against the moon: the port wing-tip. As this happens, Tom tries to identify the type. He stares at the profile through the ring-sight, but the light is too weak and the silhouette is ill defined, especially from the rear quarter. The machine continues to turn; more of the wing and part of the fuselage begin to show against the moon. Even so, Tom still can't positively confirm the type. But he'll be able to do so shortly, and he has the necessary authority to smack this intruder. This intruder who flies through our airspace uninvited, and who drops bombs on our people. What damage did he inflict back there?

At last, Tom can see the entire fuselage; now he can identify the enemy's profile. He makes a last check of aim. 'This is it,' he thinks. 'We're there now. No more time to lose.' He calls, 'Opening fire!' and firmly squeezes the gun button.

Tom squints his eyes in anticipation, but he is still startled by the sudden brilliance. Despite this, he continues to take aim, and the airframe shudders and clatters from the effect of the weaponry. The smell of cordite begins to waft into the cockpit. But then he has a sudden shock. 'I've fired too soon,' he thinks. 'The aim isn't right yet.' He keeps the gun button pressed, and feels anguish: has he made a misjudgement? Tom pulls back on the stick to adjust his line-of-fire for more deflection. The racket from the Beaufighter's cannons and machine-guns persists, and he is momentarily struck by how the once-vivid moon now looks feeble in the background, a stark contrast to the brilliant volley of fire.

At last Tom releases the gun button. It seems to him that he kept it down for too long, but his navigator confirms that it was for just four seconds. As he stares ahead, still through the ring-sight, Tom sees a minor explosion erupting from the enemy machine. Then, as he watches the intruder roll out of its turn, the wings briefly level with the horizon before the machine commences a leisurely, deliberate-looking reversal of turn, still within the globe of the moon. There's another explosion; a fire develops in the bomber's fuselage. But the aircraft maintains a gentle turn as if keen, in the dark circumstances, to stay within the comfort of the lunar globe. Perhaps the moon's light is providing a final thread of consolation, an esoteric link. Tom experiences an uneasy feeling as he watches the machine turn, seemingly ignorant of its predicament. He pictures the pilot, perhaps desperately wounded, as he gropes in his fume-filled cockpit trying to save his aircraft, his crew . . .

Then Tom sees a sudden and violent flash and he's aware of an object hurtling towards the Beaufighter. He tries to take evasive action, but he's too late. He hears a thud against the airframe, and the machine swerves. He reduces power and immediately checks the correct functioning of his aircraft, informing the navigator, 'The engine oil pressures look OK. The engine temperatures are in limits. The throttles function normally. I think debris hit our starboard wing and fuselage area, but the flight controls and the engines seem all right.'

'Look out!' cries the navigator.

Tom instinctively ducks. By now, his machine is some distance from the enemy, but still the Beaufighter is rocked. Tom stares at the enemy aircraft as it explodes. He sees flames and smoke billow out, temporarily obscuring the moon. Points of fire hurtle towards him, but they are swiftly dispersed within the veil of night. The conflagration remains suspended for some seconds before sinking earthwards, slowly at first but progressively accelerating. The remains of smoke then begin to clear away from the lunar globe.

'Not much hope for the crew!' says the navigator.

Tom manoeuvres the Beaufighter in a series of weaves as they watch. 'I don't think so.'

The aircrew still stare down, but just as the fiery remains are about to strike the ground, the navigator calls out, 'Look behind us!'

'What is it?'

'Did you not see them?'

'I can't see anything.'

'I'm sure I saw something.'

'What was it?'

'I can't be sure,' says the navigator. 'It was hard to make out clearly but, glinting in the moonlight, I thought I saw two parachutes.'

CHAPTER TWELVE

Back to Earth at Middle Wallop

'This light can be deceptive,' says Tom as he continues to fly the Beaufighter in a series of weaves and as he and his navigator scour the area below.

'I'm sure I saw something,' says the navigator. 'But I've lost sight now.'

'Can you confirm the position? Where exactly were these two parachutes?'

'Behind us, in about our five o'clock position,' says the navigator. 'But I can't see anything now.'

'We'd better keep looking, just in case,' says Tom.

However, despite their best efforts the crew fail to spot the parachutes. They see instead an inferno at ground level, the consequence of the enemy machine's final plunge, with tongues of flame reaching out from the site. These reveal spirals of smoke, the swirls supplemented from time to time with specific bursts as incendiary devices explode.

Tom speaks to Tangmere just then, to keep the controller informed.

'Flintlock have reported that they've lost you on radar,' says the controller. 'Request your present position, please.'

When this has been passed on, Tom continues to manoeuvre the Beaufighter in weaves, the crew persisting with their search. But after a while he says to his navigator, 'It's looking unlikely. I don't think we'll find these parachutes.'

'I'm sure I saw something,' says the navigator, 'but as you say, the light can be deceptive.'

'We'll still try to confirm it,' says Tom, but when the conflagration on the ground starts to die down, the crew eventually decide to discontinue their search. 'That's it, I'm afraid,' says Tom. 'If there were any parachutes, they must have landed by now.'

'I suppose we'll find out later if there were any survivors.'

'They'd have been lucky to escape from that explosion.'

'I think the ammunition must have caught. Either that or the fuel tanks blew up.'

'Perhaps both. It looked fairly impossible, but you never know. Maybe some of the crew were thrown clear, or just managed to bale out in time.'

Tom is ordered to fly in a generally southerly direction now, towards the coastline beyond Tangmere. As the aircrew leave behind the site of impact, and as the blackout once more dominates the area below them, Tom holds a steady heading while he and the navigator carry out calculations.

'We'll resume our return to base now,' he says to the navigator. 'And the fuel looks all right. We've got sufficient reserves if the foggy conditions force us to divert.'

'The flying time to Middle Wallop should be around thirty minutes in the current winds,' says the navigator. He sounds subdued as he says this.

'I'm afraid it is disappointing, not knowing one way or the other about those parachutes,' Tom says.

'It's just one of those things, boss.'

'We may find out later.'

'Perhaps.'

Tom then makes a radio call to the controller at Tangmere, requesting the latest weather report. This indicates increased amounts of local fog.

'Do you wish to carry out a QGH let-down to the airfield?' the controller asks.

'Negative,' says Tom. 'We'll get a coastal fix soon, so we'll make a D/F approach to runway two-five.' The direction finding approach system relies on the aircraft's radio calls: with each transmission a line on the controller's screen indicates a bearing that can be relayed to the pilot. The process is effective but crude; eventually a beam approach system will become available at a number of RAF airfields.

'You're presently south-east of Tangmere,' says the controller. 'Descend now to safety height, and make your initial heading three one zero degrees.'

Tom brings back the Beaufighter's throttles and manoeuvres the machine on to the instructed heading. As he descends, he catches occasional glimpses of coastal fog illuminated by the moonlight. He eases the aileron wheel to roll out of the turn, rechecks the direction indicator to confirm his heading, then alerts his navigator, 'Stand by for the before-landing checks.'

'Ready for the checks,' says the navigator who, as usual, is listening to and monitoring cockpit checks carried out by the pilot.

'Pneumatic supply pressure at two twenty,' says Tom. 'Cowling gills closed, carburettor air intake heat controls at cold.' He reduces airspeed to 150 knots before continuing. 'H – hydraulic power lever on. U – undercarriage down: indicators and warning horn checked. P – propeller speed control levers set for two thousand four hundred revs. F – fuel selected to the fullest tank. F – flaps set at twenty degrees down.'

'Before-landing checks complete,' says the navigator.

'Transmit for bearing,' says the controller. Tom presses his VHF radio transmit button. 'Turn right ten degrees, make your heading three two zero.'

In spite of his fatigue, Tom forces himself to fly with accuracy, monitoring the altimeter as he maintains the area safety height and concentrating on the correct heading and airspeed. Periodically he glances out of the cockpit, noting how the layers of coastal fog tend to be broken up and patchy-looking in places. Away from the foggy areas, the moonlight reveals generally good visibility. In one clear patch, he notes how the surface of the sea is eerily luminous in the moon's glow. He briefly takes his gaze up towards the moon, but returns to the flight instruments when the controller asks for another radio transmission.

After further heading and height alterations, and as he draws closer to the airfield, Tom has to reduce the Beaufighter's airspeed to the recommended airfield approach speed of 115 knots. He eases the throttles back, and when requested to by the controller he double-checks the main wheels' doll's eyes. He confirms these show 'down' on a green background, and says to the controller, 'Two greens – wheels down and locked.' Tom is aware, as he makes this transmission, that for some versions of the Beaufighter the retractable tail-wheel would mean a call of 'three greens'.

'Maintain your vector of three two zero,' says the controller. 'You're clear to proceed with the approach. Be advised, we've lit the goose-necks.'

Tom glances up as he tries to spot the glow from the paraffin burners, but swirls of fog obscure them at this stage. However, by looking directly downwards he can still make out the surface of the sea.

His sense of fatigue seems relentless. He has to compel himself to fly the parameters accurately, and he realises, too, that his navigator is exhausted. This is clear from the strained tone of his voice when he says, 'On this vector, we should cross the coast near Middleton. That'll put us five miles south-east of Tangmere.'

Tom gazes below from time to time as he tries to identify when the territory will change from sea to land. At length, when this happens, he makes a further throttle adjustment to reduce to the final approach speed of 100 knots. He and the navigator then press their stopwatches: the elapsed time will indicate range from the airfield.

'Transmit again for bearing,' says the controller. Tom responds. 'Make your heading three one five. Have you an estimated range from Tangmere?'

'Four miles now,' says Tom.

He makes another small heading adjustment and rechecks his stopwatch. When he does this, he reminds himself to relax, realising that his left hand is gripping the throttles too tightly. But as he stares ahead he sees no airfield lights, just banks of fog. He makes another radio transmission.

'Maintain this heading,' the controller replies. 'You should be lined up for a left-hand finals, and you're clear to land on runway two-five. What's your range now?'

'Three miles,' says Tom.

He sees once more the fog in front, and then he glances up at the clear sky which exposes the moon and the stars. He counts down the ranges for the next two miles. When he nears the airfield boundary, he reduces the brightness of his cockpit lighting to help him pick up the goose-necks more distinctly, although he's still unable to see them by a range of one mile.

'Request another transmission,' says the controller. Tom responds. 'For a small correction, turn left on to three one zero.' After a short pause, he asks, 'Transmit again for bearing.' Tom makes a brief transmission. 'Maintain your heading,' confirms the controller.

The navigator's vision directly ahead is obscured by the pilot's cockpit; he focuses on his stopwatch, and aloud he counts down the remaining seconds to the airfield. Tom's forward vision is not restricted by airframe design, and he glances up occasionally, although chiefly his concentration remains on the flight instruments.

At last, when the Beaufighter is close to the airfield boundary, Tom can make out the goose-necks. But he's in no position to land: he's angled from the runway, and he's too high for a 'dirty dive'. He moves the throttles forward to the rated gates to initiate overshoot, and as he does so he considers whether to make a further approach to Tangmere. He agrees with his navigator, though, that the lure of landing at their home airfield is not appropriate in these conditions. Diversion to another airfield has to be their most prudent option.

Tom therefore adjusts the engines appropriately: he sets 2,400 revolutions and checks that the pressures and the temperatures are normal. He moves his left hand forward to feel for the undercarriage lever and watches the doll's eyes as he raises it: black and white dazzle lines during transit; 'up' on a red background when the wheels are fully locked up. He informs the controller of his intention to divert to Middle Wallop and carries out further cockpit checks: airspeed pegged at 105 knots, flaps raised to twenty degrees. He notes the reading on the flap indicator before he increases the airspeed to 120 knots. When ready, he raises the flaps fully, and re-trims the aircraft.

'Make your vector three zero zero for Middle Wallop,' says the controller.

Tom and the navigator reset their stopwatches, and Tom climbs the Beaufighter to the route safety altitude. He's aware of the high ground of the South Downs, and when he levels at the safety altitude he brings the throttles back to the cruising gates. He eases the engine revolutions to 2,000, with occasional further adjustments to obtain a fuel-efficient airspeed of 175 knots for the transit flight; this will achieve a fuel consumption of around 100 gallons per hour. As the crew settle in to the transit flight, they carry out regular cockpit checks with ongoing fuel and navigation calculations.

'Call me when Petersfield's on your right side,' the controller says.

Tom looks outside. He sees that the fog has started to disperse already.

'We're beyond the South Downs fog barrier here,' says the navigator, and after a short interval he announces, 'That's Petersfield coming up now, boss.'

Tom acknowledges this, and informs the controller.

'Change frequency now,' says the controller. 'Call Middle Wallop.'

'Thanks for your help, Tangmere.'

Tom glances at the selector as he changes frequency, adjusting the volume control while he speaks with the controller at Middle Wallop.

'Maintain that vector,' says the new controller.

Clear moonlight now helps the crew with their navigation, and Tom glances outside, away from the cockpit instruments, when the navigator says, 'The Meon Valley and Wickham are on our left. And you might spot the cathedral ahead.'

'Request your present position,' says the controller.

'We've just passed Winchester,' Tom replies.

'We're lighting the goose-necks now.'

Tom goes through the before-landing checks, and calls the controller with 'two greens'.

'Confirm that you've set your altimeters to the QFE,' says the controller.

'QFE set.'

'You're clear to land.'

When he approaches the airfield boundary, Tom eases back the throttles, aiming for the final approach speed of 100 knots.

'All set for landing?' he says to his navigator.

'All set, boss.'

Tom focuses on the goose-necks ahead; the correct perspective will ensure a good angle of approach. He manoeuvres towards the runway, conscious that the Beaufighter's landing foibles will not allow him to relax yet. As he passes the airfield boundary, concentrating on his airspeed, he begins to ease the stick back for round-out. He grips the aileron wheel with his right hand, the throttles with his left, and inches the throttles rearwards just before touchdown, aiming for a smooth three-point landing between the second and the third set of goose-necks.

The Beaufighter sinks towards the runway; there's a thump as the wheels touch the surface. But as Tom brings the throttles to their idle position, he fails to match them evenly; the machine swings, and begins to head towards the line of goose-necks. He counteracts with rudder pedal. The aircraft straightens, and continues to decelerate as he works the rudder pedals to bring the machine fully under control. When safe to do so, he uses the wheel brake lever by his right thumb, dabbing the brakes to slow the Beaufighter to a fast walking pace.

At the end of the runway, as part of the after-landing checks, Tom raises the flaps and opens the cowling gills. He re-advances the throttles a little, using them differentially in conjunction with the brakes while he taxies towards the dispersal area. The navigator politely ignores Tom's apology for the swing on touchdown, but in response to his request for the landing time, he says, 'Exactly 0300 hours, boss. We were airborne for two hours and forty minutes.'

'We'll be seeing daylight again soon.'

Ahead, Tom spots signals from torches as a ground marshaller makes waving motions to direct the Beaufighter. Tom follows these signals, moving with caution; other Beaufighter squadrons are based here, but his visits to the airfield have been infrequent. When instructed by the marshaller, he brings the machine to a halt in a particular place. Tom applies the parking brake before he closes the throttles, checking for when the engine revolutions reach eight to nine hundred. He then presses his stopwatch.

When two minutes have elapsed, Tom glances down by his left elbow to identify the engine cut-out controls. He pulls at the two spring-loaded knobs and holds them in the up position for a few seconds; if a back-fire occurs, he is ready to release them before opening up the throttles again.

Soon, however, the drone from the engines starts to die down without back-fire. He can now complete the shut-down checks: turn off the fuel, switch off the ignition, close the cowling gills, and turn off all electrical services.

When he has completed these checks, Tom sits still for a few moments. He has to fight an urge to close his eyes, but he knows he must press on. He releases his seat straps and stretches his arms before easing himself up and out of his cockpit seat and stepping back stiffly towards his exit/entrance hatch.

Outside the Beaufighter, Tom and his navigator insert locking pins into the knuckle joints of each undercarriage main wheel. As they do this, and as they notice the ground marshaller walk towards them, they spot another figure nearby. This individual, shadowy-looking as he watches the group with his rifle at the ready, keeps a discreet distance. Tom, however, is aware of the reason: German aircrew have been known to land at RAF bases. The airfield organisation is showing good security sense in their dealings with visiting aircraft.

The ground marshaller leads Tom and his navigator towards a hangar which, in the moonlight, Tom can see has been damaged.

'That happened last year during the Battle of Britain,' says the marshaller. 'But they've done some temporary repairs.'

As they reach the hangar, the aircrew are directed towards an office. They squint their eyes against the sudden dazzle of lights, a shocking contrast to their accustomed conditions. The group remain standing as the duty officer, an army captain, keeping one hand close to his revolver holster, introduces himself.

'As you know, gentlemen,' says the captain, 'I need proof of identity. If you would kindly oblige, please.' When satisfied with the credentials, the captain becomes more relaxed. 'Thank you. Please, sit down. We've organised some tea for you.' He gestures to an orderly. 'We'll arrange accommodation when you're ready. It's been a bad night. The news has been coming through. It's estimated that five hundred enemy bombers have dropped thousands of bombs on London. You've been kept busy by the sound of things.'

'We've had to do our bit,' says Tom.

'I'm sure,' says the captain. 'We admire your efforts.'

'Perhaps we should have brought down more.'

'When there are so many, some are bound to get through. But can I ask how many you intercepted?'

'Two.'

'Both shot down?'

Tom nods, and the captain hesitates before he continues. 'You look exhausted,' he says.

'It's been a long night.'

'We salute you, gentlemen,' says the captain, staring at the aircrew. 'The nation owes you a debt of gratitude.'

'We just do our duty.'

'It's rather more than that,' says the captain. 'The PM made his comments last year about the Battle of Britain pilots, but this phase of night bombing is also demanding on the RAF.' The captain hesitates again, but he has a sincere tone as he goes on. 'And surely none of us can fully appreciate the skills, and the degree of courage, needed by you night-fighter crews.'

'G/CDR. T.G.PIKE. D.F.C.   219 SQUADRON

A charcoal portrait of Wing Commander T.G. Pike, DFC★ drawn by 'Orde' and dated
2 August 1941.

Tom and Althea sit perched on the running-board of a small family car in 1929.

Full dress uniform, complete with sword, on Tom and Althea's wedding day at Potter Street Church in Essex.

A picture of Althea taken on a picnic in 1930.

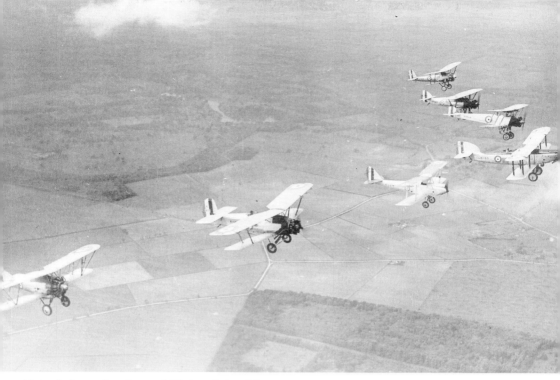

Aircraft from the Central Flying School based at Wittering, rehearsing for the 1930 Hendon Air Display in which Tom participated.

RAF Wittering in 1930.

The Central Flying School Aerobatic Team seen at RAF Wittering in 1930. Flying Officer Thomas Pike is second from the left from the right.

Flight Lieutenant Thomas Pike when a flying instructor at 4FTS in Egypt in March, 1936. He stands on the right in the white flying suit.

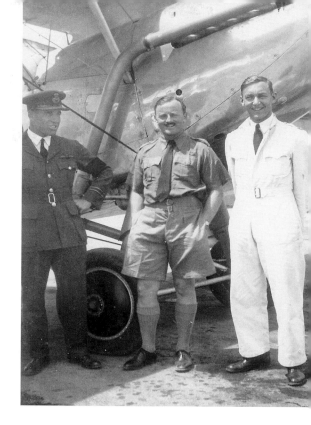

Flight Lieutenant Thomas Pike is seen seated in the centre in this unit photograph taken in 1936 whilst at 4FTS, Abu Sueir, Egypt.

An aircrew member (name unknown) of 219 Squadron tightens the straps of his parachute harness as he waits at readiness with other crews in the night fighter crew room.

Picture taken of a tired and pensive Wing Commander Thomas Pike after an operational mission.

Although flying as an operational pilot, the desk-work of the CO was still part of his job.

A 219 Squadron Beaufighter lifts off from the runway at Tangmere ready to join the queue for incoming 'trade'.

A typical scene in the night fighter crew-room. Note the dark adaptation goggles worn by aircrew to protect their night vision.

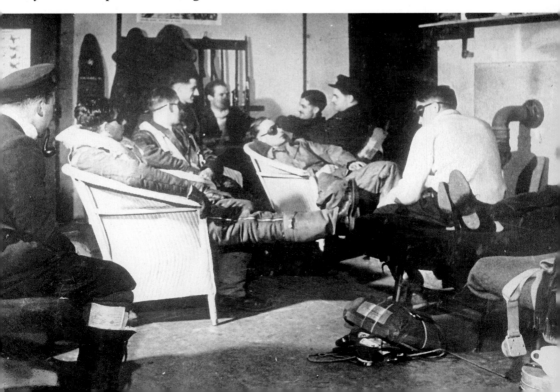

Silhouetted against the late evening sky, a Beaufighter stands ready for night-time action at Tangmere in 1941.

What will tonight bring? 219 Squadron crews remain on standby.

No. 219 Squadron's tally increases. A sixth Luftwaffe 'kill' is scored below the cockpit of this Beaufighter.

Accompanied by the squadron engineering officer the CO checks for damage and oil leakage under the engine nacelle of a 219 Squadron aircraft.

The CO and his navigator discuss the night ahead. Note the row of rifles in the background.

Crew on stand by. In the top left corner of the photograph you can see the 'war-prize' propeller of a Heinkel III, previously shot down by the CO.

A lone 'Beau' takes to the evening sky above Tangmere. The wartime introduction of double summertime extended daylight hours well into the late evening.

219 Squadron aircrew members in discussion.

The eyes that pierced the night skies above southern England in 1941.

A cheery wave from the legendary Douglas Bader, CO of the day-fighters based at Tangmere. The two wing commanders (Pike and Bader) became firm friends at this time, although Bader's ambition to fly a night mission in a Beaufighter was not realized before he was shot down in August 1941.

Aircraft recognition silhouettes and drawings adorned the walls of the crew-room. Identification of enemy and allied aircraft types was a vital factor in aerial combat.

May 1941; aircrew members and their wives at a lunch-time drinks party in the officer's mess garden at Tangmere. Wing Commander and Mrs T. G. Pike are either side of the station commander (smoking a pipe).

Air Marshal Sir Thomas Pike seen here in August 1956 when he was Air Officer Commander-in-Chief Fighter Command.

A portrait of Marshal of the Royal Air Force Sir Thomas Pike as Chief of the Air Staff, 1961.

CHAPTER THIRTEEN

The Reward, Saturday, 3 May

Her hand is placed elegantly through his arm as Tom escorts his wife through the officers' mess at Tangmere. He comments on how graceful she looks.

'Where did you manage to find that dress?'

'I have my sources,' says Althea with a smile. 'This one I keep for very special occasions. See, it's got all the latest features – pointed collar, padded shoulders, and softly gathered here.'

'Did you make it yourself?'

'Actually, I bought this one.'

'I thought you made your own these days.'

'Occasionally I have to push the boat out.'

'There's talk that they'll bring in clothing coupons next month.'

'Then I'll have to get down to even more needlework. Unless, that is, we're going to walk around semi-naked.'

'Which reminds me,' says Tom.

'About?'

'About your favourite ditty.'

'Which one is that?'

'Something about Spain?'

Althea clears her throat. 'There was a young lady from Spain, who began to undress in the train. A naughty young porter . . .' Althea hesitates. 'Saw more than he ought ter . . .'

'And?'

'And begged her to do it again.'

'Olé!' exclaims Tom as they both start to laugh.

By this time, the couple have walked through the mess and reached a door leading into a back garden. A number of officers are gathered

there, standing in groups as they chat, but Tom and Althea are greeted
by the station commander as he walks across.

'Althea! I know it's a hike all the way from Bedford, but these
lunchtime socials are one of the few opportunities for our families to get
together. They make a pleasant change from some of the riotous do's in
this mess, I can tell you. It's marvellous of you to make the effort.'

'Group Captain Woodhall! Thank you very much.'

'Now let me find you something to drink. Steward?' Althea inspects
a tray with a variety of filled glasses as the station commander adds,
'Tom, our resident teetotaller. We must organise something for you.'

'These are non-alcoholic, sir,' says the steward as he points at some
glasses.

'Thank you,' says Tom. 'Just the job. Apart from anything else, I'm on
duty this evening.'

'Good man,' says the group captain.

'I've got to admire you night owls,' says Wing Commander Bader,
who has walked across to join them.

'Douglas,' says Althea. 'How are you? And how's Thelma? I do hope
she's here.'

'Wonderful to see you, Althea,' says the wing commander. 'I'm afraid
that Thelma couldn't join us today. But, as I was saying, these night
flying chaps do a pretty good job, don't you think? I don't imagine I
could stand the long, lonely nights myself.'

'I thought you wanted to join us,' says Tom.

'I must admit there's nothing much happening on the day front just
now,' says the wing commander. 'Life's pretty dull: the Jerries seem to
be saving up all the action for you and your night team. But I fancy a
flight with you one time, that's true. It's a pity you don't seem keen on
the idea.'

'There are a few problems.'

'Anyway, to be honest, I don't like the idea of flying in my pyjamas.'

'It's not so bad when you get used to it.'

'Talking about pyjamas,' says Althea, 'wasn't there some story about
a pilot flying in his pyjamas during the Battle of Britain last year?'

'A fellow called Dennis David,' says Wing Commander Bader. 'He
was scrambled at dawn, but in the rush he didn't have time to kit up
properly. So being a practical sort of a chap, he just put his flying kit
over his pyjamas.'

'Did he intercept any enemy aircraft?'

'I think the pyjamas must have put off poor old Jerry. Our man shot
down a Heinkel 111 before returning for breakfast. He was then faced
with another problem, of course.'

'Which was?'

'He had to change out of his pyjamas in order to conform with mess rules for mealtimes.'

The group laugh, then the station commander asks, 'Where are you staying tonight, Althea? And what about your girls? I hope you're fixed up?'

'Thank you, yes. The girls are staying with my mother-in-law in Bedford and Tom's booked me into a hotel in Bognor Regis for tonight. I'll catch a train back to Bedford tomorrow.'

'Well done. I'm glad it's all in hand. By the way, Tom, are you all right for transport? The taxi service can be rather unreliable at present.'

'Thanks, sir. I've got a car organised through the squadron.'

'What time do you have to start duty tonight?' Althea asks her husband.

'With this double summertime routine, it doesn't seem to get fully dark until quite late – around eleven. But I'll start duty at eight o'clock with some of the so-called early team.'

'Is that when you put on those goggle devices?'

'The fellows look like men from Mars,' says Wing Commander Bader.

'They're pretty fashionable these days, Douglas,' says Tom. 'You should try them some time.'

'Maybe, old man, if you condescend to give me a flight one evening. Other than that, I think I'll stick to the daytime ops, thank you. Anyway,' he adds with a wink, 'your new nickname – what is it? Killer? I think all this night stuff sounds a bit too daunting for us day types.'

'You'll just have to eat more carrots, Douglas.'

'Fat chance, old boy.'

At this point, Tom and Althea beg indulgence and move across the lawn to circulate among other guests.

'It's providence that the weather is so fine at the moment,' Althea says quietly to her husband as they approach another group.

'I think they're forecasting a few showers later on.'

'King George had already fled the capital . . .' An officer is speaking as Tom and Althea join the group.

'Presumably you don't refer to our king?' says Tom.

'No, sir. King George the Second of Greece.'

'Ah, yes. A bad moment indeed. But how long, I wonder, before he has to move on from Crete?'

'With the fall of Athens last weekend,' says the officer, 'probably quite soon. The swastika flies over the Acropolis now, and Nazi progression in that area looks relentless.'

'We have to be grateful, at least, to the Commonwealth and Greek troops on the Mount Olympus line,' says Tom. 'But for their efforts we couldn't possibly have saved so many Allied forces.'

'The Australians earned particular acclaim,' says a squadron leader. 'When the Greek government issued that bulletin after the fall of Athens, they made special mention of the Aussies and the way they battled their way through despite being surrounded.'

'I gather the Royal Air Force won special praise as well,' says Althea.

'The Luftwaffe had complete air superiority in the area,' says the squadron leader. 'Our pilots had a desperate job against the Stukas.'

'They displayed amazing courage against such odds. The partisans, too, showed brave resistance, but the blitzkrieg overwhelmed them eventually.'

'When the Luftwaffe employ such massive numbers – hundreds of Stukas and Messerschmitts . . .'

'The Nazis just seem unstoppable sometimes.'

'We stopped them last year,' says Tom, who looks up when he hears Wing Commander Bader come across.

'Tom, old boy,' cries the wing commander, waving one hand in the air, 'Althea, I've got something for you.'

'What on earth?'

'It's Brighton rock,' he says, displaying the sweets on the palms of his hands. 'I heard about your visit, Althea. This is a small treat for your girls. I bought a couple of sticks when I was driving through Brighton with Thelma the other day.' As they move away from the group, he continues, 'We've got to keep cheerful, you know. That lot seemed to be taking life a little seriously. We mustn't allow too much bad news to get us down.'

'Thank you for the Brighton rock,' says Althea

'Beats carrots anyway, if you ask me,' says the wing commander.

'I haven't been to Brighton for years,' says Althea, as she reminisces. 'My father used to work there when I was a child; we lived there as a family in those days.'

'It's the same old place at heart. Boring as hell, really, but there's plenty of fresh air, I suppose.'

'And the rock's good,' says Althea with a smile. 'By the way, Douglas, sorry to return to a serious theme, but what's your opinion of the exploits of these Stukas?'

'I shouldn't allow it to worry you too much,' says the wing commander. 'The Luftwaffe lack our flexible approach to life. It'll defeat them in the end, you mark my words. I've even heard that those Stuka pilots have had their ears drilled out in order to have plugs inserted.

Something about coping with the high rates of descent when they dive. What a crazy bunch.'

'They've done some terrible things,' says Althea.

'Their efficient mentality,' says Tom, 'allows them to—'

'Allows them to get away with murder,' interjects Wing Commander Bader. 'Efficient mentality is one thing, but they lack an adaptable frame of mind. It'll be the finish of them in the end. Serve the blighters right.'

They all look up when a glass is tapped, calling for silence.

'Ladies and gentlemen,' says the station commander, 'I have an announcement to make. At the risk of causing him embarrassment, I'd like to read out the following bulletin which we have just received.' Referring to a sheet, he continues, 'This is Air Ministry Bulletin number 3729 issued from the Directorate of Public Relations in King Charles Street, Whitehall. It's dated the second of May 1941, and refers to Royal Air Force awards number 207. I will read it out verbatim. "The King has been graciously pleased to approve the following award in recognition of gallantry displayed in flying operations against the enemy: Distinguished Flying Cross, Wing Commander Thomas Geoffrey Pike, number 219 Squadron. This officer, who recently assumed command of the squadron, has shown great skill in intercepting enemy aircraft at night. During his first patrol he intercepted and, it is believed, destroyed a raiding aircraft. He has since destroyed three enemy aircraft of which two were destroyed during one night. His keenness and example have had a splendid effect on other members of his squadron.'

The group captain folds up the sheet, places it in his pocket, and follows the rest of the assembled officers as they grin and applaud Tom with enthusiasm.

CHAPTER FOURTEEN

An Evening
by the Sea

As he drives at speed away from Tangmere, and as he copes with
the twisty Sussex roads heading for Bognor Regis, Tom chats
with his wife.

'The station commander's keen to have these lunchtime get-
togethers,' he says. 'Many of the families live in different parts of the
country nowadays, and this is one way his officers and their wives can
meet up from time to time. And as he points out, the parties make a
civilised change from some of the affairs – near riots, some of them –
held in that mess.'

'The tensions of war have to be relieved somehow, don't they?'

At the outskirts of Bognor Regis, Tom drives along a back route
towards the sea-front. He parks, and they both stare at the local scene,
sensing a nostalgic awareness of better times. Their feelings are
tempered, though, by the sight of barbed wire furled around the sea-
front railings.

The couple step out of the car and start to breathe in the salty atmosphere. They link arms and watch the surging waves clatter onto the
pebbles. Althea points at the boisterous streams when the waters begin
to sink back, reduced to a swirling froth. She gulps the air and holds her
breath; soon, however, the next wave starts to appear. As the cycle is
repeated, an automatic round, she begins to release her breath slowly.
She laughs, and tosses her hair as she catches the familiar seaside
sounds, punctuated by the cries of gulls. The coastline is marked by the
gulls, soaring high, edged into the breeze, their heads agile and alert.
Tom watches the birds for a few moments, then looks towards Selsey
Bill following the coastal curve.

'Let's wander along the sea-front,' Althea suggests.

'The sea air will give you an appetite,' says Tom. He locks each individual car door, then looks back at the nearby Royal Hotel where Althea has been checked in for the night. 'I hope that hotel will be comfortable for you. Part of it's being used by Canadian troops. It's hard to find anywhere that's still open these days; most have shut down because of the war. As someone said at lunchtime, even Bognor's been affected by enemy action, but it'll be safer for you here than at Tangmere.'

'I'm sure it'll be perfectly all right,' says Althea. She points beyond the pier. 'Let's head that way. Then we can wander back the other way.'

The couple are still linking arms as they stroll along the sea-front.

'I can't wait to tell the girls about your Distinguished Flying Cross,' says Althea. 'Caryl will be so proud.'

Tom smiles, nods modestly, then asks, 'How are things working out at her school now?'

'There are still a few problems, I'm afraid.'

'It's just not good enough. Don't you think we should move her to another school?'

'I think we need to persevere for a bit longer,' says Althea calmly. 'It's so difficult to find good schools at the moment.' She stops, and points. 'What's happened to the pier?'

'It's been taken over by the Royal Navy. They use it for firing practice.'

'So the toy guns have been replaced by real ones?'

'I'm afraid so. And look: a section of the pier's been removed as part of this "Stop the Germans Landing" campaign.'

As the couple resume their walk, they look at a sign placed close to the pier: HMS Barbara.

'It seems everything's been taken over by the military these days,' sighs Althea. She looks along the street, and says, 'Let's carry on up here for a bit, towards Aldwick Road. Isn't that the way we drove in?'

'We took the scenic route. Remember, I pointed out Saint Richard's Church?'

'The church with the unusual tower?'

'Some people from Tangmere go there.'

'It seems odd, somehow.'

'How do you mean?'

'Oh, I don't know.' Althea pauses. 'Both sides worshipping the same god.'

'I don't suppose there are many Nazis who worship Him.'

'Do many of your people still have religious faith?'

'The war seems to have strengthened the faith of some people.'

'Is that how you feel?'

Tom ponders the question, and glances at his wife before saying, 'Yes, I think it is. It's partly a need for security. Our duties take us into a dark world, and without the back-up of religion I think I would feel too much alone, too much exposed to unknown perils.'

'It was the same in the Great War,' says Althea. 'There were some extraordinary tales – frightening, ghostly tales. Remember the cases of soldiers seeing apparitions on the field of battle? Giant, supernatural forms, holding up vast protective shields.'

'The Angels of Mons.'

'Yes, the Angels of—' They look skywards as they hear an aircraft. 'One of your machines?' asks Althea anxiously.

'It's a Spitfire,' says Tom in a calm way, 'probably setting out on patrol.' They continue their walk. 'Though the day fighters aren't very busy at present. The Germans seem intent on the night raids just now. It's causing Douglas Bader a considerable amount of frustration. He's started to take the fight across the Channel, to Cherbourg, and other places.'

'He's an incorrigible character,' says Althea with a chuckle.

'His particular form of humour is quite a tonic. And his, frankly, somewhat bloodthirsty outlook is probably just what's needed in war. He is an extraordinarily good leader, and he has this ability to practically eliminate fear from his pilots.'

'I'm sure it's the same with you and your squadron,' says Althea. 'You and he are such different characters, yet you seem to get along so well.' She pauses, then says, 'If your nickname is Killer, what's his?'

'He has the initials DB painted on the side of his Spitfire, so he's now known as Dogsbody.' Tom laughs. 'He keeps pestering me to take him up one night in a Beaufighter, but it's hardly appropriate for passengers. I don't think he'd enjoy it.'

'And what's this rumour about the paperwork?'

'He's not keen on paperwork, that's for sure. One of his pilots was in the office the other day. They were chatting away when an administrator appeared and placed some papers carefully on the office desk. "What the hell's this, Flight Sergeant?' asks Douglas. "Files for your attention, sir,"' says the Flight Sergeant. "I'll give 'em attention all right," says Douglas before picking up the files and throwing them in a waste-paper bin.'

Althea laughs. 'I liked his comments about the pyjamas.'

'His own flying dress is quite eccentric, actually. He wears a black flying suit, with a blue and white polka-dot scarf.' Tom smiles. 'The other day he was flying back across the Channel in close formation with Cocky Dundas. After a while, Douglas evidently got bored. He pushed back his canopy, took off his oxygen mask and stuffed a pipe stub into his mouth. Cocky was amazed. When Douglas started to light up, he caught Cocky's wide-eyed stare. Douglas just beamed, and made rude signs.'

'Incorrigible!' says Althea. 'What did Douglas mean about Westhampnett? Where's that?'

'It's a satellite airfield used by the day fighters. It's just a few miles to the west of Tangmere. We've moved 610 and 616 Squadrons there, and 145 Squadron to Merston; this spreads our resources in case of bombing strikes. Tangmere was badly damaged last year, during the Battle of Britain, and we still get raids from time to time. You know what happened to my room in the mess.'

'Don't remind me.'

'The hero of that night, actually, was the Roman Catholic padre. When the raid had passed, he rushed into the burning chaos, tin hat on head, and began to search for casualties. The story went around that the German bullets could be heard pinging off the padre's tin hat, while the brave fighter boys hid quaking in the air-raid shelters.'

Althea laughs again, and after a moment asks, 'Wasn't it after that raid that an article appeared in the *Sunday Express*?'

'I think it was. Douglas was keen for a special type of camouflage paint to be applied to the runways. Tangmere, in particular, stood out clearly, and the Jerries could spot the airfield too easily. Nothing seemed to be done about it, so to speed things up he contacted a journalist who wrote a cryptic article about a "certain RAF airfield". The Air Ministry was furious.'

'But it worked?'

'The runways were camouflaged within a week.'

Althea smiles, then says quietly, 'With all these night raids, I suppose you're likely to be scrambled this evening?'

'I suppose so, though we never know what to expect. But I'll try to ensure you have an undisturbed night.' Tom grins. 'And if I get back in time, I'll do my best to see you off at the station tomorrow.'

'As it's the weekend, maybe the Germans will allow you to have a quiet time.'

'I'll have a word with Goering.'

'Which reminds me. What was Douglas saying about Goering and one of his propellers in your crew room?'

'Another war trophy, I suppose. We've acquired a few just lately.'

'I remember you telling me about the German clock.'

'It's still there.'

'And the propeller?'

'In one corner of the crew room.'

'Douglas said that the machine was shot down by you.'

'It was,' says Tom quietly. 'A Heinkel 111.'

'Was that one of the casualties a couple of weeks ago, when you shot down two aircraft in one night?'

'Yes,' says Tom with a nod.

Althea grips his arm as they continue to walk slowly.

'I suppose you still have mixed feelings?' she says.

'Sometimes I do.'

'I'm sure it's the same for all the aircrew.'

'It is for some,' says Tom. 'As CO, I have to talk to them about it. One or two, in particular, have been affected, and they feel guilty about their sentiments. They think that their doubts somehow diminish their commitment to the squadron. I think it's helpful for them to realise that others, including the CO, have mixed feelings too.'

'Nobody in their right mind likes war. Except, maybe, the profiteers.'

'We can't stop now; we've just got to fight this one through, even though it may take years. We've no other choice. It would be unthinkable to capitulate to the Nazis. What future would that create for our girls, and for the next generation?'

'Capitulation's happening in France.'

'The Vichy regime is a disgrace. De Gaulle may be a difficult customer, but at least he represents decent values. Pétain and his ilk are a sham. Forward-thinking French people are disgusted by the whole set-up. As if we didn't have enough problems without Pétain.'

At that point, the couple decide to turn around and retrace their steps. 'Let's wander back,' says Tom. 'We could head towards Billy Bunter's amusement arcade at the other end of the Esplanade.'

'Billy Butlin, do you mean?'

'That's the fellow. "Mister Happiness" himself.'

'That's what we need just now,' says Althea. 'Something to cheer us up. Something to look forward to.'

'I've been thinking the same. And I've had an idea. I don't know what you'll make of it.'

'Well?'

'I wondered if we should think about buying a car.'

'Oh!'

'It seems an extravagance, I know, and there are snags. Getting enough petrol, for one thing. But it's not impossible to get petrol, and having a car again will give us more freedom. You could visit your parents more often.'

'I think it's a good idea, but can we afford one?'

'I'll have to save up. Remember, I'm paid as a wing commander nowadays. That'll help a bit.'

'A wing commander with a Distinguished Flying Cross.'

'Unfortunately, the gong won't help pay for the car.'

'How much will the car cost?'

'We should be able to buy a good second-hand one for, say, something between fifty and a hundred pounds.'

'That seems an awful lot.'

'But you're not against the idea?'

'Far from it. I think it sounds an exciting plan.'

'When we sold our other car, at the beginning of the war, it seemed the right thing to do at the time,' says Tom. 'But we didn't know then what we know now. We didn't think that the war would go on for so long.'

'We've got to try to make the best of life, even in wartime.'

'I think owning a car again would give us all a boost.'

'The girls will be most excited.'

'We'll have to get some good maps,' says Tom. 'The road signs are still chaotic. Our efforts to confuse the Germans would have been pretty successful had the invasion happened. In the meantime, though, everyone else has been thoroughly confused instead.'

'I'll look forward to driving again.'

'You're a good driver, I seem to remember.'

'Apart from gear-changing,' says Althea. 'That's such a tiresome procedure. I can't think why the car makers have to insert these wretched gear-boxes in the first place. They cause nothing but trouble.'

'You'd better write to Mister Henry Ford.'

'I'm quite good at steering, though.'

'Can you remember about the brakes?'

'What brakes?'

'We could buy an ex-army tank. It might be safer than a car. We could paint it red.'

'Or bright orange,' says Althea, inclining her head with a thoughtful look. 'On second thoughts, maybe not a tank. It would remind us too much of military things.' She shivers, and looks up. 'There's a shower coming this way.'

'Let's head for that café. Time's getting on anyway. I said the sea air would give you an appetite. Let's have a bite, then I think it'll be time . . .'

Tom's voice fades away, and they begin to increase their pace when they feel the first drops of rain. Before long they are pushing open the café door and being shown to a small table.

'This place is rather basic,' says Tom glumly.

'I'm not very hungry anyway, despite what you said about the sea air.' Althea studies the straightforward menu. 'I think I'll just have some soup, please.'

'That's not enough,' says Tom. 'You must eat properly.'

A somewhat awkward atmosphere develops between them as they grow conscious of Tom's impending departure.

'That's all I want, thank you.'

Tom scans through the menu, then says to the waitress, 'I think I'll have the mixed grill, please.'

When their order has been placed, the couple, still ill at ease, stare at the café's plain surroundings. They look through lace curtains by the front window; a group of youngsters are huddling under the awning to shelter from the rain. When the food is served, Althea toys nervously with her soup. She breaks her bread into small pieces and stares at them, feeling disinclined to eat.

At length, when Tom has finished his mixed grill, he says quietly, 'I'd better take you back to the hotel now.'

Althea nods, and tries to look cheerful. Outside, she hugs her husband's arm again as they walk towards the hotel.

'At least this rain shower has eased,' she says lightly. 'I hope the weather will be fine for your flying this evening.'

'I think the forecast is good for tonight.'

When they reach the Royal Hotel, Althea says, 'Please don't come in, Tom. I think it best if you don't come in. Maybe you should set off for Tangmere straight away.'

'Perhaps you're right. But you should go inside, it's chilly out here. Wave to me from your bedroom window.'

Althea falters before she reaches out to give her husband a last hug. She closes her eyelids as she holds him tightly for a few moments, then eases him gently away. At the last instant she clasps both of his arms. She's aware of the cry of gulls above, and as she gazes into his eyes and feels her own eyes slowly welling up, she hesitates again. She releases her grip and quickly turns away, unwilling to prolong the moment, heading straight for the hotel without looking back.

Tom walks to the military car, his mind so preoccupied that he barely notices the seaside clamours, the surging waves, the clatter of pebbles, even the salty atmosphere and the barbed wire around the sea-front railings. As he unlocks the car and steps inside, he can have no idea of how his flying activities during the night ahead will decide the fate of these exposed and fragile assets.

CHAPTER FIFTEEN

Saturday Night Out

om's emotions are in turmoil. He winds down the car window and returns Althea's hand-waves as he drives away from the Royal Hotel. He finds it so hard, so disconcerting, to leave his wife like this. Althea shows formidable pluck, and she puts on such a brave face, but somehow this makes the problem even harder. At least when he's at work Tom is active and absorbed. But for the families, the waiting and the uncertainty, the suspense – surely it must be almost unbearable at times, perhaps even worse in a way than the aircrews' feeling of tension while they wait for a scramble order.

At length, as Tom continues to glance in his rear-view mirror, he gives a final wave goodbye as Althea's last words echo through his mind. He slowly winds up the car window and begins to turn away from the sea-front area.

Tom feels for a packet of cigarettes and a box of matches, and he slows the car as he fumbles with them. He eventually succeeds in lighting up, and with relish he inhales a deep breath of cigarette smoke before he begins to accelerate the car again. He'll be on duty shortly; he has to attune his mind to what lies ahead. He glances at his watch; he should have over an hour of available time when he gets to the squadron. He'll have to check over his aircraft, then he can do a few administrative jobs before starting operational standby.

When Tom turns into the camp area at Tangmere airfield, his car is checked and searched by guards, who salute when they have inspected Tom's identity pass. 'Thank you, sir.' One of them raises a barrier, and salutes again as he waves the car through.

In the 219 Squadron area, Tom ensures his cigarette is extinguished before he steps out of the car. He stretches his arms as he gets out, then locks the car doors before making his way towards the CO's office.

'How did it go, sir?' the squadron senior engineering officer says as he spots Tom walking by.

'Pretty good, thanks,' says Tom. 'Thank you for organising the car.'

'Not at all, sir. Any time.'

'Have you been to Bognor recently?'

'Not for a week or so.'

'There are plenty of Canadians about, and some Polish servicemen.'

'I've heard that Bognor's becoming quite cosmopolitan.'

'A shock to their system, no doubt. How are things here?'

The squadron leader hesitates before saying, 'I wasn't going to trouble you with it just now, but we've had a problem, actually.'

'Oh?'

'But I don't want to hold you up. I expect you've got to get organised for flying this evening.'

'Have I got my usual machine?'

'R2253 – yes, I believe so, though ops will have to confirm that.'

'OK. But I've got a bit of time in hand. Perhaps we should go to my office to talk.'

The two men hurry towards the CO's office, and as they enter the squadron leader is direct. 'I'm afraid there's been some trouble involving one of our airmen. We've had a call from the police in London.'

'London?'

'Our man was due for some leave, so he decided to go up to London. Unfortunately, he wasn't fixed up with any form of accommodation. He reckoned to try one of the underground stations – Green Park, I think.'

'One of the better ones, pretty clean and with facilities, I seem to remember from my time in London last year.'

'I wouldn't know,' says the squadron leader. 'The details are still a bit sketchy, but you're aware, I expect, of these spivs who operate around the Tube stations?'

'Indeed,' says Tom. 'You often see these shady characters hanging around the stations. They're the dregs, and quite unscrupulous. They save up the good positions along the platform, then charge two shillings and sixpence. These petty crooks, in their way, are as bad as the big-time war profiteers.'

'That was evidently the attitude of our airman.'

'Along with many others.'

'As I say, the details are still sketchy, but the policeman told me there'd been a fight.'

'Is our man OK?'

'He was beaten up and, confused, started to wander the streets. He ended up in a back street where he eventually slumped down near a pub. Passers-by thought he was drunk, so they ignored him. But when the air-raid sirens started up a warden tried to help him to a shelter.'

'Good fellow. So are they sending the airman back now?'

'That won't be possible, sir.'

'Go on.'

'The air-raid warden had some difficulty trying to help our man and they couldn't move quickly. They were just a short distance from the shelter when the bomb struck. The warden was killed outright, but our man was still alive when they found him. He managed to tell his story before they took him off to hospital. But unfortunately his condition deteriorated in the hospital, and I'm sorry to say that he didn't pull through. He died a few hours ago.'

'My God,' gasps Tom.

'I'm sorry to be the bearer of bad tidings.'

'These Tube touts are a disgrace.'

'I suppose the police are too preoccupied to clamp down on them.'

Tom hesitates, then asks, 'Have you been in touch with the next of kin?'

'We're dealing with that now, sir. We're waiting to hear about the next of kin's wishes for his funeral.'

'Poor fellow,' says Tom. 'As if we can afford to lose good people at the moment.'

'Sorry to have to bother you with such matters.'

'Keep me in the picture please,' says Tom. 'But unless there's something else, I must get ready for flying now.'

'Good luck tonight, sir.'

Tom stands up to leave his office, but remains absorbed in thought as he walks to the operations room. Inside the room, he spots the duty operations officer gesticulating with one hand while he speaks on the telephone. 'De Valera & Co. provide a pretty good beacon,' he is saying. 'But I've noted the message, and I'll pass it on to the CO – he's just come in.' The operations officer replaces the receiver as he says, 'That was Tangmere ops, sir.'

'Are they getting worked up?' asks Tom, his mind quickly attuning to operational matters.

'A tip-off from HQ 11 Group. They're warning again about the current thrust of raids towards Liverpool.'

'So-called neutral Eire giving trouble?'

'The Irish make no blackout efforts at all, so the German pilots have a first-rate navigation aid as they fly up the Irish Sea. The bright lights of Ireland point conveniently towards Liverpool – the key centre in the Battle of the Atlantic.'

'It's ironic that Liverpool houses such a large population of Irish people.'

'And it's a scandal that the authorities in Eire don't interfere with the IRA. The dissidents work unimpeded with spies parachuted in by Germany.'

'Churchill has protested to his Irish counterpart, but De Valera's evidently afraid of feeling the force of German arms against his country. So the Irish lights keep shining, and German submarines quietly refuel in obscure bays along Ireland's southern coast.'

'And it's not just the Irish giving us problems at present.'

'Meaning?'

'I was thinking about the Welsh. We've had these reports of beacons placed on hill-tops in various parts of Wales. The Irish keep their lights on, and the Welsh nationalists provide the beacons. Can you believe it? If you ask me, they should send in the army to round up these traitors.'

'It's preposterous that they can get away with it. And, meanwhile, the citizens of Liverpool have to suffer such hardship. The French have to contend with the Vichy regime, but it seems in this country we're just as plagued with fifth columnists and general miscreants. Did you hear what happened to one of our airmen in London?'

'The engineers were talking about it; something about a scam on the London Underground.' The operations officer looks up as he hears someone approach. 'Here's Sergeant Austin,' he says to Tom, 'your navigator for this evening, sir.'

'Hello, Sergeant Austin,' says Tom. 'How are you? All set for tonight?'

'Evening, sir. Yes, all set.'

'There's an hour or so before we start duty.' Tom turns back to the operations officer. 'Have you allocated us an aircraft yet?'

'It's your usual machine, sir – R2253. I'll confirm with the engineers when it'll be ready.'

'If you could do that, please, then we'll check it over. The good news,' says Tom to his navigator, 'is that it's too light to bother with dark adaptation goggles yet.'

'We may not need them at all if we get an early scramble,' says the navigator.

'That's confirmed, sir,' says the operations officer. 'Your aircraft will be ready in a few minutes.'

'Thanks. In that case I'll change into my flying kit now, and see you by the aircraft, Sergeant Austin.'

When Tom has donned his flying suit, he walks to the engineering line office. Here he checks his aircraft log for the latest flight hours, any problems from the last flight, and any ongoing particulars. R2253 is normally allocated to Tom for operations, but the machine is not flown exclusively by him. He notes a report about a tendency for the navigator's exit/entrance hatch to unlock in flight, and he discusses this with the duty engineer. Tom then signs and dates the relevant sheet before he leaves the line office to walk to his parked Beaufighter, by now manned by the navigator.

As he approaches his aircraft, Tom takes time to appraise its exterior. He searches for signs of oil leakage by the engine cowlings, and on the ground beneath. He checks both of the three-bladed propellers, inspecting for marks and chips, especially along the leading edges. He scrutinises the 20mm Hispano cannon openings in the nose area, checking for indications of blockage or impairment and looks at the bulky undercarriage assembly, the brakes and the tyres. Then, as he walks towards the tail, he inspects the upper and lower surfaces of the wings, the fuselage and the tail-plane, in particular examining any repairs to previous combat damage.

When satisfied with the external checks, Tom climbs up the steps of the entrance hatch and moves forward to the pilot's cockpit, which he arranges for a quick getaway. He adjusts the seat height and places the seat straps in a convenient position and ensures that the ignition switches are set, the hydraulic power lever is on, the undercarriage lever is selected down and the pneumatic supply pressure is 220lb per square inch. Then he puts on the electrical services switch to check the undercarriage position indicators and the fuel contents gauges. He also tests the flying controls for full and free movement. When satisfied with all the checks, he turns off the electrical services switch before climbing out of his seat and stepping back to the exit/entrance hatch.

'Everything OK in your cockpit?' he asks his navigator.

'It all looks good, sir.'

'Let's check the latest weather forecast, then. After that, I'll go to my office and try to get on with some paperwork.'

'I'll be in the crew room,' says the navigator.

'I expect you'll be entertained by Haw-Haw soon.'

'I think I can guess what he's got in store for us.'

'And quite apart from this Haw-Haw fellow, I gather there's been treachery in other places, too.'

'The Irish and the Welsh seem hell-bent on giving us trouble – well, some of them do. It makes you sick when you think of our so-called kinfolk. With friends like that, who needs enemies?'

'Quite,' says Tom curtly. He gazes up at the sky before he goes inside to check the meteorological sheets. 'It looks like a repeat of last night,' he says to his navigator as they study the prognosis. 'These showers will die down eventually, and hopefully we'll have clear conditions for the rest of the evening.'

'It's looking OK.'

Tom now walks to his office where he unlocks a safe in one corner of the room. He checks inside the safe and extracts files left for him by the squadron adjutant. As he takes the files to his desk, with a wry thought he eyes the waste-paper basket. 'Perhaps Douglas Bader's got the right idea after all,' he muses. However, Tom is diligent with paperwork; he is a first-rate staff officer, and he soon becomes engrossed with the file's varied subjects. He's aware of background noise as he works: telephone conversations, outbursts of laughter, clatters from the hangar area, the occasional and shocking sound of the scramble bell. When he hears 'Germany calling, Germany calling. This is the Reichssender broadcast . . .' he checks his watch: eight o'clock. He's now on operational standby. He wonders what Althea is doing, how she's managing in Bognor, and how his two girls are coping in Bedford. He glances at their photographs on his desk top.

Tom decides to phone the operations officer. 'I'm still in my office, Bob,' he says. 'I'll stay here for a bit longer, but call me when I'm near the top of the scramble list, please.'

Tom stares out of his office window, noting the darkened sky and the approach of a rain shower. He feels for his matches and his by now battered cigarette packet. He strikes a match, lights a cigarette and inhales slowly, with appreciation. He muses on the conversations he's just had. An airman, a good man, killed while on a night out; how ironic that a man should be killed by one of the bombers his squadron has the duty to intercept. Why do the authorities in London allow these tube touts to get away with it? And what about De Valera, the Irish lights, the IRA and the Welsh nationalists? Why do we have to contend with these . . .

The papers on his desk seem to swim before Tom's eyes, but he shakes his head and forces his mind to think about the file before him. He has a powerful ability to focus his thoughts and he's soon absorbed with the file's subject matter again. As he becomes engrossed, he's less bothered by the sounds from outside, though from time to time a particular clatter disturbs him and he checks his watch before returning to the paperwork, writing notes and letters for the attention of the squadron adjutant in the morning.

Tom jerks his pen on one occasion when the sound of the scramble bell makes him jump. He looks at his watch again: it's nearly a quarter to nine, so he decides to abandon the paperwork. He returns the files to his office safe, and when the telephone rings he speaks with the operations officer. 'I reckoned it was me next, Bob. I'm just coming through.' Tom hurriedly scans around his office to make sure that all classified material is locked away before he grabs his flying gear and sets off at a fast pace towards the operations room.

Tom glances at the operations wall clock as he enters the room. It's ten minutes to nine. He nods a greeting to the operations officer and overhears his conversation on the telephone. 'The Beauty Chorus are getting busy? With their radar plot, you mean? Yes, I can hear your loudspeakers in the background. Life must be hell in that Tangmere Ops set-up. Lots of green plaques? OK, that's understood. Yes, the crew have just run outside. The CO's next in line.'

Quickly, Tom double-checks his flying kit – maps, gloves, parachute pack, Mae West. His navigator is still in the crew room, sitting patiently, and the absence of dark adaptation goggles allows him to read a magazine. As the operations officer continues to speak on the telephone, Tom's gaze drifts towards the war map: English Channel, Irish Sea, Liverpool, Eire, Wales . . .

'That was Tangmere Ops again, sir,' says the operations officer as he replaces the receiver. 'And there's a message from the group captain. He says, "Enjoy your Saturday night out."'

Tom grins and nods his thanks just as the telephone rings again. The operations officer snatches the receiver, and he's terse as he answers the call. In just a matter of seconds he bangs it down, but even before he begins to shout the scramble order Tom has started to make a dash towards the door.

CHAPTER SIXTEEN

Canadian Encounter

Althea is choked with feeling as she stares out of the bedroom window. She watches Tom drive away in his military car, and she returns his hand-waves. When he eventually disappears from sight, she stops waving and remains motionless for a few moments. She feels dazed. She's barely conscious of the seaside views as she stares out of the window. It seems so awful, she cries within herself, to bid farewell to Tom like that, just before he starts operational duty.

As she leans forward to close the bedroom window, she shivers, and snatches a final look in the direction Tom has taken. When she is in Bedford, his duties seem so detached, so remote – another world, such a particular world. A world of stealth, and of deception. A marginal world, where they operate within dark shadows. A world of violent death.

She shivers again. Tom keeps so much to himself. No wonder she can never really understand it. But tonight, if something should go wrong . . .

Eventually, Althea decides to make for the hotel's sitting room. It's well past seven by now, and at least she might find companionship there. By lingering in her bedroom she will only become depressed. She makes a firm decision: she'll take some knitting and go downstairs.

'Good evening.'

As Althea steps down the staircase, she smiles nervously when she passes a courteous gentleman. At the bottom of the stairs, she walks along a stretch of corridor towards the sitting room. A few people are in the room. Most are reading newspapers and magazines. Some are in officers' uniforms, and they casually observe Althea as she enters. Melodies from the wireless soothe the atmosphere, and a few toes tap in time to the music. Althea remembers her days as a dance teacher. That was such a different world. Had she been told then what her life would be like now, most probably she would not have believed it.

She heads for a chair next to a young woman in military uniform. The young woman looks up as Althea approaches.

'May I?' Althea points towards the chair.

'Of course – please.'

The accent is French. How unexpected; not one of the Pétain lot, Althea trusts. Tom was so vehement about them. Althea sits down, and smiles as she glances at her neighbour. She notices the young woman's graceful hands, her elegant fingers, untarnished by housewifely duties. The young woman continues to read her magazine, evidently unwilling to make conversation.

As she settles into the chair, Althea looks around the room. Everyone remains engrossed in their reading apart from a group of men who are chatting in confidential tones as they sit in the bay window area. Althea reaches for her knitting, and glances at her watch: it's past 7.30 already. She begins to study her knitting plan, supplied by Bee. Althea dislikes knitting really, but Bee is quite right: needs must. Annie, in particular, could do with another jumper.

As she knits, Althea notices that her neighbour has started to click her tongue in an irritated fashion. The young woman remains absorbed in her magazine, but from time to time she nods to herself. At one point she appears to clench a fist, and Althea looks at her in alarm. The young woman, still engrossed, waves one hand at her temple in a sudden gesture, then glances at Althea. '*Pardon*,' she mumbles in her French accent. Althea smiles, and continues with her knitting. Her mind, though, starts to race. Who is this young woman? Althea has no idea. She could be a spy. One of the Pétain traitors, disguised in an Allied uniform and sent over on a secret mission. She could be.

We're all getting neurotic. This foolishness must stop. Even so, thinks Althea, why should she reveal the best of British knitting techniques to a spy? Why should that scandalous Pétain brigade reap the benefit of anything? It would be absurd. It would be unpatriotic. She shakes her head: this is too ridiculous – everyone's just getting carried away.

'Excuse me, everybody.' The gentleman Althea passed on the stairs has entered the sitting room. He, too, speaks with a French accent as he politely addresses the people in the room. 'Do you good folk have any objections if I retune the wireless for a bit?' The gentleman looks around with an amiable expression. 'It's nearly eight o'clock. We could listen to Haw-Haw for a while. It might be entertaining tonight.'

Althea thinks, what is it about this Haw-Haw fellow? The man's a scoundrel and a traitor, yet he attracts the attention of thousands – no, millions of people. Althea personally can't bear his haughty voice, his arrogant manner. The others in the sitting room, though, murmur assent, and the gentleman with the French accent stoops to turn the dialling knob on the wireless.

The dance music is interrupted, and the wireless begins to emit retuning screeches. The young woman next to Althea lowers her magazine and Althea glances at the headline: PERSÉCUTION PEUPLE JUIF. My God, thinks Althea, no wonder she's worked up. What horrors are the Jewish people having to endure? The stories seem to seep out; some of them are hardly believable. What would Haw-Haw have to say about that? He doesn't make mention, of course, apart from sweeping anti-Semitic statements.

As the tones signalling eight o'clock sound from the wireless, Althea remembers that Tom is about to start duty. She feels a rush of anxiety: will he be scrambled this evening? Perhaps, as he sits in the crew room, he will be listening to Haw-Haw as well.

'Germany calling, Germany calling. This is the Reichssender broadcast . . .' Wait for it – oh dear, here he comes. 'Yesterday British troops clashed for the first time with our Iraqi friends at Habbaniyah. This foolish action involving Britain must surely be a further indication of the failed policies of your government. The British administration of Iraq has been nothing short of disastrous. Can you not see? Where are your leaders taking you? What is the aim of it all? Surely it is obvious: the policies of our Führer have reason and logic. We have clear leadership . . .'

'Tell that to the *peuple juif*.' The comment is muttered by the young woman next to Althea.

'I don't know why people listen to this.'

'A form of *curiosité* . . . fascination, I suppose.'

'Although I suppose he does have a point about Iraq.'

Althea hesitates as she glances at her neighbour. The wireless still emits the deliberate tones of the treacherous voice; the young woman scowls as she listens. Althea glimpses her blue-grey eyes, and the determined look of her square-set features. There is a starchy, correct look about her pressed flannel uniform. There is also an energy in the young woman's features, a forcefulness to her movements as she reacts to the words of Haw-Haw. '*Pah . . . fou . . .*' Once more, the wave of the hand at the temple, the young woman's good looks darkened by a frown. Eventually, though, her expression relaxes and she tidies the magazine on her lap. At last Haw-Haw has stopped and the wireless is being retuned again.

'You're from Canada?' Althea has sighted the insignia on the young woman's uniform.

'*Oui*, Quebec.'

'You don't have to endure Haw-Haw over there, I suppose?'

'Terrible . . . *terrible*.'

'How long have you been based over here?'

'Oh, not long.'

The young woman remains vague, anxious not to be drawn into conversation. Althea, though, feels a sudden pity for her. The young woman seems restless, and lonely.

'My name is Althea.' Althea speaks lightly, on impulse, as she holds out her hand.

'Beatrice.'

The young woman smiles briefly as she returns the handshake, but Althea senses that Beatrice is not her real name.

'I'm making this for my younger daughter.' Althea picks up her handiwork. 'But I hate knitting, really.'

'I've never tried it.'

Althea hesitates. 'Quebec must be very beautiful. Though I haven't been there.'

'It is beautiful.'

She seems so nervous, so much on edge, thinks Althea. She isn't keen to converse yet there's something about her that is, somehow, saddening.

'I had a cousin who went to university in Quebec,' Althea says, deciding to persist a little. 'I think the establishment was called Laval. My cousin loved it there.' Althea smiles. 'He sent me letters describing the picturesque old town above the St Lawrence River. And he wrote enthusiastically about the fine views of the Notre Dame mountains.'

Althea stops. She thinks she can detect a flicker of emotion on her young friend's face. I mustn't upset her, thinks Althea; that would be unkind.

Althea checks her watch again. Nearly twenty to nine; she wonders what Tom is up to at that second. Perhaps he's airborne already; a few flights have already passed overhead. Presumably they were friendly, or we would have heard the air-raid sirens go off. Perhaps Tom is flying over the sea, already in violent combat with an enemy machine. Perhaps he's about to press the gun-firing button. Perhaps, instead, the German has Tom in his sights. Perhaps it is the German who is about to press the firing button. Perhaps . . .

Oh no! Just her luck – a dropped stitch. That's the penalty of day-dreaming. Althea will have to scrutinise Bee's instructions again. This knitting is nothing but a nuisance, an intensely tedious pest. Althea looks down as she slams the knitting onto her lap. She feels her eyes begin to fill up. If only . . .

'Althea?'

Althea looks up sharply, aware of being observed. The blue-grey eyes study her with concern. Althea's own vision remains blurred.

'Are you OK? You seem a little . . .' Still the steady gaze of those eyes.

'Do I? I'm so sorry . . .'

'It's OK.' The young woman begins to fold up her magazine. She seems to have made up her mind as she says, 'Would you care for a short stroll, *peut-être*? Some fresh air?' The French accent, so distinctive, has a sympathetic tone.

Althea hesitates. 'Thank you. That would be pleasant. Will we need coats, I wonder?'

'Maybe. There are some rain showers, and it's getting a bit cold. I meet you in reception, in, *quoi*? Five minutes?'

'That's a nice idea. *Merci*.'

Althea rises from her seat. As she follows her young friend out of the sitting room, and as the two go in different directions towards their own rooms, Althea briefly wonders if she is doing the right thing. Is this really advisable? But then, why not? After all, this is supposed to be a seaside resort, and a brief spell of fresh air will surely do her good. Nevertheless, as she hurries towards the stairs she tells herself firmly that she must try to ignore the note of caution now sounding at the back of her mind.

CHAPTER SEVENTEEN

'Bloody Jerries Bloody Bognor'

As the crews run outside, the duty officer yells instructions above the clang of the scramble bell. Tom soon spots his navigator and the ground crew, as they all sprint towards parked Beaufighter number R2253.

Tom makes directly for the entrance hatch that leads to his cockpit, where he eases himself into the pilot's seat. His earlier cockpit preparations expedite the preliminaries; carefully placed seat straps help him to strap in quickly before he puts on his flying head gear and oxygen mask. He swiftly checks the cockpit controls: ignition switches, hydraulic power lever, undercarriage selector, pneumatics. He selects the electrical services switch to 'on'. He sets the fuel controls: inner tank fuel cocks, suction balance cock, drop tank cock. He positions the throttles three-quarters of an inch open, and the propeller speed control fully forward.

Tom glances outside and gives a prearranged signal to the ground crew as they watch him expectantly. The ground crew have to turn each engine by hand through at least two revolutions; this guards against hydraulic shock damage. Then, for the first engine to be started, they operate a Ki-gass priming pump, monitoring the suction and delivery pipelines. When these indicate full, the crew start to prime the engine, applying seven strokes for the air temperature of the early May evening. They eventually give a thumbs-up sign to Tom, who straight away switches on the ignition and makes a final check around the cockpit before he presses the starter and booster coil push-buttons.

The Beaufighter's first engine begins to sputter into life. Tom, meanwhile, monitors the cockpit gauges. As soon as he is satisfied with the readings, he gives a further hand signal and the ground crew move across to the other engine to repeat the start procedure. When both engines have been fired up, Tom runs them at their lowest steady speed. The ground crew simultaneously ensure that the Ki-gass priming pumps are screwed down, and that the ground starter battery is disconnected.

Tom gradually advances the twin throttles, and the Beaufighter's distinctive engine note begins to rise. He monitors the engine gauges and holds a reading of 1,000 rpm to allow the engines to warm up. During the warm-up process, he lowers and raises the flaps to test the operation of the hydraulic system. In turn, he tests each engine's magneto, and the functioning of the vacuum pumps.

Meanwhile, the ground crew remove the undercarriage safety locking pins and hand them to the navigator for stowage. They then confirm that all entrance hatches are closed and securely fastened. Tom checks the brake and the pneumatic supply pressures before saying to his navigator, 'Everything's OK in my cockpit. Are you ready?'

'All ready, boss.'

'There's still plenty of daylight, so we'll do the before-take-off checks as we taxi out,' says Tom, who then presses his radio transmit button to call air traffic control. The airfield is busy this evening; radio silence is not practical.

'You're clear to taxi,' says the controller.

Tom signals to the ground crew, ordering removal of the wheel chocks. The ground crew run underneath the Beaufighter, tug the wheel chocks away, and dash clear of the machine again as they wave thumbs-up signs. Tom reacts by slightly advancing the throttles to ease the aircraft forward. He tests the machine's brakes, then advances the throttles to pick up speed for the taxi out.

Soon, Tom begins to move the aircraft along the taxiway at a fast pace and as he does so he says to his navigator, 'Stand by for the checks.' Using the standard mnemonic system, he then calls out, 'H – hydraulics . . . T – trim . . . P – propeller speed control levers . . . F – fuel . . . F – flaps . . . C – cowling gills . . . C – carburettor air intake heat controls.'

'Checks complete,' says the navigator.

As the machine draws close to the runway entrance point, the controller gives clearance to line up and take off. Tom manoeuvres the rudder pedals as he lines up, kicking them positively left and right to ensure the tailwheel is straight before he applies the brakes. Soon, his left hand begins to inch the twin throttles forward, and he notes the engine response.

'Ready to go?' Tom slides back the throttles again as he speaks with his navigator.

'Affirmative, boss.'

Tom immediately releases the Beaufighter's brakes and applies coarse movements to the rudder pedals as he opens up both throttles. The engine note quickly begins to rise, and he watches the airspeed indicator while the machine picks up speed. He pushes the control column forward, anticipating the Beaufighter's tendency to swing, and aims to lift the tail as early as possible to improve rudder control.

As soon as the tail-wheel has lifted from the runway, Tom begins to ease back the control stick while the Beaufighter accelerates towards the take-off speed of ninety knots. When the machine's main wheels have lifted off, he continues to scan the airspeed indicator, and when practical and safe he operates the selector lever to raise the undercarriage. As the machine approaches the recommended climb speed of 150 knots (172 mph), he adjusts the nose-up attitude. Above 300 feet, he ensures the flaps are raised, sets the hydraulic power lever off, and continues with minor control inputs to hold the climb attitude.

'Take up a southerly direction towards Bognor,' orders the controller. 'Beyond Bognor, follow the coastline due east.'

Soon, Tom eases the control stick forward, operates the trimming tab controls and brings the throttles back as he levels the machine at 1,200 feet. He then carries out further cockpit checks and maintains a good lookout, searching for other aircraft at the same time as observing the general weather conditions. He also takes the opportunity to look at the small villages and the twisty roads along which he has recently driven, noting the contrast between the flat countryside towards the coast and the hilly areas of the South Downs behind him. In all directions, individual fields display patterns of spring crops and ahead Tom sees that a rain shower is affecting the coastal region around Bognor Regis. The visibility at his present altitude, however, is sufficient to allow him to maintain visual contact with the surface.

'Confirm our airborne time.'

'2108 hours, boss.'

Tom continues to scan ahead, and as the aircraft approaches the northern outskirts of Bognor Regis the Beaufighter is shaken by turbulence near the shower. Beyond the town's suburban outreaches, when the shoreline becomes visible, he begins to make out a few figures walking along the sea-front. He notices that they seem to be well wrapped up as they cope with the squally rains and he rocks the Beaufighter's wings in spontaneous salute when he spots some of them wave.

'Sturdy souls,' he says.

'Who's sturdy, boss?'

'Didn't you see them? Some folk are braving the walk along the promenade.'

'They're probably sceptical right now about the famous Bognor "cure".'

Tom glances down again. 'Of course,' he says with a chuckle. 'The late king had views on that, didn't he?'

'He certainly did. He refused a return visit to the place. And on his deathbed, didn't he make some comment about "bloody Bognor"?'

'Something like that.'

The Beaufighter is positioned over the sea by now, so Tom turns the machine to the left and takes up an easterly heading. The rain shower is still affecting the area and the visibility remains reduced, though he's able to make out the surface of the sea as he peers forward. When the rain drives against the Beaufighter's windshield more forcefully, he glances inside the cockpit, on the right side of the instrument panel, and locates a rheostat switch that he rotates in order to operate the windshield wipers. However, he can see the visibility improving just a few miles ahead, beyond the edge of the shower. 'I'll be able to turn them off again soon,' he says to his navigator, conscious that the wipers will damage the windshield if used injudiciously.

At length, as the rain begins to ease, Tom switches off the wipers and adjusts the throttles to increase airspeed. He is still flying over the sea and from time to time he looks at coastal towns on his left side, including Felpham, Middleton and Littlehampton. As the visibility improves he can make out the urban sprawls of Worthing and Brighton in the distance.

He is about to make another comment to his navigator when the Tangmere controller says, 'Blue One Eight, confirm your altitude.'

'We're still at twelve hundred feet.'

'OK,' says the controller, 'stand by.' Then, 'We've just heard from Flintlock: you're to climb now to angels one five and call them on pre-briefed frequency.'

'Understood,' says Tom. 'Thanks for your help, Tangmere.'

He advances the Beaufighter's throttles again and scans the airspace ahead while the machine starts to climb. He checks the airspeed indicator and makes regular small attitude changes to maintain the climb speed of 150 knots. Tom glances at the radio selector as he alters the frequency and adjusts the volume by turning the bulky control knob on the cockpit's left side as he checks in with Flintlock.

'Good evening, Blue One Eight,' says the Flintlock controller. 'Be advised, there will be two other aircraft holding above you at angels one six and one seven respectively. Both machines are the same type as yourself.'

'That's understood,' says Tom. 'Confirm we'll be operating over the Worthing beacon.'

'Affirmative. Just three of you tonight, so far.' On occasions, six or more aircraft would be stacked overhead a beacon.

'Only a minor queue for action this evening,' mutters the navigator.

Tom still searches the sky as his aircraft climbs, and as the machine draws near to the Worthing beacon he eventually catches sight of the other two Beaufighters circling above. To initiate level-off at the instructed 15,000 feet, he begins to ease the stick forward and the throttles back and re-trims the aircraft. He calls the Flintlock controller again to confirm the Beaufighter is levelling at angels one five and carries out more cockpit checks while he settles the machine. He co-ordinates his position with the aircraft above, observing them against the clear backdrop of the sky. As he continues to scan the surrounding airspace, he notes that the general shower activity appears to be dying out.

'It looks as if the weather man was right about this evening,' he says to the navigator.

'His forecasts haven't been bad lately,' the navigator replies. 'But we should sort out these controllers. We spend too long going round in circles, if you ask me.'

'Blame the Jerries.'

'I suppose we can blame them for everything,' says the navigator. He hesitates before saying lightly, 'Just to pass the time, we could think about something cheerful.'

'Did you confess to being a Welshman?' says Tom, still monitoring the position of the two aircraft above him. 'I trust you're not going to break into song?'

'I'm a member of a male voice choir,' says the navigator with a chuckle. 'I could have a bash at a Welsh folk song or two. Or even Flanagan and Allen, if you insist.'

'Maybe,' says Tom as he turns his aircraft in a left-hand routine and as he makes corrective manoeuvres to keep the others in sight.

'Maybe?'

'Maybe later. When we get back.'

The navigator laughs but makes no further comment. Tom glances at the aircraft clock but still maintains a close eye on the others as, like birds of prey, they circle, ready for action.

As the circling routine becomes recurrent, Tom begins to ponder the news about his squadron airman. The event seemed so cruel, doubly unjustified. Mr Brenden Bracken's publicity machine and government propaganda, painted an image of a united nation, steadfast against a common evil. It sounded good but matters were hardly that straight-forward. The war had produced positive aspects including, for one thing, the breakdown of tedious social barriers. But other, more devious problems were emerging as criminal minds, fifth columnists, so-called pacifists, and sometimes people displaying just plain cowardice—

'Blue One Six, this is Flintlock.' The controller's voice sounds terse.

'Go ahead,' says the top-cover Beaufighter.

'Blue One Six, stand by for trade.'

The pilot of Blue One Six acknowledges and Tom looks upwards, noting that the machine is holding its position for now. To the east, in the distance towards Kent, the aircrew see signs of anti-aircraft activity as puffs of smoke burst into the sky.

A few minutes pass before the controller says, 'Blue One Six, from Flintlock, vector zero nine zero. There's a bandit at angels one eight, on reciprocal heading.'

The top Beaufighter at once applies a high angle of bank and Tom sees the machine begin to shrink into the distance as it peels away.

'Sounds like . . .' The navigator falters, then goes on, 'On that heading, by the sound of it, they're making for Liverpool, or maybe Southampton.'

'Who knows?'

'Probably Liverpool again, poor blighters.'

Tom initiates another turn, and at the same time he continues to co-ordinate his position with the remaining Beaufighter. He glances once more at the aircraft clock: 2135 hours – nearly thirty minutes airborne already. By now he's lost sight of Blue One Six, but he stares up at Blue One Seven, still circling a thousand feet above. He makes another positional adjustment and looks due east, noting the increasing activity of the ground artillery units.

During his next positioning turn, Tom looks due north, towards Horsham and Crawley, with London beyond. He then looks to the west, eyeing the east–west line of the southern coast of Britain – the line to be followed, no doubt, by the German bombers. Tom notes the various coastal towns he has recently overflown, all of them potential targets for the bombers. In the middle distance he can make out the distinctive shape of Selsey Bill. Tom stares at the unique headland before taking his eyes northwards, following the coastal contour towards Bognor Regis.

'Bognor,' he says quietly.

'Where, boss?'

'Bognor,' says Tom as he continues to stare at the flat area between Tangmere and Selsey Bill. 'I was just thinking about Bognor.'

'The Jerries can't be interested in Bognor, surely?'

'They've attacked it before.'

'Bloody Jerries. What's the point of attacking a place like Bognor?'

'A very good question,' says Tom as he ponders the town where he has a personal interest this evening. 'Bloody Jerries,' he says. 'Bloody Bognor.'

CHAPTER EIGHTEEN

A Salute from
the Sky

Althea goes up the stairs, heads directly for her room and fumbles with the key as she hurriedly attempts to unlock her bedroom door. She enters the room and puts her knitting on top of the bed. She picks up her overcoat and her scarf, then re-locks the door before heading back to the staircase, reaching the reception area just ahead of her walking companion.

'It was a little stuffy in there,' says Beatrice with a nod towards the sitting room as she pushes open the hotel's front door. 'Which way shall we go?'

'This afternoon, I walked with my husband past the pier – just over there.'

'Ah, *bon*. Let's go in that direction, then.'

As they set off, Althea pulls her coat's collar closer around her neck. The evening chill feels uncomfortable, accentuated by blustery winds ahead of a rain shower. Gulls still soar above, their melancholy cries mixed with the systematic crash of rollers. Althea and Beatrice lean into the wind as they head for the sea-front.

'Your husband – he works in this town?' asks Beatrice, softly clearing her throat.

'He works at the nearby airfield, Tangmere. Do you know it? He's a pilot there.'

Althea checks herself. Perhaps she should not have said that. The young woman seems more companionable now, but one can't be sure. She could still be a spy. Oh, what nonsense; can't people even have a civil conversation these days? Surely it's a time for common sense; matters have gone too far. We must at least try for some form of normality.

'And you? You're in the Canadian army?'

Beatrice nods, but says nothing. She shivers in the cold of the wind, then slows her pace as she hears the sound of an aircraft approaching overhead.

'Ooh la la . . .'

They gaze up at the aircraft.

'Your husband, *peut-être*?'

Althea looks at her watch: just before nine o'clock. 'That's a Beaufighter,' she says. 'It could be him, I suppose.'

'Your husband,' Beatrice hesitates. 'He must be a very brave man.'

Althea glances at her companion. Those blue-grey eyes seem so calculating, so dedicated; they reveal such wariness as they look at you, and as they sum you up. My God, thinks Althea, with sudden understanding. This young woman – she *is* a spy; I'm sure she's a spy. But I don't think she's an enemy; I think she's one of ours. She's here on a special mission, probably about to be parachuted into France. She'll be sent over to help those incredibly courageous resistance workers. She'll be fighting against the Nazis and those disgraceful Pétain collaborators.

'He *is* a very brave man,' says Althea. 'We're all so proud of him. This war seems to bring out the best in some people.'

'And the worst in others,' says Beatrice. 'The confusion of war,' she adds as they resume their stroll.

They face into the wind as they walk, and from time to time they look up to observe the agitated gulls. They stop walking at one point and Althea angles her head as she hears the sound of another aircraft above the rush of the sea and shingle. They look skywards and watch the machine as it flies closer.

'Did you see that?' cries Beatrice.

'It's another Beaufighter.'

They both wave at the machine.

'*Mais oui*. What is the time?'

'It's just after . . .' Althea checks her watch. 'Ten minutes past nine. Why do you ask?'

'You must ask him later. That machine, how you say? Move its wings?'

'Perhaps the pilot rocked his wings in reply to our hand-waves.'

'*Peut-être*, this time, it really *was* your husband. But don't worry. You must not worry. I think your husband . . . I think he will be OK. You must not worry. That will not help him.'

'I wish it was that easy,' says Althea, in a quiet voice.

As the Beaufighter flies away, and as the engine note fades into the distance, the walkers set off again. They proceed along the promenade, remaining silent for a spell, immersed in their own individual thoughts. 'She's right, though,' muses Althea, 'there's no point in worrying. That won't help him.' Beatrice is reflective too, her mood betraying her own uncertainties. Raindrops, whisked about by the shower, start to saturate the sea-front area. The two ladies, however, seem barely conscious of this, or of the turbulent breezes that disturb the gulls. When the sound of the Beaufighter can be heard no longer, Beatrice's problems begin to absorb her. As the women walk, and as they stare at the pavement in front of them, their heads still bent towards the wind, Beatrice is unaware of her companion's disagreeable rush of feeling. She fails to notice her unsteady progress, her subdued manner, even the teardrop on her cheek.

Althea eventually wipes her cheek with a handkerchief. She then glances back over her shoulder, her eyes narrowing as she squints upwards, straining for a last glimpse of the Beaufighter. Even though the engine note can't be heard any more, she hopes the machine may come back this way. It would be so exciting if it really was flown by Tom.

'He is gone,' Beatrice says quietly, aware now of her friend's emotional feeling. 'But he will be OK. Sure. Try not to be upset.'

'You're being kind to me,' says Althea, dabbing her cheek. 'Thank you.'

Beatrice shrugs and smiles. She gazes back towards the pier and halts for a moment as she adjusts her military overcoat. Then the two walkers set off again, gripping their scarves around their necks.

'*Mais quelle chose*. Maybe we should seek – *quoi?* – shelter?'

'Let's turn round. We could go back the other way, towards the amusement arcade. We haven't walked very far yet and it would be nice to get some more fresh air. With any luck this shower will die out soon.'

'What is this amusement arcade?'

'It's run by Billy Butlin – you probably haven't heard of him. His nick-name is "Mister Happiness".'

'Perhaps he should change his nickname during the war,' says Beatrice with a half-laugh. 'Maybe "Mister Miserable" would be better just now.' She looks at Althea and feels a sudden sympathy. 'Your husband,' she says quietly, 'was he OK when you saw him this after-noon?'

'Yes, thank you. He seemed fine, though naturally it was difficult when he had to leave for duty. Saying goodbye is never easy in wartime.'

'No, it certainly is not. Your husband: at least when he's at work, he'll be among his colleagues, and he'll be busy. In a way it is harder for the families – waiting, wondering.'

'That's so true.'

'And your husband, is he a famous pilot? Has he a nickname?'

'It's funny you should ask that. He has a nickname, but not a very nice one. We were talking about it at lunchtime. My husband's a quiet man, and a modest one. He's a very good pilot and he's had a lot of success with his flying recently, so much so that they've just awarded him a medal. But I'm not supposed to tell you very much.'

'Oh, I understand. But, anyhow, that is good news.'

'It is. And for what it's worth, he's been nicknamed "Killer".'

'That's not so bad,' says Beatrice with a chuckle. 'I've heard much worse.'

The couple walk back towards the pier and begin to quicken their pace.

Before long, Beatrice says, 'Let's go up there, along that side street. We might get a little more protection from this awful British weather.'

'I suppose we could try.'

The women stride across the Esplanade and head for the side street, The Steyne. They walk past a pub and as they do so they hear a flood of sounds: the hubbub of voices, cackles of laughter, a singer and pianist coping valiantly.

'At least some people aren't allowing the war to get them down.'

'There seem to be a few of your compatriots in town.'

'Yes, there are,' says Beatrice in a noncommittal way.

'I live in Bedford with my two daughters. We don't get many Canadians there.'

'When the war's over, you should go with your family to see your cousin in Quebec.'

'Unfortunately, he's no longer there. He's involved in fighting the war.'

'Everyone is affected by the war now,' says Beatrice. 'Everything has changed. The world will never be the same again. Mister Hitler has seen to that.'

'Mister Hitler has a lot to answer for, has he not?' says Althea. 'For one thing, my husband being in his present danger.'

'And for another, my being in this place,' says Beatrice as they both glance up into the sky again. They see no aircraft this time, just the soaring gulls. 'They seem – *quoi?* – calmer now,' Beatrice notes, pointing at the gulls.

'This shower is clearing,' says Althea. 'Hopefully we should get some respite.'

'Until the next shower comes along.'
'Just a temporary calm, I suppose.'
'*Certainement*. The calm before . . .' Beatrice falters.
'I expect you're right,' says Althea. 'Just the calm before the storm.'

CHAPTER NINETEEN

Waiting for Trade

Tom has to judge the right moment. And when he initiates a turn above the Worthing beacon, easing the Beaufighter's control stick to the left, he has to monitor the machine's turn and slip indicator in conjunction with the artificial horizon to achieve a steady turn at rate one. He checks surrounding airspace during the manoeuvre, constantly on the lookout for enemy aircraft. In addition, he has to ensure good station-keeping to synchronise with his fellow Beaufighter. He notes pockets of smoke drifting across the sky to the east, marking the efforts of ground artillery. Even to the north, he can see the first signs of anti-aircraft fire.

'Poor old London,' says the navigator.

Tom watches the activity of anti-aircraft guns for a few moments, then his eyes flick automatically to the aircraft clock: 2145 hours. 'We've been airborne over thirty minutes already.'

'Time flies when you're up here. My God . . .' Beyond Horsham, the navigator can see a pall of smoke, the swirls mixed with bursts from the ground artillery. 'Look at that.' They stare at the scene, and listen to the increasingly agitated exchanges between pilots and controllers. Tom and his navigator remain silent as they observe, but after a while the navigator says, 'Why don't they make use of us?'

'Perhaps we're being held in reserve.'

'Why did they use Blue One Six so soon, then?'

'Presumably there's a master plan.'

'And one assumes the Jerries have got their own master plan for tonight.'

'Who knows what's on Goering's mind?'

'London and Liverpool again, no doubt. Poor devils.' After a second or two, the navigator adds, 'Weren't you in London last year, boss?'

'I was,' says Tom.

'Then you can commiserate with them.'

'I can indeed,' says Tom. 'Although it's been bad enough at Tangmere recently.'

'It must have been even worse in London. And apparently the set-up for air-raid shelters isn't good in London, though I find that hard to believe. Could you use the Tube system? Safe enough there, I imagine.'

'You could try the Tube, though it was often overcrowded. Some people would spend most of the day queuing for a place at night.'

'And if you couldn't find a place?'

'You just had to look for the nearest suitable surface shelter. At the Air Ministry we had our own shelters.' Tom checks due north again, towards London, and at the same time he notes the other Beaufighter starting another turn. 'At the beginning of the war everyone rushed to the shelters at the first sound of an air-raid siren. But people stopped that eventually. They got complacent, I suppose.'

'Look.' The navigator points out another pall of smoke, this time in the area of Crawley.

'At least it sounds as if the enemy is being chased, judging by all this radio chatter.'

'Surely Flintlock must make use of us before long?'

'We'll hear soon.'

Tom turns the Beaufighter and glances again at the aircraft clock: 2150.

'I've only visited London in peacetime,' says the navigator. 'I don't think I'd like to go there at the moment.'

'You heard what happened to one of our airmen last night?'

'What a dreadful business.'

'Stay well out of London seems to be the moral of that story, though I imagine the same could be said for most cities.'

'Cardiff, near my home, hasn't exactly been spared by the Germans,' says the navigator. 'I heard a tale recently which in some ways was quite heartening. A six-year-old boy was found buried in rubble after a bombing raid on Cardiff. He'd been entombed for three days and he was in a bad state. But there was an amusing side: they found him because he was singing. His poor voice was hoarse, but he managed to keep going anyway. When he was asked about it, he said, "My dad was a collier, see. He always said that when a miner was trapped, he sang."'

'Brave lad,' says Tom with a chuckle.

He glances again at the pall of smoke above Crawley but just as he is about to make another positioning turn he hears an unusual screeching sound behind him. He half-turns towards the navigator's cockpit and hears the navigator say, 'I think there's a problem with my exit hatch.'

Tom tries once more to look behind him.

'The exit hatch has . . .' The navigator's voice trails away and Tom can just spot him as he moves towards the hatch.

'OK. Stand by,' says Tom.

At once he retards the throttles, eases back the control stick and adjusts the trim tabs as he reduces airspeed below 175 knots.

'The hatch release lanyards have worked loose,' says the navigator, speaking breathlessly. Tom further reduces the airspeed, and eventually the screeching sound begins to quieten. 'I think that's it,' says the navigator, sounding calmer. 'Hang on, boss, while I confirm it.'

'I'll hold this airspeed for now.'

'I'm trying to see . . . I can't be sure. As you mentioned, this thing's been giving problems.'

'We'll get the engineers to check it out again later,' says Tom, once more attempting to glance back at the hatch, the crew's main exit point for parachute bale-out.

'OK, boss. That's fixed it, I think. You can increase speed now.'

Tom advances the throttles again and works to return to his position in sequence with the other Beaufighter. He listens to the exchanges between aircrew and controllers which are still crackling through the radio and thinks about the exit hatch predicament. He recalls the technical log entry he read before flight, remembers reports he has seen recently about a more general problem and makes a mental note: his senior engineering officer must seek a solution from the specialists at Fighter Command.

As Tom muses on this, he gazes due west again, in the direction of Portsmouth and Southampton. 'At least, so far, there are no signs of any bombs over there,' he says.

'Over where, boss?'

'Due west, towards Southampton.'

'I assume the mayor's pushed off already.'

'The mayor?'

'The local papers are full of it. They're scathing about the fellow, who apparently leaves his office every afternoon heading for a country retreat. Thousands have taken to following his example. The "trekkers" move beyond the sirens' wail and sleep in cars and buses. Whole streets become deserted and civil organisation's virtually non-existent. Things have become so bad that our chaps, RAF officers, have taken over. Meanwhile—'

'Blue One Seven, this is Flintlock.'

'Go ahead,' says the pilot of the top-cover Beaufighter.

'Blue One Seven, another aircraft's just been scrambled from Tangmere; he'll be joining you soon. You're instructed to climb up one thousand feet, to angels one eight. Acknowledge.'

'That's acknowledged.'

'Blue One Eight, did you copy that?'

'Affirmative,' says Tom.

'Confirm that you're still in visual contact with Blue One Seven.'

'We're in good contact.'

'Understood. When clear, climb to angels one seven. The next aircraft will join at angels one six in five minutes.'

'OK, Flintlock,' says Tom, advancing the aircraft throttles as he carefully watches the Beaufighter above.

The signs of anti-aircraft artillery are still criss-crossing the skies in erratic patterns. But as the crews comment to each other about this, they are interrupted by the controller again.

'Blue One Seven from Flintlock.'

'Go ahead.'

'Blue One Seven, stand by for trade.'

'That's acknowledged.'

'Signs of action at last,' says Tom's navigator.

The aircrew discussions become intermittent after this. They wait for the controller's further instructions and when he next speaks there is a note of excitement in his voice.

'Blue One Seven, make your vector one zero zero. There's a bandit at angels one eight.'

When the top Beaufighter applies a high angle of bank, Tom's navigator stares due east, then due west, his gaze following the line of the coast. 'Looks like another one for Liverpool, ' he says quietly.

As the navigator assesses the general picture, Tom, too, glances below, then looks due east, in the direction taken by Blue One Seven. When his fellow Beaufighter becomes imperceptible, just a distant speck, Tom looks the other way, towards Bognor and Tangmere, before his eyes instinctively check the aircraft clock again: two minutes before 2200 hours. The next Beaufighter should take up position at any moment.

Tom stares in the vicinity of Bognor for some seconds, then looks inside his cockpit for a further scan of the flight instruments. As he checks the artificial horizon, he makes a small attitude change, then retrims the machine to hold an accurate height of 17,000 feet. As he does so, there is a call.

'Flintlock, this is Blue One Nine.'

'Go ahead,' says the controller.

'Blue One Nine, shortly levelling at angels one six, ready to take up position over the Worthing beacon. I'm visual with the other machine.'

'His call-sign is Blue One Eight, and with him in sight you're cleared overhead the Worthing beacon.'

Tom begins to make out the profile of the joining Beaufighter and he sees further smoke traces created by ground artillery units; by now the anti-aircraft activity appears to have spread to the western side of London. Below him, in the clear daylight, he can distinguish lines of barrage balloons in specific areas, and he notes that the weather conditions remain good. 'At least the showers seem to have petered out,' he says to his navigator.

'Blue One Eight, this is Flintlock.'

'Blue One Eight holding angels one seven and visual with Blue One Nine below,' says Tom.

'Blue One Eight, stand by for trade.'

CHAPTER TWENTY

Talking of Bombs

As Althea and her companion stroll through the streets of Bognor Regis, Beatrice asks about wartime life in Britain. 'In Canada, we're far from the front line,' she says, 'but we're curious. How do you cope with the bombing? What's it like living with the threat of being bombed every day?'

'We've learnt to be adaptable, I suppose. After a while, you just accept certain things as inevitable. Look at that, for instance.' Althea nods towards an air-raid shelter near the town hall. 'I don't suppose you see many of those in Canada.'

'It could be useful: we could hide from the next shower,' says Beatrice with a laugh. 'But the shelter's not very big, only enough for twenty-two people according to the sign.'

'More could be squeezed in at a pinch, I expect.'

'Or we could go back to that pub. We could hide in the cellar.'

'Alongside the beer barrels?'

'It might be quite cosy.'

'I wonder what the ARPs would say.'

'ARPs?'

'"Air Raid Precautions" – the air-raid wardens. They can be quite bossy.'

'I'm sure there are many strange places to hide from Mister Hitler.'

'Particularly in London. My husband has told me some extraordinary tales.'

'He worked in London?'

'Last year, yes. He told me about the air-raids there, and how people managed. Things were especially bad during the Battle of Britain, but even so, a lot of people stopped using the air-raid shelters after a while. There weren't enough anyway, and the shelters themselves were too small and stuffy. There was no privacy, and people got fed up with it. They tried to lead as normal a life as possible in their own homes.'

'I suppose you can hardly blame them.'

'Then one or two of the shelters received direct hits, which knocked people's confidence. And when some of the hospitals were hit as well, that was even worse.'

'*Mon Dieu.*'

'There was a grim incident last year when a nurses home in London was hit by a bomb. Some medical students living in the basement ran upstairs to help and they managed to evacuate a women's ward, moving patients around in the dark. And the patients themselves were brave: some made jokes; others stayed silent; some prayed. The worst part came when another bomb landed nearby. But despite the danger, the students carried on working, deeply affected by the stifled cries of fear and dismay from their patients.'

'People must have felt angry – keen for revenge.'

'That incident seemed to affect the whole nation.'

'*Certainement.*'

'After a while,' Althea continues, 'people start to take the bombs, you know, personally. It's silly, of course, but they begin to think that a particular bomb is headed for a particular person. I live in a quieter part of the country, but my husband's niece, who works in London, has told me about it.'

'What did she say?'

'She told me about a recent experience. She was aware of bombs in the distance, but nothing close by, although the bombs began to fall closer and closer. Eventually, when she heard the whistle of a bomb directly above, she said she just went numb. "This is it," she thought. "This one's for me." She threw herself to the ground and covered her ears. When the bomb exploded, she said it was the oddest feeling, as if the air was falling apart. There were spurts of flame all around, like a giant firework. Then, quite suddenly, everything seemed to go quiet for a few moments, apart from pieces of earth showering down. Eventually, when she got up, her mouth was full of grit and dirt.'

'What did she do then?'

'She ran over to assist the poor people who had been hit. Some were buried. Their cries for help were . . .'

'Did help come quickly?'

'She said the emergency services came pretty quickly. Everyone lent a hand to dig away the rubble, though it seemed to take for ever. One thing she mentioned was the tea. She said she will always remember it: gallons of the stuff appeared from nearby homes. You were awash after a while.'

'I wonder what the British would do without their tea.'

'There was another strange thing, though. She said that after a bomb has fallen some people seem to have actually *enjoyed* the experience. It sounds extraordinary, and it's hard to fathom.'

'What craziness can be on their minds?'

'Personally, I think it's to do with people getting bored. There's so little entertainment and some people have hardly any money. At least the bombs cause some sort of action in their lives.'

'They must be rather desperate for action.'

'It's awful when you think about it. I'm sure not many feel like that, but she was saying that from time to time you hear about people who do. Most normal people, of course, have very different feelings.'

'I should hope so. *Mon Dieu.*'

'She said there was one man who lived near her who really didn't appreciate the bombs. He was disabled and diabetic, and when his house was destroyed by a bomb he lost his wheelchair and his insulin. However, he was a determined character and he found the strength to crawl half a mile to the nearest hospital. He searched around for help, and eventually he found a doctor who gave him an injection, got a new wheelchair, and generally sorted out the poor man.'

'All this action in London. What about the rest of the country?'

'London's been worst affected, I suppose. But everywhere's been involved in one way or another. I have a friend, for instance, who was posted to south-west England, miles from London, and supposedly away from all the action. But she's written to tell me how the war has still affected them. She's a doctor, and she was called up to join the Royal Medical Corps, though she didn't really want a posting down there.'

'She would rather be in London?'

'Some people like to be where the action is. But you have to do your duty, wherever you are. She was telling me about her first job, when the driver got lost. All the road signs had been removed and my friend was hopeless at map reading. She sent the driver to ask a group of villagers for help, and when he returned the driver was grinning. "They won't tell me," he said. At this, my friend and the driver both burst out laughing. They laughed so heartily that the villagers softened, evidently thinking that the strangers' reaction could hardly be that of Germans in disguise.'

'Surely the Germans aren't down there?'

'Who knows? But my friend got fed up there in the end and she volunteered for overseas work.'

'Did they send her to Canada?'

'No,' says Althea with a chuckle, 'they sent her to North Africa. But she had a rough passage: her convoy was attacked during the sea voyage. She said that when the emergency bell started to clang, she had to rush to her allotted station at the stern of the ship. She was stopped at one point by a naval officer who told her to go back. "I can't," she said. "I'm the medical officer for the poop deck." "My God," said the naval officer, "what *is* the army coming to these days?"'

'Typical male reaction.'

'She eventually got to her post and hid at the stern of the ship while they were being attacked by a German aircraft. She told me the anti-aircraft men had been in the London blitz, and they were cracking jokes as they fired away. Their jokes were interrupted, though, when there was an almighty explosion and flames leapt up from one side of the ship. The gunners had succeeded in shooting down the German aircraft, which then struck the ship.'

'I suppose that if the gunners could cope with the London blitz, they could cope with most things.'

'But there was another odd thing.'

'To do with the ship?'

'The ship survived and so did my friend. No, I was thinking about a feeling, a certain type of feeling you get when an air-raid is over.'

'A feeling of relief, no doubt.'

'It's more than that. Often the raid goes on into the small hours, and naturally you can't sleep properly until it's all over. Then you might sleep for a couple of hours before you wake in the morning. That's what I'm thinking about: the reaction on waking up. It can seem as if the whole thing never really happened – as if it was just some sort of a dream. The birds will be singing and the trees will look green, the sky blue. It somehow seems impossible to believe that the night before was red with fire and smoke and deafening with noise.'

'Everyone must get so tired,' says Beatrice.

'Listen . . .'

The walkers suddenly slow their pace and remain silent as they try to identify a particular noise. They look at each other as the drone of engines becomes recognisable. Then the two stop walking and gaze up into the sky with anxious expressions. An aircraft is in the vicinity and from the pitch of the engine note they realise that the machine is close by, and about to get closer.

CHAPTER TWENTY-ONE

An Exchange of Fire

Tom hurriedly goes through the standard cockpit checks before combat and continues to orbit the Worthing beacon as he and his navigator watch the manoeuvres of the newly joining Beaufighter.

'Our man gave an accurate ETA,' says the navigator, 'on the dot of 2200 hours.'

'Only the best in 219 Squadron.'

'Blue One Eight, from Flintlock.'

'Blue One Eight,' says Tom. 'We're still at angels one seven, and we're in visual contact with Blue One Nine.'

'OK, Blue One Eight, we have a target for you now. Make your vector two eight zero.' The controller speaks in a calm but urgent manner. 'There's a bandit at angels one eight, on a northerly heading. Looks like he's targeting London.'

As Tom turns towards the west, he advances the Beaufighter's throttles to gain 3,000 feet. He searches for other aircraft as he climbs and glances at his clock when the navigator mutters, 'We were held there for forty-five minutes that time.' Tom eases back the throttles when he approaches 20,000 feet and confirms his new height with the controller.

'Turn right ten degrees,' says the controller. 'Make your vector now two nine zero. You're clear to flash weapon.'

As the navigator activates the Beaufighter's radar, he stares at his scopes and starts to call, 'Looking . . . looking, but no contact yet.'

Tom, meanwhile, searches visually as he flies on the instructed heading.

'Any contact?' asks Flintlock after a while.

'Nothing yet. No contact, radar or visual.'

'OK. Turn further right on to three two zero. You're closing on the target from his right side. You're some way behind, catching up very slowly.'

Tom sets the Beaufighter's engines for maximum performance. He places the propeller speed control levers fully forward and advances the throttles. He monitors the available boost to see if the indicator falls to plus 7lb per square inch or less; this reading will require him to bring the throttles back to the rated gates. When he realises that the rate of closure is still too slow, he says to the controller, 'Confirm the bandit remains at angels one eight.'

'Affirmative.'

'In that case I'll have to descend to pick up airspeed.'

'Understood.'

Tom eases the control stick forward and leaves the throttles at their set position. As the airspeed builds, 'Beaufighter whistle' starts to shriek through the airframe.

'Stand by!' cries the navigator suddenly. 'Confirm our present altitude.'

'Nineteen thousand five hundred feet,' says Tom.

'I'm just beginning to pick up a faint return.'

Tom scans ahead but the camouflaged machine is hard to spot from the rear. 'Nothing seen visually,' he says.

'Stand by,' repeats the navigator as he continues to work at his radar controls. 'I think . . . *contact*!'

'Is our heading still OK?'

'He's slightly on our right. Turn right ten degrees.'

'Still nothing seen visually. Although . . .' At that moment, Tom thinks he can faintly make out an aircraft silhouette ahead. 'Confirm you're holding good radar contact.'

'Radar contact still good.'

'Do you need further help from Flintlock?'

'No further help required.'

Tom then calls 'tally-ho' to the controller, who replies, 'Blue One Eight, you're clear to smack.'

'We're closing steadily now,' says the navigator as he begins to count down the ranges.

Tom focuses on the silhouette, which becomes more distinct as the Beaufighter catches up. He tries to work out the aircraft type, which he thinks is a Ju 88. He manoeuvres to gain a better view but he still finds the rear profile hard to positively identify.

'We're now at eight hundred yards,' the navigator informs Tom.

'He's making no attempt to evade yet – his course is steady.'

'OK. We're continuing to close. He's nearly at seven hundred yards now.'

'I've still got him in visual contact,' says Tom. 'It's a Ju 88.' Now he can see the outline clearly: a pencil-shaped fuselage with a bulbous, ungainly-looking cockpit positioned between two engines.

The navigator continues to call the ranges and by the time he says, 'Three hundred yards,' Tom has begun to squint through the Beaufighter's ring-sight. He double-checks that the gun button is set to fire.

'Two hundred and fifty yards.'

Tom keeps the throttles at full power. He glances at the airspeed indicator from time to time, but his main focus is through the ring-sight. He's still aware of anti-aircraft flak in the distance, but not close by. He listens anxiously to the final stages of his navigator's commentary and lightly covers the gun button with his thumb.

'We're closing slowly,' says the navigator. 'We're approaching two hundred yards now.'

Despite the intruder's steady course, Tom's accurate line-up and ranging remain crucial. As he squints through the ring-sight he makes constant minor adjustments to position. Streams of pale smoke from the bomber's engines by now appear alarmingly close. Tom is struck by the thought that close proximity to the target is unnerving enough at night, but in daylight it can seem even worse. He nevertheless continues to focus through the ring-sight while he concentrates on his aim which, at this close range, is disturbed by turbulence from the bomber's wake. As the Beaufighter is rocked, Tom struggles to re-settle his aim. 'Steady . . . steady . . .' The process is facilitated by the Ju 88's lack of evasion, although the wake turbulence is still a problem. At least a turn, or a strong cross-wind, would help to disperse the vortices. Tom works again to fix his aim. His timing has to be right: premature attack will give away his position of advantage.

Eventually he is satisfied. Tom makes one last check of the safety switch before crying out, 'Opening fire!'

Tom squeezes the gun button and his peripheral vision immediately picks up flashes from the Beaufighter's weaponry. There's a crashing sound from the cannon and the usual strong whiff of cordite. The airframe shakes and he has to work at the flying controls to maintain an accurate line-up through the ring-sight. The vibrations cease abruptly when he releases the gun button which he has kept down for just two seconds.

Tom holds his position for a few more seconds. He sees a flash and a cloud of smoke from the enemy's right engine; then the aircraft swerves and begins to decelerate. There's an imminent danger of collision, so Tom pulls up sharply. When he levels off again, he dips the

Beaufighter's wings in order to observe. He sees the Ju 88 resume a steady course, sparks flying as the engine fire develops, and he wonders if the machine might explode. He's surprised, though, when the sparks start to die down.

'He must have operated his fire extinguisher,' exclaims the navigator.

'We may have to reposition for another cannon burst.'

For the moment Tom holds station, but as he does so he becomes aware of a different form of fire: aggressive-looking trails from the cockpit area of the Ju 88 begin to home in on the Beaufighter.

'What the hell?' yells the navigator.

'Tracer!' shouts Tom. 'He's got his sights on us.' His heart pounds as he takes vigorous avoiding action.

'He's equipped with four machine-guns – seven point nine millimetre calibre.'

As Tom advances the throttles, and as he banks steeply, he begins to lose sight of the enemy.

'Can you still see him?' he asks the navigator eventually.

'Negative. I've lost him.'

Tom then asks the controller, 'Have you any radar contact?'

'Sorry, Blue One Eight. I'm still checking but he seems to have disappeared from my screen.'

'We're still looking visually, but we've lost him too.'

Some minutes pass while the crew search and eventually their attention is drawn to an area a few miles to the west where they witness an explosion at ground level. Tom turns his machine towards the flames and the spirals of black smoke.

'Can you work out the position of impact?' he asks the navigator.

'Stand by, boss.' The navigator fumbles for his map, which he studies before saying, 'There's Midhurst over to the west. That's Pulborough down there. I reckon the crash site's just by Petworth. Luckily, it doesn't look highly populated.' The navigator continues to study his map and after a moment adds, 'He must have flown along the Channel for his initial approach, before he turned due north.'

'That seems to be their tactic just now. They fly in low over the water, then climb up as they cross the coast.'

'That one chose to cross the coast rather close to home.'

'Where, exactly?' asks Tom.

'Close to Bognor.'

Tom stares in the direction of Bognor for a moment. His mind starts to race, but his thoughts are interrupted when the controller says, 'Blue One Eight, can you confirm that the bandit was smacked?'

'We believe so, Flintlock,' says Tom. 'We're going to investigate smoke near Petworth. We think this is the bandit we engaged, but we'll check it out.'

'Proceed with that for now, then stand by for further instructions.'

When Tom reaches the crash site, he levels at 2,000 feet, adjusts the Beaufighter's throttles and flies a slow orbit as he inspects the crash site beneath. A ball of fire created by the initial impact has started to die down and now an ugly gush of black smoke streams upwards in a corkscrew effect. Drifts of smoke, caught by the wind, become gradually more prominent across the area as the crew search. They look for signs of survivors, but see none, though they see figures running up to the spot.

'The local Home Guard doing their stuff?' says the navigator.

'I think they're farm workers.'

'I don't suppose they'll find any survivors.'

'But those farm hands are brave individuals. Look – they're trying to search the wreckage.'

Tom has already selected his gun button to 'safe' and his navigator has reloaded the Beaufighter's cannon. As they check the site, their observations helped by the double summertime system, they note that the hour is well past 2200. Above the smoke drifts they can see the first colours of sunset, although these are still faint at present. The daylight conditions may help their task, but they feel keen to move away; they are glad when their search is ended with the controller's words, 'Blue One eight, you're instructed to return to the Worthing beacon now. Hold there until further orders.'

Tom acknowledges, and turns on to a south-easterly heading.

'Climb to angels one two, and maintain,' says the controller. 'Be advised that Blue One Six, the same type as yourself, is over the Worthing beacon at this time. He's patrolling at angels one three. Blue Two Two may be joining soon, but we'll confirm that shortly.'

'That's understood. We're climbing now.'

Tom advances the Beaufighter's throttles and checks the airspace above and all around, still searching for other aircraft. He soon begins to make out the conspicuous line of England's south coast when he over-flies the Arun River and Harrow Hill. Eventually, as he flies beyond Storrington, Tom scans ahead for the other Beaufighter. When he spots his colleague, a small speck in the distance, he notes the machine's disciplined orbital routine.

As he approaches the Worthing beacon, Tom eases back the throttles to level off and he reports his position to Flintlock. He glances back towards Petworth, now some twenty miles away, with spirals of smoke still marking the site of fatality.

'It'll take a while to burn out completely,' says the navigator, adding with a sigh, 'It's a strange set-up.'

'Meaning?'

'Just that we seem to spend ages going round in circles, followed by bursts of sudden activity. Now we go back to waiting again.'

'And back to wondering how long they'll keep us here this time.'

While the crew carry out their orbit, Tom, as usual, makes adjustments to his position in order to maintain station with the other Beaufighter. He and his navigator remain silent now, their minds filled with their recent experience. Duty has been done, but is not yet complete. The radio, still alive with the excited chatter of aircrew and controllers, confirms that waves of bombers continue to approach. The implication is clear: the Beaufighters' vigil must be ongoing.

CHAPTER TWENTY-TWO

The Home Front

'I'm sure that's a Beaufighter,' exclaims Althea, pointing upwards. 'Although I'm not very good at identifying aircraft.'

'It's like the one we saw earlier,' says Beatrice as they gaze at the machine flying overhead, towards the coastline. 'The one we thought might have been flown by your husband.'

'I wonder if he's flying at this moment.'

'Try not to worry,' says Beatrice soothingly as they resume their walk, and as the aircraft flies off into the distance.

'It's best to concentrate on the good times,' says Althea with a sigh. 'We were talking about North Africa just now. We were posted there before the war, when my husband was a flying instructor. We lived near Cairo with our baby daughter, Caryl.'

'How old is she now?'

'She's just had her ninth birthday. And my other daughter's two.'

'It must be hard bringing up children in wartime.'

'There are so many problems, especially with schooling. We moved to Bedford because it's a reasonably safe area and we're near my mother-in-law. But Caryl's found it difficult to settle. She's unhappy at her new school. They're short-staffed and some of the other children aren't kind to her.'

'Will you move her?'

'We may have to.'

'Where will you go?'

'We may have to go back to Essex, where my father lives. He's near North Weald aerodrome.'

'Is that not dangerous, near an aerodrome?'

'That's why we moved away in the first place. North Weald aerodrome was badly hit by bombing raids last year during the Battle of Britain.'

'Did you have an air-raid shelter where you lived?'

'My father had an Anderson shelter built at the bottom of his garden and we became adept at dashing down there. At first it seemed quite fun, though the novelty soon wore off. It was pretty bleak inside the shelter. There was a foul smell – permanently musty and earthy – and it filled up with water when it rained. The girls always seemed to have colds.'

'Perhaps it was better to stay in the house?'

'We thought so too in the end, so we built a sort of safe house under the stairs. It was an improvement, but still not very satisfactory. When we heard the air-raid sirens start up the household would scramble downstairs to the safety zone. Caryl used to complain about the feeling of fear in the pit of her tummy.'

'I'm sure everyone felt the same.'

'It somehow helps, though, when you know that everyone's affected in the same way. If we did hear the sound of bombs dropping, we'd all cling together and pray. Sometimes we'd go to the Anderson shelter if things got really bad. I made the girls siren suits, which they could slip on quickly.'

'They're very fashionable. Even Mister Churchill wears one.'

'One time we were caught out,' says Althea. 'It was in the afternoon, and I'd taken the girls for a walk to the local shop just up the road. We reached the shop safely, but as we were making our way home we heard the air-raid sirens start up. We tried to hurry but it was too late. Before long we heard the noise of several aircraft approaching, so we hurled ourselves into the nearest ditch.'

'Were you OK?'

'It was all right at first, but then a bomb landed close by. The girls got very upset. They started to sob and I found it hard to console them. We had to hide in the ditch for ages, but eventually the aircraft went away and we managed to dash home. We were very shaken up. And I broke one of our precious eggs when we fell into the ditch. Now that really *did* annoy me.'

'That was careless,' says Beatrice with a chuckle.

'It was lucky, I suppose, it wasn't all the eggs. Although, it *is* an ordeal trying to make the rations stretch. Even so . . .' Althea's voice trails away.

'*Oui?*'

'It's just so difficult with a young family, knowing what to do for the best. From the point of view of rations, we were probably better off in Essex. We got to know local farmers and there was a certain amount of bartering. People tried to help one another out. We were affected by shortages, I know, but there's generally more give and take in the country areas than in the towns.'

'Especially London, I imagine.'

'I've heard that the rules are applied strictly in London. This was especially true with the system we had at the beginning of the war. Ration books were marked when people collected their weekly entitlement, and that was that.'

'So they changed the system?'

'They introduced the points system. It gave us a bit more flexibility. Points were allocated to certain items and you had to hand over coupons if you bought something. At least we could save up for special occasions.'

'Is it not complicated?'

'You just have to put up with it. When you first move, you have to pick a particular grocer's shop. You register there and then it pays to stay on the right side of the owner: you'll get first choice if there's a shortage of anything.'

'Will you have to re-register if you move?'

'Yes, unfortunately. Last time I had to queue for ages at the Food Office. There are so many forms these days. And if it isn't forms, it's *uni*forms. Men in uniform, women in uniform. Soldiers, sailors, airmen, Home Guard, ARPs – goodness knows what else.'

'I'm in uniform.'

'That proves my point.'

'I don't enjoy wearing uniform, though it's easier in some ways. But I suppose we should wear pretty dresses whenever we can.'

'It's hard to find anything nowadays. A lot of women in this country have taken to wearing dungarees. You can buy these Chiesman things in the shops, but they cost twelve and six – a ridiculous expense when you consider how awful they look.'

'I expect people have to learn to make their own clothes. They have to become good at needlework.'

'It's helpful for birthdays and for special occasions. And it's especially helpful at Christmas time.'

'I'm sure you have to be inventive. Were you together last Christmas?'

'We were lucky. It was just before my husband started his present job, and he managed to get leave. It was hard, though, with the shortages of everything.'

'The spirit of Christmas doesn't seem very appropriate in wartime.'

'I'm sure it was a lot better in Canada.'

'We could get things and we could go places. Even so, it didn't feel right somehow, knowing what was happening in the world.'

'Were you with your family?'

'I was,' says Beatrice. 'We were in Quebec.'

'We were in Bedford and we tried to make things as normal as possible. We had home-made crackers and my mother-in-law managed to get hold of a joint of pork. Our girls made streamers and paper-chains. We managed to buy a few Christmas cards and we made some more by hand.'

'Isn't that the motto in this country? "Make do and mend".'

'It's the reason I've taken up this wretched knitting. I admit that I don't enjoy it one bit. Though I suppose it's a form of entertainment. Do you think we should head back to the hotel now? It's past ten already.'

'OK, *oui*,' says Beatrice, with a shrug.

'Though I don't suppose there's much going on there.'

'We could listen to Haw-Haw again.'

'He's a madman. So is Quisling, not to mention a few others. They're best ignored, are they not? Most normal people want to do their bit and to try to make something of their lives even in wartime. Entertainment is hard to find, though.'

'What about the dance halls?'

'The Embassy dance halls? I don't expect there are many down in this part of the world.'

'They're centred around London, I suppose, like most things in this country.'

'That's probably true,' says Althea. She laughs and continues, 'There was a recent story about one.'

'A dance hall?'

'One of the Embassy dance halls in London. Some friends were enjoying a night out there but they found themselves in the middle of an air-raid when it was time to go home. There were no buses or taxis, so they decided to walk. They had to go past burning buildings, fire engines, hoses, the lot. The bombs were still falling and there was shrapnel flying about. They couldn't find shelter anywhere so they started to dance. They were waltzing in the streets and singing. Eventually they bumped into a policeman who appeared from a side turning. "Be quiet," he said, "you're causing a public nuisance." "What about the public nuisance caused by these bombs?" they asked, and fell about laughing.'

'And the policeman?'

'He left them alone after that.'

'The famous British reserve,' Beatrice says with a chuckle. 'But it seems to be changing.'

'The war is breaking down barriers. Even on the trains people seem more willing to speak with one another. And if you're shopping – you have to queue for *hours* sometimes – people talk about their experiences of an air-raid, or they swap recipes.'

Althea and Beatrice slow their pace again when they hear the sound of another aircraft. They listen carefully as they try to identify the type, but the machine is flying over the sea this time and the engine note is distant.

'I don't think that one's a Beaufighter,' says Althea anxiously. 'It's not far to the hotel from here. Perhaps we should go back there now.'

'*Mais oui*,' says Beatrice as, for the second time, the two suddenly stop walking.

They stand still for a few seconds. Then they look at each other and nod. They resume their walk, taking up a fast pace, occasionally breaking into a run. Even when they become breathless they maintain their momentum, spurred on by the howl of an air-raid siren which now accompanies the clatter of their footsteps.

CHAPTER TWENTY-THREE

Frustrated Intercept

Tom holds his aircraft at 12,000 feet as he flies in sequence with the Beaufighter a thousand feet above. As the crews circle the Worthing beacon, awaiting further orders from the controller, at one point Tom hears his navigator say, 'There's an aircraft down there, boss. Just this side of Littlehampton.'

'Confirm his height,' says Tom.

'Almost at sea level. He's on an easterly heading, following the coastline.'

'I've got him now,' says Tom, at once reporting the aircraft's position to the controller.

'We know about that one,' says the controller. 'He's one of ours.'

Tom stares down at the distant machine as he tries to distinguish the type. 'It's hard to identify at this range,' he says. 'Though it looks as if it could be a Lysander.'

'I think it could be,' says the navigator as he gazes down. 'Maybe he's on a special mission, about to parachute spies into France.'

'That'll be kept hush-hush then.'

'Typical of Lysanders,' says the navigator. 'Although stories leak out from time to time. A chap on our squadron knew the pilot of one that crashed in France recently.'

'Did the crew survive?'

'Both the crew survived – the pilot and the agent he was flying. They were rescued by the French resistance, though I heard the agent was badly hurt.'

'Poor fellow.'

'We heard, actually, that "he" was a "she".'

'A female agent? That needs a special type of courage.'

'They're very special types. Again, it's hush-hush, of course, but there are rumours that extra agents are based in Bognor just now, ready to be sent across to France. They're French-speaking Canadian troops and they'll be employed in the fight against the Pétain regime.'

'Good luck to them. They'll need all the help they can get.'

Tom and his navigator remain quiet for a spell as they observe the Lysander progress towards Brighton and from time to time Tom performs routine cockpit checks. As he monitors the airspeed, occasionally he moves the Beaufighter's throttles to adjust the engine revolutions as he and the aircraft above him fly at a fuel-efficient cruising speed.

At one point, when another positioning turn has been completed, the navigator asks, 'Did you hear about the Miese case, boss?'

'The what case?'

'Lieutenant Miese, the Messerschmitt pilot shot down near here.'

'Miese's Messerschmitt? What happened?'

'He was part of a bomber escort last November. They were attacked by Spitfires off the coast of Bognor. Miese's aircraft was hit but he managed to bale out despite serious burns. During the descent he found two Spitfires circling round him – our fellows were waving.'

'He was fortunate. When the roles have been reversed, some German pilots have been rather less friendly: they've opened fire.'

'I've heard that too.'

'An amazingly cowardly thing to do. So what happened to this man?'

'He landed by parachute by the beach at Felpham and he was arrested by a local policeman. Crowds of nearby folk began to appear and they formed a circle as people just stared in awe. I think they expected him to have two heads or something. Miese was obviously in a lot of pain, so he wasn't a threat. The policeman rolled up his parachute for him and applied first-aid until an ambulance with an RAF doctor appeared. The doc took him off to the hospital at Littlehampton.'

'The German was lucky to get humane treatment.'

'When he was fit, he was interrogated by one of the squadron intelligence officers. I think Miese was amazed when he was told the name of his CO, and the names of other pilots on his squadron, 4/JG2. He was even given his take-off time.'

'The Lysanders and their agents must have been doing their stuff.'

'Evidently so,' says the navigator. 'And talking of Lysanders, that one's just about to disappear from sight.'

'They've chosen their timing with care.'

'To reach their destination at sunset?'

'Doubtless.'

Tom initiates another turn as he watches the distant Lysander. To the north-west he can see that black smoke still marks the sky above Petworth. He notes that in addition to this and other specific spirals, a general shadow of smokiness has begun to form, especially over London.

'I think our fellows have brought down a few tonight,' he says.

'Though it seems that bandits are still reaching their targets.'

'It's frustrating that we don't catch more.'

The crew stare at the scene below them as they discuss this, but the controller, as if he has overheard, suddenly interjects.

'Blue One Six and Blue One Eight, this is Flintlock. Both aircraft stand by for trade.'

'Blue One Six, understood.'

'Also Blue One Eight,' says Tom, who reacts by quickly running through the pre-combat checks: confirm cannon . . . gun button selection . . . ring-sight. 'How long have we been kept here this time?' he asks his navigator.

'It's 2235 hours, boss, so nearly thirty minutes, although—' There's a sudden resumption of the screech from the navigator's cockpit. 'It's my hatch again!'

Tom reduces airspeed, and speaks with Flintlock.

'Blue One Eight, I'll have trade for you very shortly,' says the controller, who then hesitates before going on, 'Blue One Six, from Flintlock . . . I say again, Blue One Six: make your vector zero seven zero. There's a bandit at angels one three. We think he's still climbing.'

Tom glances up and watches the Beaufighter above turn away steeply.

'Blue One Eight from Flintlock, are you ready yet?'

'Stand by, Flintlock,' says Tom.

'I'm sorry, boss. It's still stuck. I can't fix it properly.'

'Flintlock from Blue One Eight, we've still got a problem.'

'Can you take up a heading of zero five zero while you sort it out?'

'That OK with you?' Tom asks his navigator.

'OK, boss. But don't increase speed yet.'

As Tom turns the Beaufighter, he maintains minimum safe airspeed. When he rolls out on the instructed heading, he looks again at the smoky haze above London. The layer is slowly spreading to areas near Crawley and Redhill. Tom scours the sky, but he is unable to spot any enemy aircraft at this stage.

'Your target is on a northerly vector, Blue One Eight,' says the controller. 'He's just crossed the coast by Brighton. He's at a range of fifteen miles. Maintain zero five zero.'

As Tom acknowledges this, he looks to his right, searching for the
enemy machine. He still monitors his flight instruments to hold an
accurate heading and his left hand anxiously grips the throttles. He
keeps these well back for minimum safe airspeed. On the horizon,
ribbons of red and yellow have become more distinct as they point
up the sunset and above distant cumulus he can see a translucent
moon.

'Blue One Eight, your target is at fourteen miles. He's still on your
right side and you're converging slowly.'

'Confirm his height.'

'We estimate he's at angels one four. Repeat, angels one four.'

Tom then asks his navigator, 'OK with you if I start a slow climb?'

'Yes, boss. Just keep the airspeed as low as you can manage, please.'

'Flintlock from Blue One Eight, I'm starting a slow climb.'

'Understood. When you've fixed the problem, I'll turn you towards
the target for a ninety-degree interception.'

Tom raises the aircraft nose and advances the throttles a little,
scrutinising the airspeed indicator to ensure minimum safe airspeed
and continuing to search visually for the enemy machine.

'Still no contact,' he says to the controller.

'Your target is now at thirteen miles.'

Tom stares to his right, then tries to look behind him, towards his
navigator's cockpit. He is desperate to proceed with the interception,
but he appreciates that his navigator should not be harassed with over-
regular progress requests.

'Your target is now at twelve miles,' says the controller.

Tom is frustrated by the lack of contrails behind the enemy machine:
the bombers fly at optimum height for concealment, making their
camouflaged paint hard to spot. Tom thinks about the Ju 88 he shot
down just thirty minutes ago and he wonders if the next machine will
be a similar type.

'Target now at eleven miles.'

In his mind, Tom tries to work out the profile of the interception. The
convergence will be slow on his present heading, but when he turns
towards the other machine, and when he increases airspeed, the rate of
closure will pick up rapidly. He stretches his hands over the throttles in
a nervous movement, adjusts the aircraft's pitch attitude and re-trims
the flight controls as he continues to gain altitude.

'Passing twelve thousand eight hundred feet,' he tells his navigator.

'Target at ten miles,' says the controller.

'We're still looking and still climbing, Flintlock.'

'Sorry, boss. This hatch still isn't right yet,' says the navigator.

'OK. Keep trying.' Tom listens with anguish to the whine caused by the defective hatch. The noise, though different to the Beaufighter's 'whispering death', is just as unnerving. 'Do your best,' he says to his navigator.

The navigator, though, does not reply.

CHAPTER TWENTY-FOUR

The Worries
of War

An air of panic spurs people running for shelter. Althea and her
companion dash towards their hotel, encouraging each other
along. Eventually, as they near the sea-front, they hear the
warble of the air-raid siren start to die down. They hasten into the hotel
where the receptionist, too, seems in a state of excitement.

'We weren't sure if you'd come back here,' she says, 'or look for an
air-raid shelter somewhere.'

'We couldn't find many,' says Althea, sounding out of breath.

'They're very limited, I'm afraid. Most of our guests remain here in
the hotel if there's an air-raid warning.'

'Have you heard any news about the aircraft that overflew just now?'

'It was a German bomber according to the local ARP. The machine
approached from the sea, then went that way' – the receptionist waves
her hand – 'due north towards London.'

'It was frightening, anyway.'

'The ARP wants guests to stay on the ground floor until the all-clear
has sounded. The sitting room is rather crowded, but there's more space
in the dining area if you wish.'

'Thank you. Let's go there.'

The two walkers loosen their neck scarves and remove their coats.
Beatrice takes off her military hat and they walk along a short corridor
towards the dining room.

'Who would expect a blitz on Bognor?' she says.

'At least the authorities seem to be looking after us,' says Althea, as
she and her companion enter the dining room.

A number of guests are seated around the dining tables; Althea
and Beatrice head for a table where an older man sits alone. He
half stands as the two select chairs and greets them with courtesy

before asking, 'Were you caught outside when the siren went off?'

'We went for an evening stroll,' Althea replies. 'A little fresh air.'

'The famous Bognor "cure"',' he says. 'Although I'm not convinced personally.'

'You're not local, then?'

'I'm from London,' he says. 'I came here for a break.'

'Well deserved, no doubt.'

'We've managed to keep going. We've survived, though I'll admit that life in London has not been exactly pleasant of late.'

'Especially in the East End?'

'I've not been to the East End for a while. I work on a different patch as an ARP. But we've all had our problems; it's not been easy for anyone.'

'Bognor's not turning out to be much of a break for you.'

'At least I'm used to this.'

'How long have you been an ARP?'

'I decided to volunteer when I had to give up my business interests about a year ago. I was too old for the military, so I thought I'd serve as an ARP. It seemed the best option. We all have to do our bit for king and country, don't we?'

'It will be good for us to know there's an ARP to look after us and to make us do the right things. You must tell us about life in London. My friend from Canada here and I have been talking about it.'

'In some ways, I'm missing London already.'

'A glutton for punishment?'

'Probably,' he says with a laugh. 'I'm not exactly home-sick or anything, but I suppose I must feel a bit like these evacuee kids, poor little so-and-sos. At least I'm old enough to fend for myself. Some of the stories you hear about these children.'

'It's sad,' says Althea. 'But there've been good stories too, although, some of the things you read!'

'What happens to the children?' asks Beatrice.

'You see these pictures of youngsters lined up at railway stations, each clutching a bag of worldly possessions and a few tins of food. Sometimes the children have to queue all day, just waiting their turn to be called forward.'

'It seems so brutal,' says the man. 'The kids don't really understand what's going on, and naturally they get upset when they have to hug their mums goodbye. And some of them never see their mums again.'

'I heard one tale,' says Althea, 'which my husband told me about. The billeting officer wore an air force officer's uniform, though he was actually a schoolmaster who ran the local training corps. By the end of one particular afternoon all the children had been assigned to homes, apart from one girl. The billeting officer said to her, "You'd better come with me, I suppose," and took her to his own home in suburbia. They were a middle-aged couple with no children of their own and they were just so unkind to this poor girl. She wasn't properly fed and she was even restricted from going upstairs. "You'll wear out the stair carpet," she was told.'

'Oh my goodness.'

'Apparently, the man always went around in his air force uniform. One day, she had a letter from home: her mother wrote to say that her brother had been killed in the war. It was dreadful. When the girl was summoned for tea, she was silent at first and sat quietly without revealing her news. During tea-time, though, the man started to read the local paper, whistling through his teeth as he scanned the list of casualties. "Only a fool gets himself killed," he said at one point. At this, the girl exploded. She leapt to her feet and started to shout at him. She told him he was a jumped-up, cowardly buffoon, a nothing-man in his peacock clothes who thought himself too good for the poor bloody infantry, where he might get blown up and run around like a headless chicken. And that's what he was – a mindless, brainless, heartless, strutting turkey-cock, not even good enough for the pot.'

'*Mon Dieu*. What did the turkey-cock do?'

'He just stood up and left the room without a word.'

'And after that?'

'After that, things went from bad to worse. He started to abuse the girl. It went on for a long time because she was far from home, alone in a strange place with nowhere to turn.'

'*Zut alors!*' exclaims Beatrice. 'What a terrible tale.'

The London man grabs their table as Althea, in her agitation, knocks against its side. 'I'm so sorry,' she says.

He straightens the table again before leaning towards his new companions. 'I heard about another case,' he says in a lowered voice, 'about two boys taken in by a vicar and his spinster sisters somewhere in the West Country. It was a cold household, so they said, in spirit as much as anything else. They wouldn't even let the mums visit.'

'Why on earth not? Some people!' Althea rolls her eyes heavenwards.

'One of the boys became ill so the vicar sent for the doctor. But the doctor didn't turn up until the next day. When he finally did turn up, he said the youngster had bull-neck diphtheria. By then, though, it was too late: treatment needed to be quick or it was no good.'

'So, *quoi*? What happened?'

'The poor little blighter died, that's what happened.'

'*C'est tragique.*' Beatrice shakes her head. 'This war . . .'

'Another wasted young life,' says Althea.

'There've been plenty of those lately.'

'Especially in London, I suppose,' says Beatrice.

'Yes . . .' The London man falters. 'You're right. Although, well, people have got – kind of – hardened to it all. Mister Hitler and his blitz . . . well, you know, it has *united* people. With one or two notable exceptions.'

'As an ARP, though, you must have to cope with some awful things,' Althea says.

'It probably sounds heartless, but again, you do get hardened to it.'

'So when are you on duty?'

'Normally I report for duty at eight o'clock in the morning, then work right through for twenty-four hours. The part-timers join us in the evening and they work through until six the next morning. Then they have to do their normal job.'

'All of you must be so exhausted.'

'A full twenty-four-hour shift isn't what you might describe as fun.'

'I should think not. And what do your duties entail?'

'You want all the gory details?'

'Only if you . . .'

'First of all,' he says with a chuckle, 'it's a case of donning protective clothing: waterproof leggings and jacket, and tin helmet. And I have an armband with ARP on it and a whistle and a rattle. It's a bit like going to a football match.' He laughs. 'After that, I walk up and down the street checking on blackout, looking for bombs, for people in trouble and that sort of thing. We work in groups of four, with one ARP manning the bunker and the rest walking the streets. During an air-raid, we take cover, but you have to be ready to react quickly and to send a message if anything drops on your patch.'

'*Très dangereuse.*'

'When the war first started, everyone ducked for every little sound. But after a while folk got used to the noise and they could tell if a bomb was near or far. If it's a long way off, you feel a judder; if it's in the next street, the glass shatters and it feels as if the building has been picked up and put down again. It's a thing you've got to live through before you can really understand it.'

'My husband worked in London last year,' says Althea. 'He made the same comment.'

'If a bomb *does* drop on your patch, you have to locate it as rapidly as possible. It doesn't take long, though, because you see a cloud of dust, and usually someone runs up to tell you about it. Then you dash to the bunker, or send someone else to report it. The warden in the bunker has to ring for the fire brigade, and for the other services.'

'It must be such a problem trying to carry on with what you might call a normal life in London.'

'It's strange, really. People cope somehow. I mean, we still get milk deliveries and the post.'

'Is that right?' says Althea. 'That sounds most surprising.'

'It's most surprising how we *do* carry on as normal in some respects. I'm not saying life's comfortable or anything – far from it. I mean, for one thing, people are generally, you know, hungry most of the time.'

'Don't you have soup kitchens?'

'We do, but they're not always very well organised. A lot of people will go for days without anything hot to eat. Gas, electricity and water are all restricted, so cooking is difficult. Bread's usually in short supply and some shops have been bombed out. Improvisation is the key. People have to bake their own when they get a chance.'

'I know a recipe for eggless cake,' says Althea.

'A cake without eggs?' says Beatrice. 'I thought that was impossible.'

'It works quite well. You need four cups of flour, one of milk and one of sugar. Also four teaspoons of baking powder and a pinch of salt. Mix the flour and the sugar before adding the other ingredients. Leave the cake to rise for ten minutes, then use a greased tin for baking. That's it – the job's done.'

'Perhaps I'll try it one day,' says Beatrice doubtfully. 'Do you use butter to grease the tin?'

'I should think not! Butter's much too precious. But you can use liquid paraffin – it's more or less tasteless.'

'What do your girls think of this cake?' asks Beatrice.

'I made one the other day which they enjoyed.'

'You just have to make the best of what's available,' says the man.

'What about fruit?' asks Beatrice. 'Do you get any for the children?'

'Hardly any,' says Althea. 'The last time I managed to get hold of bananas, the children looked quite bemused. When I started to peel one, Caryl asked me why I didn't cook it first.'

'Poor kid,' the man says with a laugh. 'But don't your ration books give you priority for the children?'

'Supposedly there's priority given to the younger one – there's a green book for her. For my nine-year-old there's a blue book which gives some priority, though less than the green book. But it doesn't exactly help if the shops haven't anything to sell. As I was telling my friend from Canada, in the country areas we sometimes resort to bartering.'

The man nods in sympathy at this remark. Althea glances towards a dining-room window; with the mention of her family, she feels a sudden jolt of nostalgia and a desire to be alone for a few moments.

'It's a little stuffy in here,' she says as she slides her chair back.

'I suppose that should . . .'

The man's voice trails away as he watches Althea stand up and walk with determination to the window. She tugs at the bottom handles, pulling the sash device upwards. She wonders if she might hear more aircraft, but as she takes a breath of sea air she feels a sense of relief: there's no aircraft noise, just the cry of gulls mixed with the other familiar sounds of the seaside. Althea realises that her mind, though, is never far from thoughts of aircraft and the immediate activities of her husband.

CHAPTER TWENTY-FIVE

A Heinkel Outwitted

'Fixed now?' cries Tom as the whine from the defective hatch ceases abruptly.

'Stand by, boss.'

'Well?'

'I think it's OK now.'

'I'll increase airspeed as soon as you're ready.'

'Stand by.' The navigator tugs at the locking lanyards, then says, 'OK, boss, you can increase speed now.'

Tom advances the Beaufighter's throttles and informs the controller that the machine is serviceable again.

'Turn right on to zero nine zero,' says the controller. 'Your target's at nine miles. You're clear to flash weapon.'

As the navigator stares at his radar and says, 'Looking . . . looking . . .' Tom applies the required heading correction and continues to scan ahead visually. When his compass indicates an easterly heading and as the Beaufighter's airspeed begins to pick up, the controller says, 'Your range is reducing fairly rapidly now.'

'Stand by,' says the navigator. 'I'm getting a faint return. Confirm our height.'

'Thirteen thousand five hundred feet,' says Tom. 'We're just below the bandit.'

'OK,' says the navigator as he studies his scopes. After a few seconds, he cries, '*Contact!*'

'I've got him visually as well,' says Tom.

'Maintain this heading for now,' says the navigator.

As Tom calls 'tally-ho' to the controller, he anxiously watches the other machine draw closer. He stares at the enemy bomber and as the rate of closure appears to accelerate he tries to identify the type.

'I can't confirm it yet,' he says to the navigator, 'but I don't think it's a Ju 88 this time. I think it's a Heinkel 111.'

'We're closing fast. Our range is under five miles,' says the navigator, mindful that good crew co-ordination is ever more crucial as the Beaufighter nears the target. The navigator remains responsible for the profile of the interception; he still uses his radar, but the pilot will use any available daylight to pass on visual information.

'He's maintaining a steady course,' says Tom. 'I suggest we level at this height.'

'OK, then. Hold this heading and height for now.'

'He's slightly above us and I still have visual contact. I don't think he's seen us yet.'

'He's now at three and a half miles. Any signs of evasion?'

'Nothing yet. He's still on a steady course.'

'Hold this vector, then. I estimate he'll cross in front at a range of two thousand yards.'

'I can positively confirm the type as He 111 now,' says Tom.

'Are you climbing?'

'Negative.'

'Hold this height.'

Tom ensures the selector is at 'fire'. His thumb lightly strokes the gun button as he squints through the ring-sight. With the enemy machine almost at right angles, an accurate heading is critical. He monitors his direction indicator with anxiety and watches the right to left relative movement of the target, although his turn-in will be under the instructions of the navigator if the Heinkel keeps this constant course.

'Two and a half miles' range,' says the navigator. 'He's still closing fast. I'll call for a hard left shortly.'

Tom's observation of the enemy machine is helped by the background clouds and he catches a fleeting glimpse of the moon mixed up with the colours of sunset. He experiences a sense of incredulity. 'Surely this crew will act soon?' he thinks to himself. The outline looms progressively larger.

'His vector's steady,' he says to his navigator.

'Hold it. Don't turn yet. His range is just over two thousand six hundred yards.'

'Still no attempt at evasion?' thinks Tom. 'With a four-man crew, one of them must see us soon.' He wonders at the enemy's reputation for inflexibility, but he knows that their crews, like his own men, are exhausted.

'We're just approaching two thousand five hundred yards,' says the navigator. 'I'll be turning you left very soon.'

'He's seen us at last!' interjects Tom. 'He's started to turn.'

'He's at two thousand four hundred yards now.'

'He's turning towards us. I'm going left.'

As he says this and as he initiates a hard turn, Tom fully advances his throttles. The He 111 now has a high angle of bank; the machine starts to rush towards the Beaufighter. Tom knows he will have to use fine judgement before his next move. He delays until the last second, then levels the Beaufighter's wings and hauls the control stick towards his stomach. As he initiates a counter-manoeuvre and as he pulls his machine upwards, he feels the effect of 'g' pin him to his seat. He twists his head to keep the enemy in sight and monitors the airspeed indicator as his speed begins to decline rapidly. The Beaufighter starts to judder, but just before stalling Tom rams the aileron wheel and the rudder hard left in a co-ordinated movement. The machine now turns in a steep wing-over and its nose begins to drop. The machine descends, and as the airspeed builds up again the Beaufighter judders fiercely while Tom pulls the stick hard back. But even though he is operating to the limit, he has to fly with finesse: his Beaufighter is a converted bomber, not a Spitfire.

As the enemy machine turns, the pilot now fighting for his life, Tom notices small contrails stream from the wing tips. While each machine maintains a gyrational struggle to out-manoeuvre the other, a so-called circle-of-joy begins to form. The He 111 may persist in attempts to out-turn its adversary, but Tom's wing-over has given him a lead. He uses this to his advantage.

'We're slowly gaining,' the navigator yells. 'I've still got AI contact. We're at five hundred yards.'

Tom stares at the camouflage paintwork on his opponent's airframe. He notices the black crosses daubed on the wings and on the fuselage. A steady stream of smoke flows from the twin Daimler-Benz engines as the German pilot holds his throttles forward and Tom is aware of the Heinkel's gunner inside his perspex bubble. At any second Tom expects to see flashes of tracer from the bubble, but they fail to materialise; perhaps the angle is too steep.

'Range now four hundred yards,' says the navigator.

Both machines are beginning to lose height, forced down by the manoeuvres.

'We're descending through twelve thousand feet,' says Tom, still stroking the gun button with his thumb. His eyes are focused through the ring-sight as he follows the Heinkel. He views the slightly swept wing form and the distinctive and rounded cockpit area with a sense of grim determination, trying to work out the deflection needed. He glimpses the black crosses again – those crooked crosses of Nazi infamy – and this seems to spur him on. 'Keep pulling . . . come on, Tom . . . keep fighting . . .' Tom clenches his stomach muscles against the 'g' forces.

'Range three hundred yards,' cries the navigator.

Tom continues to worry about the deflection angle. 'One ring deflection?' he wonders. 'No . . . not enough. Two rings' deflection?' Still he keeps his thumb just gently touching the gun button. As he persists with his aim through the ring-sight, suddenly, sooner then expected, he hears his navigator.

'Two hundred yards!'

Tom makes a final check of deflection. 'One ring to start with . . .' he decides. There's no time to lose, so he presses the gun button, even though he's still worried about the deflection angle. He keeps the gun button pressed and the Beaufighter's airframe judder is promptly supplemented with the force of the machine's weaponry. Then Tom decides to increase his deflection angle; he pulls back even harder on the stick. He can see no effect on the He 111, so he keeps firing. He makes further adjustments to the deflection angle until, at last, he can see a series of hits. These seem minor, so he keeps pressure on the gun button, the effects of the Beaufighter's cannon continuing to jolt through the airframe.

Tom knows he will run out of ammunition soon. For a few more seconds he holds down the gun button, but then, quite abruptly, he's out of ammunition. He continues to track the target, and as he does so he observes two small fires on the He 111's top fuselage. The machine rolls out of the turn as it takes up a westerly heading. Tom manoeuvres away from the gunner's line-of-fire and holds a safe position to observe. The fires look insignificant, although Tom notes the development of a flow of smoke. When the intensity of this smoke increases, Tom readjusts his position.

'We're going down steadily,' the navigator calls out, 'through ten thousand feet shortly.'

'OK,' says Tom. 'We'll hold this position as we follow it down.'

'Look!'

'I've seen them: two parachutes – two of the crew have baled out.'

'It's a four-crew Heinkel. There must be two left on board.'

'His rate of descent is increasing. And he's heading towards the coast.'

'He's heading directly for Bognor!'

'Quick, man. Have you reloaded the cannon?'

'It's done. I've just reloaded.'

'We'll have to catch up to fire another burst.'

'His rate of descent is accelerating now,' cries the navigator. 'And he's still pointing directly at Bognor. Hurry!'

CHAPTER TWENTY-SIX

Take Cover,
Take Cover

Althea shivers as an evening chill seeps into the dining room. She stares out of the hotel window, glancing up and down the deserted streets. With no signs of human life, the promenade's bleak atmosphere is monopolised by the gulls and their doleful cries. 'There's a doorway over there,' she thinks. 'Is that someone hiding?' She stares at the doorway, looks left and right again, but she can't see anyone. She observes the soft shadows that, in the dwindling light, are gradually enveloping houses along the sea-front, then looks up at the sky and the gulls. As she gazes upwards, an animal – a cat, she thinks – makes a sudden movement. Althea jumps as she hears the creature scamper across the promenade. 'Poor thing. It must be terrified.'

Althea looks back at her companions, still seated at the dining-room table. She notices Beatrice check her watch and she spontaneously does the same: nearly ten minutes to eleven. Althea observes the horizon as she looks up again, studying the translucent moon and the clouds, the distant cumulus tinged with the colours of sunset. She wonders at the kaleidoscope of hues, then her eyes focus on the gulls again. She watches their movement as they cope with their environment, soaring into the wind, indifferent to man-made problems, to global events, to the world at war, to the obnoxious Mister Hitler. She thinks about the 'peace in our time' fiasco. Mr Chamberlain – an absurd man out of his depth, unable to face reality. His hollow promises were absurd, her present situation is absurd. She feels a mix of irritation and nostalgia as reflections work through her mind.

Her mood softens, though, when her thoughts begin to dwell on personal events. She goes back in time – nine years, ten years, no, eleven years ago. 'Eleven years,' she thinks. Recollections flood her mind. She thinks about flying, about Tom, about Hendon; she recalls Tom's flying display. It seems so long ago, so many years – the mock dog fights, the aerobatics, the noise, the kite balloon. A kite balloon, a commotion – a curious commotion. There was jostling among the crowds. 'I fainted . . .' Althea steadies herself against the window frame. The kite balloon's shadow and a sense of foreboding; Tom's moment of glory. She holds her breath for a second or two. Moment of glory?

'Althea?' Beatrice calls to her companion. 'Are you OK?'

Althea doesn't reply at once and her smile is feeble when she turns around. She looks at Beatrice and at the others in the room, most of them absorbed in their reading matter. She catches sight of a newspaper, casually cast aside. 'Do it now!' urges an advertisement. 'Order your Kendarp air-raid shelter – estimates free – Ockendens of Littlehampton: phone Littlehampton 700.'

'Just what we need,' says Beatrice with a half-laugh as she spots the paper while moving across to join her friend. 'Perhaps better than the public shelters?'

'Better than the ones we saw earlier.'

'They weren't very impressive.'

'We should search for a Kendarp, then.'

'We'll have to go for another stroll.'

'The present situation is hardly conducive.'

'*Quoi?* Where's this British sangfroid, this stiff upper lip?'

'Even the British have their limitations.'

'They seem to be doing all right against the odds.'

'We're law-abiding, and we don't want the ARP to shout at us.'

'We should speak to him kindly. Maybe he'll direct us.' Beatrice chuckles as she says this.

But she's interrupted just then. The pair glance at each other and frown when they pick up a sudden and unusual sound from above. For some moments they remain silent, listening to the racket of an approaching aircraft. The noise becomes gradually louder and more high-pitched. They glance at each other again, before they instinctively decide to hurry away from the window. As they do so, they pick up another sound – a distinctive whistle. And what's that clatter? Such a particular noise, just like the crack of firing cannon.

'What *is* that?' cries Beatrice.

Althea's attempt to reply is checked by a male voice and she is shocked by his urgent and anguished tone. He bellows again, and her movements freeze. Her eyes grow wide; hairs tingle at the back of her neck. For some seconds she feels rooted to the spot as she listens to his shouts, which are coming from the direction of the promenade.

'Take cover, everyone!' screams the voice of an ARP.

Althea and others within hearing distance are galvanised into action now. They dive under tables and chairs as they hear him blow a whistle, the shrill signal contrasting with his yelled instructions, repeated over and over.

'Take cover! Take cover!'

CHAPTER TWENTY-SEVEN

Too Close for Comfort

S he wakes with a start, but Althea remains still for some seconds, momentarily confused by strange surroundings. As she glances sideways to check her watch, she notices how a breeze causes the blackout curtains in her hotel bedroom to flap out of position. She stares at the curtains and at the early-morning mists that spill into her room. These movements and the cries of gulls outside, cause her suddenly to feel apprehensive. She begins to recall the anxieties of the night before, remembering the events with unease. Her restlessness makes her decide to get up and look out through the window.

Through the dawn mists she can just make out the pier, reduced in status but still solid and somehow dependable as its truncated remains defy the efforts of tidal surges and the potential efforts of invasion forces. Last night, when she walked past the pier in company with that young Canadian woman, the troubles of them both seemed overwhelming. For Althea, knowing that her husband was close by and on operational duty, there was particular anguish. When she was in Bedford, the practicality of distance meant that her own life, the events of the moment, the difficulties of bringing up youngsters, resulted in a remoteness from his day-to-day activities. She knew Tom preferred it that way, but nevertheless she felt guilty about her isolation from his flying activities, and how this gave them an almost hypothetical quality.

Last night, though, she was brought frighteningly close to the realities. The frequent drone of aircraft overhead, the wails of the air-raid sirens and the yells of ARPs were rarely heard in Bedford. But last night she was part of the actuality of front-line life. She could not know for certain at the time, but even so she had had a feeling that Tom was airborne. And now, following the telephone call, she knew for certain.

The lunchtime drinks party at Tangmere had been typical of such affairs: officers in amiable discussion as they tried to create a weekend atmosphere in spite of wartime constraints. Most seemed to defy the gloomy war picture, or at least to try to, with high spirits, laughter and badinage, if not the high jinks evidently taken to excess on some occasions. But the news about Tom's medal had been far from typical, the esteem in which he was held by his fellow officers reflected by the warmth of their applause. He had accepted the award with modesty, in characteristic fashion, and on behalf of his team. Nevertheless, all the officers were aware of his individual efforts and of how his dedication had provided the spark to turn around the results of his squadron.

But there had been a cost. It was understandable, but even so Tom was unusually anxious. He looked thin, his face was drawn and pale, and it was rare for her to have time with him alone these days. The walk along the sea-front yesterday had been a special opportunity, although there was always so much to discuss, and so little time. And then, nagging at the back of her mind was the anticipation of the parting, which became worse as the moment approached. There was no easy solution; she just had to learn how best to cope, and to remember the unique situation faced by the airmen. The contrasts were stark: one instant strolling arm in arm along the sea-front, the next in airborne combat. The sailor and the soldier had their own particular hazards, but at least they operated in more consistent environments. The airman had to be adaptable in ways not faced by the other fighting services.

Althea sees some figures walk near to the pier. 'Perhaps one of them is the ARP, the individual who gave those warning shouts last night,' she thinks to herself. 'It's possible that he's still on duty; these characters seem to work such long hours. He certainly did his duty last night, although as it turned out the enemy machine apparently veered away at the last minute.' It was intriguing to hear about it from Tom. He was guarded in what he said, restricted by wartime confidentiality, but even so she was amazed by what he told her. He gave a few details, perhaps too many, because she had felt convinced that their conversation was cut short by someone monitoring the line.

It was some time after midnight when she took the call. Her companions in the dining room had observed with curiosity when she was summonsed by the hotel receptionist. Her subsequent conversation was awkward, not helped by a poor line and that sense of being over-heard.

'It's good to hear your voice,' Tom said, but there was a pause after this, and a moment of apprehensive silence.

'Are you all right?' Althea said at length, trying to speak confidentially.

'Yes, I am. But I can't say very much, other than to mention that there was some trouble this evening.'

'Trouble?'

'I spoke to the hotel people just now. They told me about the air-raid warning.'

'The all-clear is sounding as we speak.'

'I can hear it in the background. But I know why the air-raid warning was given.'

'You do?'

'I was airborne at the time.'

'I had a feeling.'

'A feeling?'

'That you were flying. Did you see any enemy machines?'

'Yes, I did, but . . .'

'What can you tell me?'

'Just that I engaged a bomber that was heading directly for Bognor. At one point we thought it would hit the town, but it veered away at the last minute and crashed just to the north, at Eastergate. I saw two of the German crew escape by parachute, though the rest of the crew – another two people – were killed.'

'I think we heard you. We were in the hotel.'

'You weren't in an air-raid shelter?'

'We were in the hotel dining room hiding under tables at that stage.'

'Aren't there any proper air-raid shelters?'

The line had started to crackle then and she could just hear Tom say something about 'the poor line', but further conversation had proved impossible, so eventually she had just said 'Goodbye, Tom', hoping that he would hear. The receptionist made some comment about the un-reliable telephone system, and as Althea returned to the dining room the all-clear siren began to die down. Everyone was dispersing by then, hurrying to their own rooms, keen to seek rest at last.

But sleep can be difficult after such an experience and despite her fatigue Althea retained an annoying tendency to wake early. Perhaps this is natural with such events at the forefront of the mind, although, as she observes outside now, the events seem a world away. 'The seaside scenes are so placid,' she muses. 'It's hard to relate them to the violence and the tensions of last night. However, these are past; today is another matter, and life has to go on. Which reminds me: soon I'll have to catch the early train up to Victoria.' Althea must leave behind the world of Tangmere, that world of extremes. The aperitif? Drinks parties at lunchtime. To follow? Deadly conflict against German bombers.

Her husband would not be pleased, but she is glad, on reflection, about her experience of last night. If nothing else, she has gained an inkling of what is involved, of the hazards Tom faces. Everyone has to face dangers at the moment, the civilian population and military personnel alike. But the immediacy of the dangers the night fighter pilots face, the tangible and at the same time the intangible nature of their duties, seems hazardous to the point of being barely credible.

Althea moves away from the bedroom window, mulling this over in her mind as she does so. She knows she mustn't allow herself to become morbid, but the matter is too important, too prominent in her mind, to be easily and immediately dismissed. After last night, she has a notion now of the perils dutifully confronted by the night fighter pilots and their navigators night after night. These seem impossible for the layman to comprehend – duties even she, with her husband directly involved, cannot properly understand. She must try, of course, and she must be sympathetic about moral and other issues when he needs to discuss them. She must be the tower of strength in the background; he must be allowed to carry out his duties while she supports him to the best of her ability. This has been the rule she has been trying to follow already, but in future she will have to do so with more determination and invariably without question or argument.

She frowns when she realises the implications of this line of thought, though she tells herself not to become introspective; she has other things to worry about just now. She frowns again as she searches around her room, seeking out the clothes impatiently discarded last night, cast aside in her fatigue and keenness for rest.

But she knows she must be staunch, even more so than in the past, and she must be pragmatic. She must face up to the day ahead and to the life ahead – a life that has assumed, somehow, an unexpected and daunting slant. She sighs as she begins to dress, aware that she sees the future through different eyes, and aware that the turmoil in her mind is unsettling her.

Before long, Althea begins to pack her suitcase in preparation for her journey home. However, she is still preoccupied. She muses and she reasons with herself, as she moves around the room, though she cannot be aware of the true significance, the far-reaching impact, of the prospects in store. She cannot know about the wider implications or about the extraordinary nature of the future she will be duty-bound to accept.

Before leaving the hotel she takes a last look out of her bedroom window. The sea mists are still wafting across the Esplanade in ethereal waves. From time to time the pier is obscured, then some hidden force prompts its re-emergence and the spindly legs, the truncated form, the military presence are re-exposed. As she stares at these images, she imagines the toy guns replaced by real ones. She thinks about the surrounding apparatus of war: the air-raid shelters, the sirens, the ration books, the forms, the uniforms, the ARPs . . . Is that really the ARP from last night? The figures have assembled into a group; they seem to be in conversation.

But she must hurry now. The sea mists are about to envelop the figures; the ARP and his friends are about to disappear. Time presses; times move on. She turns away from the window, and gives the room a final check. Then she places her overcoat across her arm, lifts her suitcase and heads for the bedroom door. But as she does so Althea still wonders if she is altogether prepared for the journey ahead.

CHAPTER TWENTY-EIGHT

Nights
to Remember

The time approaches eight in the evening, and although they are on night duty, fine weather enables a number of 219 Squadron aircrew to sit outside as they wait on operational standby. The men are in convivial mood: dark adaptation goggles are not needed yet and the good weather seems conducive to general conversation. Tom is one of those on standby, although he is in his office just now dealing with a backlog of paperwork. Earlier in the day he flew to Watchfield and his navigator, Sergeant Austin, is now being quizzed by the other crews about the pilot's 'blind flying' course run there.

'Is it true they use Anson aircraft?' asks one of the pilots.

'It's true,' says Sergeant Austin. 'When we looked at the set-up today, we were shown round one. The CO had his doubts: he felt that the course would be more effective if the exercises could be flown with operational machines.'

'When's he doing the course?'

'Next week.'

'So what did they say?'

'That the operational machines aren't suitably equipped yet, and that the Air Ministry is reluctant to release them from front-line service.'

Sergeant Austin looks across at the line of squadron Beaufighters neatly parked on the dispersal area, entrance hatches lowered, preliminary checks completed, the aircraft poised to receive the aircrew when scrambled. His gaze lingers at his own aircraft, R2253, the same machine he flew on three operational missions last month as the CO's navigator.

His thoughts dwell on the first of these sorties, the night of 3 May, when they shot down a Ju 88 bomber near Petworth. He remembers the aftermath of this action, and how the remnants burnt in a field as he and the CO observed from their Beaufighter. He recalls how, during the interception, they approached from the rear quarter and the bomber had made no attempt to evade. They had closed to 200 yards before opening fire, after which the CO had pulled up sharply to prevent a collision. And when the Ju 88 had returned fire, forcing the CO into a series of avoiding manoeuvres, visual contact with the enemy had been lost. At length, however, they had spotted spirals of black smoke rising from a field near Petworth and at that point the excitement of the chase had evaporated. Suddenly there was a new perspective.

They had flown to the scene in order to observe, and as they'd stared down, they'd experienced a rapid and poignant change in attitude: now they felt a need to help the trapped aircrew. There had been little conversation with the CO at that stage, but he knew that the CO had feelings similar to his own. The CO had continued to overfly in an orbit and when they saw figures running up to the site, the aircrew noted the frantic but futile attempts at rescue. Later, apparently, there were newspaper reports – the farm workers had felt guilty about the failure of their efforts. The workers probably didn't even know at the time whether those they were trying to rescue were Allied or Axis, friend or foe. Would such knowledge have influenced their energies in any case? The question was surely secondary to the vital priority: life or death in their hands. And they had no resources other than their hands – bare hands. There must have been a sense of great desperation.

Eventually, when he and the CO were ordered to return to patrol, they were glad to move away from Petworth. But there were problems with the aircraft hatch as they orbited the Worthing beacon, the problem being resolved only just in time – just in time to intercept that He 111. When they became engrossed with the technicalities of the next interception, their attitude changed again, soon returning to one of concentrated pragmatism. Sergeant Austin recalls quite distinctly, however, the feeling of dread when he and the CO realised that the machine they had shot at, and had crippled, was heading directly for Bognor, although it veered away at the last moment.

'Perhaps they could try out the Whittle machine,' says another of the pilots, whose comment brings Sergeant Austin back from his reminiscences.

'The Whittle machine?'

'This Gloster E28/39. It's a bit hush-hush, but word's leaked out – there was a successful flight at Cranwell last month. Whittle, Watchfield: they're both experimental; perhaps the two should go together.'

'They both begin with "w", I suppose,' mutters Sergeant Austin.

'Anyway, what's the great secret about the Whittle machine?'

'He's invented this so-called jet engine – an engine that operates without propellers.'

'No propellers? Sounds like a mad idea. It'll never work.'

'Apparently his engine can produce nearly a thousand pounds of thrust, and potentially a lot more.'

'It'll never catch on.'

'They say that's where the future lies, old boy. And there's a race against Jerry to see who can produce the first operational machine.'

'No contest on that score. Anyway, what good will it do Jerry? He's got enough Stukas and Messerschmitts already.'

'Yes, but they've had their day, it seems – outdated already. And talking of Messerschmitts, what are we supposed to make of the one that crashed in Scotland last month?'

'Himself, Rudolf Hess, was on board.'

'Even old Haw-Haw didn't know what to make of that one.'

'So what did he say about it eventually?'

'That Hess, the poor fellow, Hitler's trusted deputy, was suffering from hallucinations.'

'He'll be suffering from rather more just now.'

'Maybe he had a plan: maybe he wanted to spy on our Whittle machine.'

'Pity he landed in the wrong country, then.'

'Talking of plans, perhaps there's a master plan,' says George, a pilot new to the squadron, but with previous experience on Beaufighters. 'Perhaps they're going to fit our Beaus with jet engines.'

'That's not a bad idea, George,' says Sergeant Austin. 'Where did you hear that one? On your last squadron? Where was it, by the way?'

'29 Squadron, a premier outfit based at Digby.'

'Quite near Cranwell, then.'

'Nearer than Scotland.'

'Poor old Jerry – his navigation was always a bit suspect,' observes one of the pilots.

'But when did you join the premier 29 Squadron, George?' asks Sergeant Austin.

'At the beginning of last year, though we didn't get our first Beaus until September.'

'So you've gone from 29 to 219 – quite appropriate really.'

'They posted me here to join you lot when 29 moved to West Malling recently.'

'And the jet engines with them?'

'Forget about the jet engines. When those first Beaus arrived to replace our Blenheims, we were struck with awe and wonder by the huge size of the Hercules engines. The engineers were running around like scalded cats. Some of them even managed to injure themselves during the general excitement.'

'How did they manage that?'

'It was during engine run-ups. With the Blenheims, a couple of riggers would hang on to the tail. But with the Beau's, the fellows were blown away by the slipstream.'

'Invigorating.'

'We had a few other difficulties, too. For one thing, it took us a little time to learn the knack of engine priming. A bit too much and the engine wouldn't start, or else a sheet of flame would shoot out of the exhaust. And we had a lot of trouble with the early radar sets.'

'We still have that small difficulty.'

'Then we had tail-wheel problems: they would shimmy on the landing run – most alarming. The Bristol company had to send specialist engineers who stayed for several months while they checked and modi-fied the stern frames.'

'And what was that rumour about the paintwork?'

'Black. It's usually been black, but they couldn't decide on the type of finish. They settled eventually for a sooty non-reflective paint.'

'The least conspicuous in moonlight, I suppose,' says Sergeant Austin.

He stares again at the line of Beaufighters, each aircraft with that brutish aura of the no-nonsense fighting machine. None of the sleekness of the Spitfire here, or the pleasing shape of the Mosquito. Just beyond the line of parked Beaufighters, he can see into the squadron hangar. Some of the hangar aircraft are on jacks as engineers probe into under-carriages, work on the pneumatics, adjust the hydraulic systems and deal with electrical looms dangling down like monstrous spaghetti. Engine cowlings have been loosened or removed and step ladders are needed to allow mechanics to scrutinise the complexities of the giant Hercules engines. Sergeant Austin observes specialist airmen standing on separate steps placed by the front of the machines as, with serious expressions, they gaze into the mysterious gadgetry of the radar. He assumes they know what to look for, though sometimes these radar sets can seem a law unto themselves.

That point was firmly made last month, just a week after the Petworth incident. The occasion is imprinted in his memory. He and the CO had been scrambled from Tangmere and were about to set up patrol at 18,000 feet when the controller suddenly changed his orders.

'Head south, head south!' he cried. 'There's a bandit approaching Selsey Bill.'

The CO turned immediately, but there was difficulty with the Beaufighter's radar: the equipment refused to co-operate and no blip was picked up. As a consequence the controller had to guide them on to the target, resulting in a long tail chase. When the Beaufighter eventually caught up, the bandit was in the vicinity of Guildford. However, the Beaufighter's radar worked eventually, allowing them to close up to and identify an He 111 heading towards London. They succeeded in shooting down the intruder and as the machine plummeted they observed one of the crew escape by parachute, but just one. Again, he remembers the prompt change of attitude when the target became helpless, just a victim.

'Talking of black paint,' says a pilot, 'take a look at that one over there.'

But when the aircrew look across at the line of nearby Beaufighters, their attention is diverted as they hear a commotion from the hangar. They redirect their gaze, and become silent as they stare at the hangar area. An airman working in the pilot's cockpit of one of the Beaufighters has dropped a tool, and he is being berated by the supervising flight sergeant.

The yells of the flight sergeant discourage further aircrew discussion for a while, but even so one of the pilots says, pointing towards the hangars, 'That aircraft has had problems with the dinghy in the front cockpit.' He furtively reaches down a hand to feel the top of one of his flying boots, checking the knife that has been secured there. He is conscious of a recent fatal accident when a dinghy in a pilot's cockpit inflated during flight. Now the aircrew have to carry special knives so they can puncture dinghies in case of premature inflation.

They can still hear the strident tones of the flight sergeant from the hangar, an ongoing impediment to the casual discussions of the aircrew, and during the conversational lull Sergeant Austin finds his thoughts returning to operational matters. As he ponders how the operational flights have such a powerful and lasting effect on the mind, he begins to reflect once more on his sorties the previous month. He thinks about the curious way these can work out. Sometimes there'll be days and days – or, rather, nights and nights – of inactivity, to be followed by hectic bursts of exertion. That was certainly the situation last month.

He and the CO were scrambled again on the very night following the interception and destruction of the He 111 near Guildford. The time was well past midnight when they were ordered airborne on that second night. As was often the case, they were told to patrol above the Worthing beacon while they waited for a target to be assigned. He recalls the long delay before they saw action. And he remembers feeling exhausted as they flew the patrol. He knew that the CO felt the same way; they'd chatted frequently to keep themselves alert. It was the day after Rudolf Hess had landed in Scotland and the newspapers were in a state of incredulity. With the Hess drama, and with the anger aroused by the recent heavy blitz, there was high excitement up and down the country. He can recall the CO's comments: 'What could have been on his mind? Hess must have been mad to try something like that. Or he must have been desperate. Maybe both.'

'Who knows what makes a Nazi tick? And who found him anyway?'

'According to the first reports, a local ploughman. Evidently he had a broken ankle.'

'The ploughman or Hess?'

'Hess, you clot.'

'So what did the ploughman do?'

'He took Hess home and offered him a cup of tea.'

'Sounds like a very British and a very reasonable thing to do under the circumstances.'

'Hess evidently didn't think so. He said he never drank tea late at night.'

'Churlish fellow. These Nazis haven't been very well brought up, have they?'

'Hess said that he'd got an important message for the Duke of Hamilton and insisted on meeting him at once. Hess then suggested compromise peace proposals, but they were immediately rejected.'

'No negotiations with Nazis. Quite right too – the blighters can't be trusted one jot. So what happens to Hess now?'

'He's made a prisoner of war, I suppose.'

As they chatted, and as they maintained position above the beacon, Sergeant Austin remembers how, despite good moonlight and the distant glow of fires caused by enemy bombing, the conditions seemed uncannily dark that night. The blackout was rigorous in every direction. The aircraft compass had to be checked: due north towards London; due south out to sea – both looked identical. This sameness added to a sense of unreality, and to their sense of fatigue.

The night was dark in another sense too. The nation was still attempting to come to terms with the previous night's concentrated blitz on so many British cities, including Belfast, Clydebank, Hull, Liverpool, Plymouth, Southampton and, of course, London. The Nazi High Command described the action as a 'reprisal for the methodical bombing of the residential quarters of German towns, including Berlin'. There was speculation, too, that the heavy blitz was in some way connected with the Hess saga.

As usual, London seemed to be one of the worst affected cities. The CO and Sergeant Austin had landed at Tangmere following their interception of the He 111. They were told then how the night's blitz had caused the death of 1,400 Londoners. And they were told about how the ferocity of the attack had seemed to be weakening the 'London can take it' spirit. For the first time, people were seen weeping in the streets at the signs of so much destruction.

The aircrew were told other specifics of that sad and dreadful evening; the 10th of May, 1941 would surely go down in history as one of the blackest of the war. They learnt that the chamber of the House of Commons had been reduced to rubble, and that Big Ben had been scarred (although the clock continued to keep perfect time); they heard how the British Museum was damaged by fire, and that St Paul's Cathedral, the proud building damaged last October but which had survived other raids, had been hit; and that not one of London's four largest railway stations had emerged unscathed.

They were also told that the RAF's night fighters had shot down twenty-nine bombers that night. The He 111 near Guildford was one of those bombers, and Sergeant Austin can remember the engagement vividly. And he can recollect the following night just as vividly, although the type they were vectored on to, and the circumstances of the flight, were altogether different. He recalls how they'd managed to intercept that one, a Ju 88, before the machine had even crossed the southern coast of England.

As the details, the tense minutiae of the flight, run through his mind, his hands instinctively tighten with anxiety.

'Stand by for trade,' the Flintlock controller said in his usual dulcet tones.

By then the time was around two hours after midnight on 12 May. Sergeant Austin remembers his discussion with the CO – they'd been amazed by the length of time they'd been kept on patrol without action. At last, though, something was happening, and the CO was told to maintain 18,000 feet above the beacon while they waited for further instructions. These soon followed.

'Turn on to one eight zero,' said the controller. 'There's a bandit out to sea. He's at angels one three. I say again, one three.'

The crew at once felt a surge of adrenalin and became fully alert as their hearts began to pound. And as the CO's navigator, Sergeant Austin felt an extra responsibility. He was determined not to let down the boss. He checked and double-checked the radar equipment as far as the system would allow, but still he had to wait for the magic words 'flash weapon now'. For the time being, the ground controller vectored them towards the target and Sergeant Austin could recall his desire, so urgent, to be on best form when he was finally ordered to 'flash weapon'.

'Your assigned bandit is still at angels one three and he's on a northerly heading,' said the controller.

The CO began to reduce height to 15,000 feet as he simultaneously turned the Beaufighter on to one eight zero. There was some moonlight, but even so there was a fearsome impression of blackness. As they flew beyond Brighton, out over the sea, Sergeant Austin recollects how, quite instinctively, he reached out one hand to feel for his dinghy pack.

'Maintain that southerly heading,' said the controller, 'and we'll set you up for a ninety-degree interception.'

'Levelling now at angels one five,' said the CO. 'And we're steady on one eight zero.'

'OK. Your target is forty-five miles ahead, on your right side.'

As they left the coastline behind them, the crew conversation concentrated on purely operational matters. There was a rising air of suspense that each man knew well, and knew was felt by the other. They understood that their apprehension was caused by more than any fear of the dark, of flying towards a black hole; it was more the unknown factors. Would their radar perform satisfactorily? Would they themselves? What type of aircraft would they intercept, and would there be more than one? Would the enemy evade? Would there be any return fire?

'Turn right ten, on to one nine zero,' said the controller. 'You're thirty-five miles from the target.'

The CO acknowledged that, after which there appeared to be a protracted delay. The controller gave further instructions, mainly heading information, but there seemed a drawn-out interval before he eventually said, 'You're ten miles from the target.' He then hesitated before going on: 'You can flash weapon now.'

At last! Sergeant Austin impatiently operated the radar switches. He was desperate to make use of the equipment, but, as ever, the pictures remained cluttered and confused during warm-up. He pushed his head against the rubber visor covering the scopes and he drummed his fingers fretfully, mentally urging on the radar. He was glad, at least, not to be pestered by the CO for information. Some of the pilots could become jumpy at this stage, pressing for information. The CO, though, remained calm, mindful of the system's limitations. For a while now he and the CO had been crewed together on a regular basis. They had learnt to understand each other's quirks and the personality combination had produced a good standard of teamwork.

'Maintain one nine zero.' The controller spoke slowly and deliberately as he said this. 'The target is on your right side and I see no signs of evasion. I'll be turning you right shortly.'

'OK,' said the CO. 'We're still heading one nine zero.'

'Hold that for now,' said the controller. 'I confirm that you're authorised to smack.'

'Acknowledged.'

The Beaufighter's radar picture was looking clearer at last, although Sergeant Austin still couldn't see any indication of the target.

'The radar's warmed up,' he said to the CO, 'but no sign of a blip yet.'

'You might pick him up during the turn,' said the CO.

'Stand by to turn!' interjected the controller, followed by, 'Turn hard right now. The target's heading is zero one zero. I say again, zero one zero. For a ninety-degree interception, make your initial heading two eight zero.'

'Confirm the target's height,' said the CO.

'Still at angels one three.'

'Any signs of evasion?'

'Negative, he's on a steady heading.'

'It's maybe to our advantage to descend now,' the CO said to his navigator.

'Let's go down to one thousand feet below target height.'

As the CO acknowledged this, and when the engine note altered as the throttles were brought back, Sergeant Austin monitored the altimeter (one of the few flight instruments displayed in his cockpit). His main focus, though, remained on the radar scopes as he searched for a blip. When the Beaufighter approached 12,000 feet, the CO advanced the throttles again, and informed the controller, 'We're at angels one two now.'

'The bandit's range is three miles,' said the controller, 'and he's slightly on your left, crossing ahead from left to right. Any contact?'

'Negative. I'm rolling out on two eight zero, but we still can't see him.'

'He's set on a generally northerly heading. Stand by to turn further right.'

'OK,' said the CO, speaking tersely as he concentrated on the profile of the interception.

Sergeant Austin continued to stare at his radar scopes, and the CO mentioned that he was looking up from time to time, although the moonlight was weak and the night too dark for a visual sighting at this range. His eyes had to remain chiefly on the flight instruments.

'The bandit's just crossing in front of you,' said the controller before long.

'Still no contact.'

'OK,' said the controller, 'turn hard right again.'

The CO reacted, immediately moving the Beaufighter's aileron wheel, and the engine note rose as he advanced the throttles. But Sergeant Austin, despite the urgency of his searches, continued to call 'no contact'. However, just seconds after the third such call, he suddenly glimpsed a faint blip at the edge of his scopes.

'Stand by!' he cried. As the Beaufighter turned, so the blip moved towards the centre of the scopes and became more distinct. 'I've got contact now,' he called. 'He's four thousand yards ahead and ten degrees up.'

'Tally-ho,' the CO said to the controller.

'Ease your angle of bank,' Sergeant Austin ordered the CO. 'We're approaching his line astern position.'

'OK. I'm still checking, but I can't see anything visually yet.'

'We're closing up now: he's at three thousand yards.'

'Are you happy with the rate of closure?'

'We're a little too fast. Reduce your airspeed. And hold this height – we have good separation.'

'Any signs of evasion?'

'Nothing yet. He seems oblivious of our presence.'

'Let's hope.'

As he counted down the range, Sergeant Austin knew that the CO would be searching assiduously, his eyes probably watering with the strain. They tracked the target's northerly heading, flying towards land, but their range from the coast at that juncture still exceeded thirty miles. As usual, they had to monitor the compass: over land or sea, their surroundings were equally black, equally ominous. They were anxious about return fire from the hostile machine ahead, and they were anxious, too, about the hostile void beneath in the event of bale-out.

'Confirm his height above us,' said the CO.

'He's one thousand feet above.'

'I think I'm just beginning to pick up his exhaust flames.'

'I've still got good radar contact.'

'We can start to reduce the height separation now.'

'We're less than one thousand yards now. This rate of closure looks OK.'

The CO acknowledged this, and as they continued to close he said that the exhaust flames ahead were becoming gradually more distinct, and that by now the weak moonlight was helping him to make out a silhouette. He was able to describe details which confirmed that the intruder was a Ju 88. The CO then said, 'We'll close up to two hundred yards before opening fire.'

'Understood. He's at five hundred yards now.'

When he'd said this, Sergeant Austin looked up briefly. Until that point, with his head pressed against the visor cover, he had seen just returns on his radar indicators. But when he glimpsed the shadowy, sinister profile of the Ju 88, he shrank back in his seat. He was astonished when he saw how close the machine looked. But his job was not yet complete and he quickly returned his gaze to the radar scopes. At such close range the blips were becoming fuzzy and extended; he had to use judgement, but as an experienced operator his assessment of range was accurate. With a firm voice he called, 'Four hundred yards.'

The Beaufighter's engine was fine-tuned, emitting a constant drone; unless aware of the reason, or unless warned by his pilot, the navigator wouldn't expect any change in note. Indeed, any adjustment of parameters, even the tone of voice, held significance. Sergeant Austin, his head still pushed against the visor cover, stared at the scopes, analysing the picture. He said nothing more until the due second, but when it came, his call of 'three hundred yards' was precise. As he made it, he thought he could sense a slight jerk of the aircraft flight controls, but the Beaufighter's course remained steady, the aircraft trimmed, the throttles set, the machine obedient and restrained.

But as he made the call 'two fifty yards', Sergeant Austin felt the reaction at once. He could sense the application of 'g' as the CO raised the Beaufighter's nose, and he could hear the higher engine note as the throttles were advanced. Sergeant Austin's call of 'two hundred yards' followed almost immediately and he could feel the Beaufighter being positively handled as the CO manoeuvred the gun-sight reticle onto the target. Within seconds, Sergeant Austin heard 'here goes', and a moment later he heard the crash of cannon and smelt the whiff of cordite. He tried to shield his eyes against the brilliance of light.

There was a long burst of cannon fire. When this ceased, after a fractional and unearthly hush, the crew could see almost at once that the enemy had been hit. They observed two strikes on the Ju 88's starboard engine and in the cabin area. Sergeant Austin was on the verge of shouting out, but he resisted, startled by the extreme evasive action taken by the stricken machine. The CO tried to follow, but the bomber's manoeuvres were excessively violent. In a series of steep turns, the Ju 88 eventually aimed for and then disappeared into cumulus cloud.

After that, the CO flew the Beaufighter in an orbital pattern and he spoke to the controller to keep him informed. But when he replied, the

Flintlock controller sounded agitated, still conscious, no doubt, of the severity of the previous night's blitz.

'Return to the Worthing beacon now,' he ordered. 'Hold there for further instructions.'

As they took up a northerly heading again, the crew searched behind them, attempting to spot the Ju 88 or to see evidence of its fate. But the machine's disappearance into cloud was their last sighting and they would never discover the final outcome. They would consequently claim the machine as 'damaged'.

When the Beaufighter reached the Worthing beacon, the controller soon gave further instructions: 'Divert to Middle Wallop without further delay,' he commanded. 'Tangmere's under attack.' Evidently the enemy had decided to make that airfield an object of reprisal for the night.

When they'd touched down at Middle Wallop, landing there at 0345, exactly three hours after take-off, their sense of fatigue was almost overwhelming. When the shut-down checks had been completed and as they stumbled towards the exit hatches, they barely said a word to each other. They spoke with the duty officer, who, as usual, had to routinely establish credentials. They spoke next with the duty intelligence officer to report the night's activities. Then finally, still in a state of exhaustion, they were driven to their respective messes.

Sergeant Austin frowns as he looks up, his preoccupation disturbed when one of the pilots speaks out. 'Listen to the crew-room wireless,' says the pilot, pointing behind him. 'We'll hear the eight o'clock time signal soon.'

'To be followed by tonight's rendition from Haw-Haw?' says his navigator.

Sergeant Austin glances across to recheck his aircraft, R2253, still lined up with the others. Step ladders have been placed by the machine; airmen climb them to reach across the pilot's windshield and the navigator's cupola in order to polish the perspex surfaces. Otherwise his aircraft remains untouched since the completion of the preliminary checks. His gaze lingers on the Beaufighter, with its hunched shoulders and its pug nose, the machine still solid and businesslike as it awaits the aircrew. Will he and the CO be ordered into the air tonight? Going by recent experience, probably not. They haven't flown operationally since the interception of that Ju 88. They've flown a number of practice flights to keep their hands in, but they haven't been scrambled operationally for over a month now. Tonight will probably turn out to be another quiet night.

He looks back at the hangar, by now also quiet. The furore caused by the dropped tool has died down; the supervising flight sergeant has moved to a different part of the hangar to check another airman. What's the airman doing anyway? Looks like he's handling that unpleasant distemper-like paste, that pink stuff which is supposed to help reduce the glow from the exhausts at night. The hangar, a hive of engineering activity, is opened up at present, but as dark approaches the doors will have to be closed before any lights can be turned on. As elsewhere, blackout regulations will apply.

He glances at his fellow aircrew, who have resumed their earlier conversation. One of them is holding forth again on jet engines and the Whittle machine, but as he is about to delve into technicalities, someone else holds up a hand and jerks his head towards the crew room. The aircrew are silent as they hear the time bleeps from the wireless – the eight o'clock time signal. They glance at one another when the expected voice begins to range across. 'Germany calling, Germany calling,' it cries (the voice articulates the words thus: 'Jairmany calling, Jairmany calling'). 'This is the Reichssender broadcast . . .'

But at this distance from the crew-room wireless the ramblings of Haw-Haw are hard to pick up. Sergeant Austin isn't very interested anyway, preferring to think about his operational duties – duties that mean serving his country, doing his bit, unlike the woolly-minded Haw-Haw with his contemptible rants and sly hints about the next bombing targets. Isn't it illegal, anyway, to tune in to Haw-Haw? Perhaps people listen out of inquisitiveness; perhaps the law, perversely, merely encourages this. Can there be other explanations why nearly as many listen to Haw-Haw as listen to the BBC? The aircrew may find his outbursts entertaining, but they listen to him with a sense of scorn. Loyalty to one's country is an in-built quality for them. Sergeant Austin is like the other squadron members: he's glad to play his part, to be involved and to have his duties recognised by his country. After all, these are duties for which he is in line for an award. Duties for which the CO has already received recognition.

Sergeant Austin gives a slight nod of his head, one of satisfaction, when he thinks about this. As the wireless persists with the sounds of Haw-Haw, Sergeant Austin ignores the tiresome bluster. Instead, he recollects with a pleasurable sense of respect the news, just announced, that the CO has been awarded a bar to his Distinguished Flying Cross.

CHAPTER TWENTY-NINE

Awaiting the Call
to Action

S ergeant Austin's prediction seems assured. The quiet night he fore-
    cast makes the aircrew listless, the lack of action at once welcome
    and wearisome. Their spirits are depressed anyway following the
move indoors when dusk approached. And with dark adaptation
goggles fitted, the sober atmosphere inside the crew room compares
unfavourably with the freedom of being in the open air.

Conversation, more sporadic as the night progresses, nevertheless
carries on from time to time as the aircrew try to stay cheerful. They
comment on wireless programmes, in particular a report on the BBC
that gives details of troop build-ups in and around Poland. Some of the
aircrew let out low whistles of astonishment at the correspondent's
description of how German forces, together with their Finnish and
Romanian allies, have begun to amass an estimated three and a half
million troops. One hundred army divisions, backed by tanks and sup-
ported by over 2,500 aircraft, have been observed as they muster in the
border areas. As he analyses the rumours and the counter-rumours,
the correspondent talks about the long-anticipated attack on Russia.

'No wonder life's so quiet for us these days,' says a pilot. 'Jerry's too
busy with them to bother about us.'

'We shouldn't complain.'

'It's the unpredictability.'

'Blame their leader. He's suffering another of his brainstorms.'

'God forbid. So what's going to happen in Poland?'

'Listen to the wireless. They reckon that Jerry's about to go into
Russia.'

'That's been put about for months.'

'It seems he's decided the time is right.'

'He threatened to invade this country, but it never happened.'

'We must have surprised him with the level of opposition; we were too strong for him.'

'The Russian army's over seven million strong.'

'Who knows what's on Jerry's mind? He's probably in a right old quandary, worried about the machinations of his leader.'

'But what about the so-called non-aggression pact?'

'It's probably as meaningful as that bit of white paper Chamberlain waved in the air before the war.'

'So what will Churchill do?'

'He says he's given Stalin clear warnings. And Adolf himself has given warnings – something about "flattening them like a hailstorm" – but Stalin refuses to take heed.'

'If Stalin can't cope, perhaps they'll send us over with our Beaus to help out.'

'Look what happened to Napoleon. The lessons of the past.'

'Did Napoleon have Beaus?'

'Beaus or no Beaus, the Russians will probably do now what they did then: hold out until winter.'

'What chance for poor old Jerry? We might even start to feel sorry for him.'

'Let's hope he's got some good strong boots.'

'He might find wellies useful.'

'And some nice warm overcoats.'

'Which is a very fair point. I hope he's got enough coupons.'

'Coupons?'

'Clothes rationing started a fortnight ago, remember? You'll need twenty-six coupons for a new suit, sixteen for a coat.'

'And for boots?'

'Seven.'

'No wonder Jerry didn't bother to invade us.'

'But if he changes his mind, he'll need twenty-two coupons for a coat and a pair of boots.'

'Twenty-three.'

'I haven't seen any coupons,' complains a navigator. 'Where do you get them?'

'They haven't been brought out yet,' says his pilot. 'And until they've been printed, you're supposed to use margarine coupons.'

There's laughter at this.

'It's no joke,' says the pilot.

'You'd be better off with the margarine.'

'They've run out of the stuff.'

'If you can't afford cake . . .'

'Then go up to Petticoat Lane. They don't bother with coupons, apparently.'

There's more laughter, after which the atmosphere quietens. Sergeant Austin shifts in his chair as he tries to look around him. His vision, restricted by the goggles, is still sufficient to make out the CO slumped in the next-door chair, apparently dozing. After the flight to Watchfield this morning, followed by hours of office work, it's little wonder the CO feels tired. Perhaps he should be stood down to allow him to rest properly, but he says everyone is tired; he insists on carrying on, doing his bit. With the enemy preoccupied on the Russian borders, maybe the operations officer assumes the present inactivity will persist. Sergeant Austin certainly remains confident of another quiet night, although he still feels on edge, mindful that if something does happen he and the CO will be one of the first crews ordered airborne.

The wireless programmes continue to dominate the room, though interrupted from time to time by clatters from the hangar area. There may be little in the way of operational flying, but the maintenance tasks seem ongoing; the engineers keep the Beaufighters' schedules up to date, deal with unserviceable machines, and train airmen new to the squadron. The aircrew, too, would like to make more use of the hours of waiting, but they must stay prepared – there's still the chance of a scramble. And the lack of action brings with it this unfortunate sense of lethargy, not helped by the drowsiness induced by wearing goggles.

Just before dusk, and before donning their goggles, Sergeant Austin and the CO had walked out to R2253. All the aircrew had to recheck their machines to set the cockpit lighting, adjust rheostats and carry out specific tasks to prepare for the night environment. Now the aircraft on operational standby remain undisturbed; the engineers won't interfere with these machines without permission from their aircrew.

Sergeant Austin stretches his arms and sinks deeper into his chair. He's vaguely aware of the background sounds, the musical beat from the wireless. Well-known melodies serenade his subconscious. 'Hang Out the Washing on the Siegfried Line' – the familiarity of the tune adds to the soporific atmosphere of the crew room. His eyelids begin to droop and he's almost grateful for his goggles, convenient for hiding any sense of embarrassment. He's aware of the strident tones of 'There'll Always Be an England' as they beat out from the wireless. And he's alerted when there's a break in the music, an unexpected interruption. The BBC announcer arouses interest when he introduces a special correspondent. Listeners will hear a report about the dramatic naval action of three weeks ago.

As he starts his account, the correspondent speaks in a low voice, reminding listeners of the background to the clash between the German ship *Bismarck* and HMS *Hood*. When the *Hood*'s munitions magazine was hit and when the ship blew up – literally tearing herself apart – around 1,300 men were lost. During the same engagement, the new battleship *Prince of Wales* was damaged; this ship had to put to sea so fast that a number of civilian dockyard workers were still on board.

The correspondent now focuses on the determination of the Royal Navy to retaliate: the *Bismarck*, with its so-called unsinkable design, had to be sunk at all costs. But the effort was hugely disruptive to the already stretched Royal Navy. Around a hundred vessels became involved and the correspondent describes how the action turned into the biggest sea chase in history. A combination of air and sea power eventually sealed the *Bismarck*'s fate. Torpedoes delivered by aircraft from HMS *Ark Royal*, followed by attacks from *Rodney*, *Devonshire* and *King George V* sank the *Bismarck* on 27 May.

There is an unusual hush in the crew room while the aircrew listen to this account. And as they listen to the correspondent, some of the men are prompted to wonder about naval thinking. The torpedoes launched by *Ark Royal*'s Swordfish aircraft – flimsy, obsolete-looking machines – caused crucial damage when they hit the *Bismarck*'s rudders, but the Germans put this down to chance: one in a hundred thousand. Should other torpedo-equipped aircraft (such as the Beaufighter) have been used as well? And use was not made, so it seems, of the expertise of the Royal Canadian Air Force coastal fighter unit, set up at nearby Thorney Island two months earlier. Perhaps there were good reasons, but are the admirals too independent and too fiercely protective of that independence? A hundred Royal Navy ships against one German capital ship, with one cruiser as consort. When the correspondent points out that the *Bismarck* was sunk 550 miles west of Land's End, the significance is not lost on the aircrew: this was within the Beaufighter's 1,500-mile range.

While the men ponder the facts and speculate on the tactical reasoning, some of them recall a liaison visit to the Thorney Island unit. The visit was set up by the CO and the Canadians, in turn, were glad to meet Beaufighter colleagues from another squadron and to brief them on anti-shipping techniques, which were explained in some detail. Enemy convoys would be approached at very low level, perhaps around ten feet, and without the assistance of ground-based radar. At the sighting of a target the attackers would climb to 2,000 feet. The first attack would come from cannon-firing Beaufighters – highly manoeuvrable machines designed to avoid flak. This would be followed by rocket-firing aircraft with the task of eliminating further flak. For the third phase, the torpedo-equipped Beaufighters needed a clear run: the torpedoes had to be released at precise parameters, with the aircraft level at a 100 feet and flying at 180 knots.

The aircrew now relate details of their visit to aspects of the *Bismarck* action. The men contemplate again whether sufficient consideration was given to the use of ground-based resources and whether these would have reduced the need for so many Royal Navy ships. The correspondent avoids direct opinion when he sums up his talk, but the aircrew are intrigued by the questions raised. There was little doubt, he suggests, for the need to dispense with the *Bismarck* as a matter of priority. But he re-emphasises the disproportionate amount of effort, and the knock-on effect caused by the involvement of so many ships. For the sake of one enemy vessel, virtually every naval commitment in the western Mediterranean and the northern Atlantic had to be abandoned, and this to aid a chase that went on for some 1,750 miles.

When the correspondent finishes, the BBC announces that more music will be played until the next item, the eleven o'clock news. The aircrew, meanwhile, continue to ponder the *Bismarck* story. They reflect on the fact that even Haw-Haw, generally guarded in his comments about *Bismarck*, was derisive about our use of so many vessels. He used the imbalance of forces to emphasise German naval superiority; he talked repeatedly of Germany's firm leadership and direction.

Haw-Haw may lionise German leadership but his listeners are more concerned with his recent insinuations about the blitz against British cities, threatening a resumption with renewed vigour. The warnings are received with dread, even though the mouthpiece of the German propaganda machine is considered flawed and unconvincing. Most listeners see through the transparent attempts to divert attention from the troop build-ups in Poland, although the aircrew note with particular distaste Haw-Haw's hints about the likely targets of the next air raid. The crews of the night fighters may understand the perversity of Haw-Haw, but they know as well that he still has the ability to strike fear and doubt into the hearts of many.

Seeds of doubt are planted in other ways, too: deception is felt to be practised by both sides. Folk appreciate that public morale must be kept high but they are less appreciative when the authorities seem to take this to extremes. At what point does truth become a casualty? People can go on trial for spreading alarm and despondency; intentions are misconstrued, rumours abound. Last year a correspondent wrote to anxious readers, 'Do not believe the tale the milkman tells; no troops have mutinied in Potters Bar. Nor are there submarines in Tunbridge Wells. The BBC will warn us when there are.'

But the dull talks on the Home Service, organised by the government and doubtless outside the control of the BBC, are no more convincing than Haw-Haw. The aircrew, with their inside knowledge, listen wearily to the predictable propaganda. The reports of independent observers, even the remarks and the wisecracks of comedians such as Tommy Handley, have far more influence. It's reckoned that if Hitler chose to invade between 8.30 and nine o'clock on a Thursday evening, he would have an easy time: the whole country would be tuned in to Tommy Handley's show *It's That Man Again*.

Someone says, 'The news is just coming through, fellows,' and the crew-room conversation dies down as the men listen to the eleven o'clock time signal, followed by the announcer's calm BBC voice as he reads introductory items (rumoured to be coded messages to agents). When these have been completed, the announcer goes directly to the penultimate news summary of the day. The first item causes a muted buzz of amusement around the crew room: reports that an Italian division in Abyssinia is about to surrender to British forces and that their leader, General Pralermo, will capitulate tomorrow. The general will be the fourth Italian divisional commander to be captured in that region recently.

As the BBC gives more details, the muttered aircrew comments persist. But the chatter ceases when the men catch the ring of the operations room telephone. The duty officer can be heard as he picks up the receiver, though his conversation is muffled, his words intermingled with the next item of news: 'President Roosevelt has ordered that German and Italian assets in the USA should be frozen until further notice.' The BBC voice is clear, though the duty officer speaks quietly; the aircrew have difficulty in overhearing him. His tone sounds normal and his conversation is brief. The men can relax when he replaces the receiver. The wireless dominates the room once more: a report that the Royal Air Force will reveal tomorrow that radio location has been the key weapon in the fight against German bombers.

'Isn't that meant to be classified information?' says a pilot.

'Not any more, it isn't.'

'It was probably an open secret anyway.'

'Perhaps the government wanted to give another morale booster.'

'People know that Jerry's working on a system of his own.'

'Except that Jerry's meant to be involved with other things right now.'

'If radio location—'

The navigator's remark is interrupted when the operations room telephone rings again and the aircrew strain to overhear the conversation. But the operations officer's voice remains quiet once more, and his words are hard to make out against the BBC voice, now reading the weather forecast for 16 June: 'The high pressure system currently affecting the British Isles . . .' When the BBC has confirmed that fine weather is predicted to continue, the announcer introduces the next programmed item. By special invitation, listeners will be asked to relate personal experiences with a humorous touch. The first contribution is from a newly wed young woman and begins, 'We walked from the vestry into the rectory garden to have our photographs taken. We stood there quietly while the photographer gave instructions, but as he did so we became aware of a life-and-death struggle unfolding above our heads. Suddenly, without warning, a German aircraft flew in low. I shouted to the photographer, "Look out, he's dropping bombs!" "Never mind about the bomb," said the photographer, "just smile and say—"'

The words are suddenly drowned out by the raised voice of the operations officer; this time his terse replies are heard above the voices from the wireless. The atmosphere in the crew room electrifies. Some of the aircrew, in their anxiety, half stand up. However, it is to the CO and Sergeant Austin that the operations officer shouts his instructions. And as his words echo through the building, clashing unceremoniously with the clang of the scramble bell, it is the CO and Sergeant Austin who make a dash for the door. Outside, R2253 awaits them, the preliminary checks performed, the canopies polished, the night flying checks completed. Beaufighter R2253 and crew have been called to action.

CHAPTER THIRTY

Final Combat

Their sense of shock is heightened by the need to hasten. But if Tom is surprised to be ordered into the air in the dying hour of Sunday, 15 June 1941, after so many weeks of operational quiet, he would have been even more surprised to learn how this flight will be one of such personal significance.

While the men hurry to their briefed positions, the ground crew, unhindered by goggles and bulky flying kit, reach R2253 first. They make for the right side of the machine where the external battery unit has been pre-positioned. They re-test the connections, switch on the power unit and double-check that the Beaufighter is ready: entrance hatches lowered, fire extinguishers in place, engine covers removed. The ground crew remain by the ground power unit as they observe the pilot and navigator dash towards their entrance hatches. To guide the aircrew, the ground personnel point their torches judiciously, then reposition next to the first engine to be started.

Inside the Beaufighter, the aircrew step with caution past the clutter of obstacles: Mae West lifejackets and flying suit pockets are easily snagged. But the men are practised and adept; they quickly reach the cockpits where the levers and switches, the shape of the hard seats, the position of the seat straps, and the carefully placed head gear and oxygen masks have a handy familiarity within the confined space. The two men stow their dark adaptation goggles as they settle into their cockpit seats and note the faint flickers from ground crew torches outside.

Tom checks the security of his seat collapsing lever, connects his seat straps, and dons his head gear and oxygen mask. He sets the engine controls ready for the priming procedure and gives the agreed signal to the ground crews, who begin to turn the propeller for the first engine to be started. There's another signal and the priming of the engine commences – around half a dozen strokes for the June evening. A further signal leads to the distinctive sound of the first engine spluttering into life.

Soon, when both engines have been started, the ground crew hand the undercarriage safety locking pins to the navigator and ensure that entrance hatches are securely fastened. Tom, meanwhile, calls out the pre-take-off checks, and when his navigator confirms 'all's ready', both crew look for a visual cue from the air traffic control tower. When this has been given, Tom releases the Beaufighter's parking brake catch and watches the ground crew torches which guide him as he moves away from the parking area. The moonlight helps him too, and he taxies the machine towards the runway as rapidly as safety permits. He receives a further signal from air traffic control before he manoeuvres to the take-off point.

When Tom has completed the before-take-off procedures – tail-wheel straight, brakes reapplied, engine response checks – he speaks again with his navigator. A terse 'all set' promptly follows. Tom releases the brakes and starts to ease the twin throttles forward. Both crew now monitor the take-off, listening for the protesting howl of the Hercules engines at full power, anticipating the rapid rate of acceleration, the raising of the tail-wheel, the firm control of the Beaufighter's inclination to swing, the line of flares racing past, the short amount of time before the main wheels lift off.

Tom holds the climbing speed of 150 knots. He flies with accuracy, but still feels agitated by the unexpected call to action; he has to concentrate hard on the departure procedures.

'Head south,' orders the controller. 'Make for Selsey Bill as you climb to angels one five.'

Tom readjusts the Beaufighter's climb attitude to peg the airspeed, then re-trims the aircraft. He notes the position of the moon and sees that the moonlight is revealing the generally good visibility of the night. He can clearly make out the vicinity of Selsey Bill ahead. As he approaches 15,000 feet he initiates level off and informs the controller.

'Orbit over Selsey until further orders,' says the controller.

As he levels off, Tom ensures the throttles are set for maximum fuel efficiency: engine revolutions at 2,400, cylinder temperature at 290°C, oil temperature at 80°C. He carries out further cockpit drills and is assisted by the moonlight as he rechecks his position and his general navigation. He glances again at the prominent feature of Selsey Bill, noting the distinctive sweep of the coastline: north-east towards Bognor and Worthing, north-west towards Hayling Island and Portsmouth.

Now, after the suddenness of the scramble order, the crew are glad of the lull in proceedings. They settle into the orbital routine and there's an opportunity to mentally readjust. They talk infrequently at this stage. Despite the welcome breathing space, both men are subdued –

uncharacteristically so. They wonder about the scramble and why it was prompted; they focus on cockpit procedures: fuel calculations, navigational criteria, oxygen reserves, radar and gun-sight equipment. Sergeant Austin makes use of his navigator's seat, which can be swung around; he looks forward towards the pilot, then swivels his seat to check the aircraft's rear quarter. He ponders and he worries. The conversation is restrained and he is bothered.

For one thing, he is contemplating some recent bad news, news that will disturb the squadron as a whole and which will affect him in particular: in just a matter of weeks the CO will leave the squadron. This news, still rumour at present, says that the CO will be promoted and posted to another staff job. Another staff job! Surely good pilots should be kept in cockpits, not hidden away at Headquarters 11 Group? The CO no doubt has a fine career ahead of him, but this is wartime – what are the priorities? Sergeant Austin concedes that 11 Group will benefit from someone of the CO's experience, that they need a person of ability to be in charge of night operations. But what happens then?

He cannot be aware, of course, that the CO will spend a mere four months at headquarters; that he will then move to North Weald where he will be appointed station commander to resolve a particular discipline problem; that after six months he will return to 11 Group as senior officer in charge of administration; that, following this job, he will be posted to the Mediterranean theatre of operations, in charge of the mobile operations room; that he will end the war as an air commodore at the headquarters of the Desert Air Force. And Sergeant Austin can have no perception that within ten years the CO will have become one of the youngest air vice marshals in the history of the service; that in fifteen years' time he will be shaking hands with his present adversary, Luftwaffe General Kammhuber, in charge of German night fighter defences; that in fewer than twenty years' time the CO will be appointed Chief of the Air Staff and will be promoted to the most senior air force rank, Marshal of the Royal Air Force; that he will witness atomic bomb tests at Christmas Island and that, like other servicemen who observe these tests, he will develop a cancerous tumour (the link will be officially denied); that this will lead to neuro-surgery that will fail; that as a consequence, after several months of lingering excruciation, frightened nurses at Halton hospital will summons his wife to his bedside; that she will reach him with just minutes to spare before his passing; and that, in an ironic twist, this will occur at night-time during a violent thunderstorm.

'Confirm you're still at angels one five.' The controller's voice eventually interrupts the cockpit silence.

'Maintaining angels one five,' says Tom, 'overhead Selsey.'

'OK. Stand by,' says the controller. 'Call Flintlock now as pre-briefed.'

Tom glances at the radio control box and changes frequency before saying, 'Flintlock, good evening. We've just been handed over by Tangmere.'

'Good evening. That's understood. There'll be trade for you shortly – stand by for trade.'

'OK. The visibility is exceptionally good this evening.'

'You might need it,' says the controller. 'Make your vector now one four zero.'

'Shall we maintain this height?'

'Angels one five should be OK.'

All seems uncannily quiet as they turn: little in the way of searchlight activity; no discernible anti-aircraft fire; the radio frequency pretty much to themselves. Perhaps this scene, the unusual and unexpected atmosphere, is the trigger for Tom's train of thoughts. Later in his life he will make oblique references to this, although in general, like many of his contemporaries, he was reticent about his war experiences. If someone chanced across the subject it would be met with brusqueness; the matter was best avoided. Very occasionally his guard would slip but if inner feelings were divulged, this was probably unintentional. It was perhaps accidental, therefore, when the significance of this particular flight was revealed, although at the time, of course, other than by premonition he could not himself have known.

'Turn port,' says the controller, 'make it one one zero.'

The crew focus on their job.

'Your target's crossing from right to left,' adds the controller before long. 'Make your vector zero eight zero.'

'Any joy?' Tom asks his navigator.

'Nothing yet,' says Sergeant Austin.

'Turn further left,' says the controller. 'Make it zero five zero. The target is a little below you.'

'Still no luck,' says the navigator to his pilot. 'There's some interference on my scopes.'

'We can't see him yet,' Tom says to the controller.

'OK,' says the controller. 'Go hard left now on to zero one zero. The bandit should be two miles in front.'

Tom turns the Beaufighter, but he turns too far: as he rolls out, his compass indicates a northerly heading so he eases the aileron wheel to take him back ten degrees. 'We still can't see him,' he says to the controller.

'Hold your present heading,' says the controller. 'The target's slightly right of you. You're closing on him quite swiftly.'

'Affirmative!' says Sergeant Austin abruptly. 'I have radar contact now. Reduce your airspeed. He's at one mile, closing rapidly.'

But as Tom brings back the twin throttles, the navigator's countdown of range is fast – too fast.

'Confirm we still have height separation,' Tom asks his navigator urgently.

'Yes, but I think we're overtaking . . .'

'Stand by,' says Tom. 'I've got him visually now: he's below us on our starboard side. I estimate his range at five hundred yards.'

'I've got him visually as well,' says Sergeant Austin, who has removed his head from the radar visor. What he sees causes butterflies to run riot in his stomach. 'Watch out!' he cries. 'He's turning towards us!'

'He's passing beneath.'

'He could open fire at any second.'

'Stand by! I'm reversing this turn,' says Tom.

The navigator feels 'g' as the Beaufighter is manoeuvred.

'I've still got him visually,' says Tom. 'I think it's an He 111.'

'I agree with the type,' says the navigator as the moonlight helps him make out the profile of the engines – the shape of the bulbous fuselage sitting high on the wing-line.

'OK, I'm closing up.'

'Looking for him on radar again,' says the navigator.

'He's still evading,' cries Tom, 'but we're just about within firing range.'

The navigator continues to feel 'g', then a series of lurches as the gun sight is brought to bear.

'Here goes,' says Tom. 'Opening fire!'

A crash of cannons, and the acrid smell of cordite fills the interior of the Beaufighter. There's an interval of silence, an air of shock; time is momentarily halted.

The navigator suddenly exclaims, 'His starboard engine is on fire!' Then adds, 'But I think it's going out.'

'I'll have to reposition for another burst.'

Once more the Beaufighter pitches firmly while Tom takes aim. Within seconds, there's the repeated sound of cannons rattling through the airframe.

'His other engine's been hit!' cries the navigator. 'He's well alight now. He's going down!'

'I'll try to follow.'

Tom banks the Beaufighter steeply, lowering the machine's nose but the stricken bomber accelerates away from him. He attempts to follow, but he cannot keep up and at 3,000 feet he levels the Beaufighter and the crew scour the area. They see two bright flashes.

'He's jettisoned his bombs,' says the navigator. Two minutes later he exclaims, 'Look over there! That must be him!'

Tom flies towards the scene but the fire has gone out before he can reach it. He speaks to the controller, who says, 'The bandit's gone down in the sea? Confirm his bearing.'

'We estimate two three zero from Brighton. Do you want us to search?'

'Negative,' says the controller. He pauses for some moments. 'Head for the Worthing beacon,' he goes on. 'Hold there for now.'

When the Beaufighter reaches the beacon, there to be held for another hour, the prevalent atmosphere of quiet soon returns, this time clashing with the turmoil in the minds of the crew. The searchlights remain docile, the anti-aircraft activity non-existent, the radio chatter leisurely. And in the cockpit of R2253 the awkward silence endures: the contemplation of changes ahead amid a conglomeration of images in their heads. Why that particular Heinkel on that particular night, with that particular crew? Poor devils. As for R2253 and its crew, they did their duty. Another 'good show'.

With that torment still in the back of the mind Tom maintains patrol and as the minutes pass, as the prevailing quiet persists, he reflects on his activities of the last few months. He thinks about his tally, six enemy aircraft destroyed, two probables and one damaged. Other images recur; he feels bemused, gratified, daunted, even somewhat fearful, for he's a religious man. As he turns the Beaufighter in obedient orbit above the Worthing beacon, he can ruminate and he can speculate, for he's an ambitious man. He cannot know that this was to be the last combat flight of his life. He cannot predict the extraordinary prospects ahead, the full bounds of the new show that awaits. When he's finally cleared to take the Beaufighter back to Tangmere, there to land at 0130, this show is now over.

Index